Food Science
Laboratory Manual

Karen Jamesen, M.S., R.D.
Assistant Professor
Foods and Nutrition
Purdue University

Pearson
Education

Merrill,
an imprint of Prentice Hall
Upper Saddle River, New Jersey   Columbus, Ohio

Cover art/photo: Alfred Pasieka/Science Photo Library
Editor: Kevin M. Davis
Production Editor: Patricia S. Kelly
Design Coordinator: Karrie M. Converse
Text Designer: Beth Dubberley
Cover Designer: Russ Maselli
Production Manager: Pamela D. Bennett
Illustrations: Diphrent Strokes
Director of Marketing: Kevin Flanagan
Marketing Manager: Suzanne Stanton
Advertising/Marketing Coordinator: Julie Shough
Editing and typing contributions: Marcia Stanley, M.S., R.D.; Joey Hall; Kelly Douds; Dawn Haan

This book was set in Times Roman by Beth Dubberley and was printed and bound by Banta Company. The cover was printed by Phoenix Color Corp.

Contributions for previous editions by current and retired Purdue University faculty.

Pearson
Education

© 1998 by Prentice-Hall, Inc.
A Pearson Education Company
Upper Saddle River, NJ 07458

Printed in the United States of America

10 9 8 7 6 5 4 3 2 1

ISBN: 0-02-360192-2

Prentice-Hall International (UK) Limited,London
Prentice-Hall of Australia Pty. Limited, Sydney
Prentice-Hall Canada Inc., Toronto
Prentice-Hall Hispanoamericana, S.A., Mexico
Prentice-Hall of India Private Limited, New Delhi
Prentice-Hall of Japan, Inc., Tokyo
Pearson Education Asia Pte. Ltd., Singapore
Editora Prentice-Hall do Brasil, Ltda., Rio de Janeiro

PREFACE

This laboratory manual was developed to guide the students in their quest for the scientific principles involved in the attainment of food quality. The manual includes application experiments to allow observation of quality changes: both physical and chemical. Experiments are followed with questions to help the student identify changes and explain the causes.

The manual was developed for a one-semester introductory scientific food class although it could easily be adapted to two semesters. The large variety of experiments available on each topic will give the instructor the flexibility to adapt to one or two laboratories per week and to laboratories of varying lengths. The experimental approach promotes the scientific study of foods. Experiments that illustrate the major concepts are indicated with this symbol—❖. Other experiments and formulas are included for use at the discretion of the instructor.

Ingredients used in the food industry are included in some of the experiments. These give the student exposure to products available to the food industry to solve technical problems identified in food processing. Many of these ingredients have been included in the fat-free or reduced fat formulas. Sources of these ingredients are identified in the Appendix.

The experiments in this manual have evolved over many years and through the hands of many retired and current faculty at Purdue University. The input of each person has been invaluable in achieving the result of this manual.

TABLE OF CONTENTS

GOALS

1. To identify physical and chemical properties of fresh and processed foods.

2. To identify and gain an understanding of the chemical and physical changes that occur in foods due to storage, heat, freezing, pH change, additives, and other forms of processing.

3. To become familiar with ingredients and their functionality available for product formation.

4. To observe and describe changes in foods due to cooking, processing, and additives.

5. To identify the composition of a wide variety of food products.

6. To prepare, taste, and identify the quality of a wide variety of processed and unprocessed foods, including foods from a variety of cultures, that are available on the market.

7. To describe or define terms relating to food composition, such as cellulose, pectins, amylose, amylopectin, enzyme, solution, emulsion, colloidal dispersion, pigments, coagulation, denaturation, and syneresis.

8. To describe and perform basic food preparation techniques used with each type of food product.

9. To define terms used in basic food preparation, such as saute, simmer, scald, fold, and knead.

10. To use a variety of food preparation and food evaluation equipment.

11. To identify changes in nutrient quality of foods following storage, cooking, or processing.

12. To use British (traditional American) and metric measuring systems.

13. To identify and produce an excellent standard of quality for food products.

Food Handling, Laboratory, and Measurement Practices

Goals: To know safe and sanitary food handling procedures and to understand the rationale for practices used with foods.

To know measuring equivalents and methods for measuring ingredient quantities and heat.

Objectives: To maintain sanitary laboratory conditions.

To maintain safe food handling procedures.

To measure ingredients accurately.

To measure heat accurately.

PROFESSIONAL APPEARANCE

*   Attire clean. To assure cleanliness, laboratory coats or uniforms are worn only in the food preparation area.

*   Shoes have enclosed toes and heels to provide safety.

*   Hair is covered with hair net or lab cap to maintain food sanitation.

*   Jewelry is not worn to prevent contamination to food or loss in food.

*   Personal items and books are stored away from preparation area.

LABORATORY PROCEDURES

*   **Hands should always be washed** with soap and water before any food preparation. Because the potential for food contamination is easily carried into the lab through persons working with food, this precaution is mandatory.

*   Always fill tasting spoon from mixing or serving spoon. **Never taste from serving or mixing spoon or place tasting spoon in common serving dish.**

*   Always wash fruits and vegetables and can lids before using.

*   Refrigerate food products promptly after use.

*   Always wash dishes with **hot soapy water, sanitize by heat or chemicals, and rinse with hot water.**

*   Never place knives in dishwater.

*   Rinse thermometers after use. Be careful that thermometer is not cracked. Be especially careful with mercury thermometers; check with instructor on handling of mercury if thermometer breaks.

*   Know location and use of fire extinguisher.

MEASUREMENT
British and Metric Measures and Equivalents
Equivalents (Volume)

1 t	= 4.9 ml		2 c	= 1 pt (473 ml)
3 t	= 1 T (14.8 ml)		4 c	= 1 qt (946 ml.)
16 T	= 1 c (237 ml)		4 qt	= 1 gal
4 T	= 1/4 c		2 T	= 1 liquid oz or 1/8 c
8 T	= 1/2 c		8 fl oz	= 1 c or 1/2 pt
12 T	= 3/4 c		2 gal	= 1 pk
5 1/3 T	= 1/3 c		4 pk	= 1 bu

Equivalents (Weight)

1 g	= .035 oz
1 oz (avdp.)	= 28.4 g
1 lb	= 454 g

Each *volume* listed below is equivalent to 1 lb (avdp.) or 454 g.

All-purpose flour	4 c
Cake flour	4 1/2 c
Lard, margarine, butter	2 c
Hydrogenated fats	2 1/2 c
Granulated sugar	2 c
Brown sugar, packed	2 1/3 c
Confectioners' sugar	3 1/2 c

Symbols for Measurements and Weights

Tbsp or T	= tablespoon		fg	= few grains (very light sprinkle)
tsp or t	= teaspoon		pt	= pint
c	= cup		qt	= quart
bu	= bushel		gal	= gallon
pk	= peck		oz	= ounce
g	= gram		spk	= speck
kg	= kilogram		lb	= pound
ml	= milliliter		fl	= fluid
l	= liter		fd	= few drops
°F	= degrees Fahrenheit		°C	= degrees Celsius

Conversions: Celsius and Fahrenheit

Temperature $°F = 9/5\ T°C + 32$ Temperature $°C = 5/9\ (T°F - 32)$

	°F	°C
Freezing	32°	0°
Refrigerator	43°	7°
Boiling	212°	100°
Slow oven	300°–325°	149°–163°
Moderate oven	350°–375°	75°–190°

Microwave/Convection Oven Directions
To set microwave on various power levels:

100%:	10 High
80%:	8 Med
70%:	7 Med–Low
10%:	1 Low

Measuring Equipment

Measuring Cups

Conventional British Cups: 1-C Measure
> A 1-c measure has 8 fluid oz capacity.
> Types: A. cup line at the rim
>   B. space above the 1-c mark.

Fractional Cups: 1/2-, 1/3-, 1/4-C Measures
If standardized, these permit more nearly accurate measurements for solid foods than can be obtained in the cup with subdivisions.

Metric Cup
Liquids are measured metrically in a metric cup with 25 or 50 ml markings or in a graduated cylinder. Glass or plastic cups allow for accurate volumetric measure.

Scales and Balances

Dry materials are measured by ounces or metrically by weight in grams. Weight is a more accurate measure for some dry ingredients than is a volumetric measure.

How to Measure Staple Foods by Metric or British Methods

Flour, Sugar, and Other Dry or Solid Foods

Measurement of these foods is most conveniently and accurately measured by weight. When volumetric measures are used, all measurements should be level. Cut level with the straight edge of a spatula or knife. Small quantities—less than 25 ml—are measured by teaspoon, tablespoon, or weight.

Solid food materials are best measured in fractional cups or 1-c measure with the cup line at the rim. If not available, care must be taken to level food to the subdivision mark as accurately as possible.

White flour:	Sift before measuring by volume and spoon into measuring equipment. Don't pack.
Whole grain flour:	Stir before measuring by volume.
Sugar:	
Granulated:	Spoon into measuring equipment; omit sifting unless lumpy; level.
Confectioners:	Roll out lumps if necessary. Spoon into measuring equipment. Don't pack; level.
Brown sugar:	Pack into measuring equipment. Level.

Liquids

Glass or plastic cups with milliliter or ounce division lines are used. Use measuring cup with lip. Place cup on flat surface. Fill to desired level and read at eye level. Meniscus should touch line. Scrape heavy liquids from container.

Fat

Solid Fats
Solid fats should be removed from the refrigerator long enough before measuring to permit them to become plastic. Very hard fats are difficult to measure accurately.

a. Solid Pack—Weigh or press the fat into the cup (fractional cups are most desirable) so that air spaces are forced out (level).

b. Water Displacement—used with standard measuring cup with lip above the 1-c mark. Cold water is placed in the cup, leaving space equivalent to the amount of fat to be measured. Fat is added to the cup until the water and fat reach the 1-c level. Be sure that the fat is entirely covered with water. The water is then drained off.

Oils
Follow directions for liquids.

Measuring Experiments

Goal: To practice measuring techniques.

Objectives: To use standardized equipment and procedures when measuring food materials.
To identify causes of inaccurate measuring.
To identify the most accurate measuring procedures.

Experiment 1

Objective: To compare volume and weight measures.

Procedure: Measure and then weigh in grams (454 g = 1 lb).

Results:

Variable	Weight (g)	*Standard
1. 1 c unsifted all-purpose flour		125 g
2. 1 c minus 2 T unsifted all-purpose flour		115 g
❖3. 1 c sifted all-purpose flour, lightly fill cup by means of a spoon (no packing or shaking); level top with edge of a straight knife or spatula		116 g
4. 1 c sifted all-purpose flour packed and tapped into a cup with a spoon		
5. Same as 3—use cake flour		96 g

*Standards from *Handbook of Food Preparation*, 9th Edition, p. 182, by American Home Economics Association. Published by Kendal/Hunt Publishing Co.

Conclusions: The method in variable 3 provides the most accurate measure, achieving closest to 115 g.

Why is flour sifted before measuring?

Why is flour not packed or tapped into a cup?

Is measuring by weight rather than by volume more consistently accurate when measuring flour? Why?

Experiment 2

Objective: To practice correct procedures for measuring fat, sugar, and water.

Procedure: Measure with volume measures and then weigh in grams. Use procedures outlined previously under "How to Measure Staple Foods by Metric or British Methods."

Results:

Variable	Weight in Grams	Class Variation	*Standard g/c
❖1. 1/2 c hydrogenated fat: solid pack			204
1/2 c hydrogenated fat: water displacement			204
1/2 c hydrogenated fat: melted, filled, level			218
❖2. 1 c brown sugar			201
3. 1 c granulated brown sugar			153
4. 1 c granulated sugar			201
5. 1 c water			237

*Standards from *Handbook of Food Preparation,* 9th Edition, pp. 175, 195, by American Home Economics Association. Published by Kendal/Hunt Publishing Co.

Conclusions: Which is heavier: 1 c hydrogenated fat or 1 c melted hydrogenated fat?

Was it necessary to pack brown sugar into a cup to obtain the standard weight?

Experiment 3

Objectives: To recognize when a precision balance is necessary for accurate measuring.
To correctly use a trip balance or top-loading electronic balance.

Procedure:
1.   Weigh 3.4 g NaCl on dietetic scales.
2.   Place weighing paper on a trip balance or top-loading electronic balance, either weigh or tare to 0.
3.   Add previously weighed NaCl. Notice discrepancy in weight.
4.   Calculate the percentage error.

	Desired Weight	Weight on Dietetic Scale	Weight on Balance	%Error
❖NaCl	3.4 g			

Conclusions: Which method must be used to accurately weigh small weights of ingredients?

Use of the Thermometer

Objectives: To read the thermometer accurately.
To determine temperatures related to terminology below.

I. Calibration of Thermometer
A. Fill a saucepan 1/2 full of water.
B. Boil water.
C. Center thermometer in water and record the temperature at which water boils. Read at eye level.
D. If reading is lower than 100°C, add the difference to all future thermometer readings of that thermometer.
E. If reading is higher than 100°C, subtract the difference from all future thermometer readings.

❖**II. Procedure:** Have a saucepan 1/2 full of water. Follow variables as listed below.

	Variables		Results	
Water	**Thermometer**		**Directions for Thermometer Reading**	**C° F°** **Temp.**
1. Boiling rapidly	bulb completely immersed but not on bottom of pan		eyes on straight line with top of the mercury column	
2. Boiling slowly	same		same	
3. Water held over boiling water until temperature is stabilized (double boiler)	same		same	
4. Simmering	same		same	80–90° 180–210°
5. Pressure cooked water 15 lbs	maximum thermometer suspended		read maximum thermometer after removal from cooker	

Conclusions: Where in a pan of water must bulb of thermometer be placed to read thermometer accurately?

What is the temperature of:

Rapidly boiling water?

Slowly boiling water?

Simmering water?

Water in top of double boiler?

Water boiling under 15 lbs pressure?

What errors in using a thermometer could result in reading temperature inaccurately?

Effect of Container Material on Heat Transfer

Procedure: Place 2 c (250 ml) water in each of the following oven-proof and cook-top-proof utensils of same shape and size. Make sure all water is same temperature.

    2 aluminum
    2 aluminum with copper bottom, all copper, or iron
    2 glass

Place one utensil of each material on a surface heating unit of same size. Turn burner on high and take temperature each minute. Record the temperature.

Turn on the oven to 400°F (204°C). Place one utensil of each material with water in it in oven as near the center as possible. Take the water temperature after 10 min and after 20 min.

Oven

Utensil	Temperature		
	5 Min	**10 Min**	**20 Min**
Glass			
Aluminum			
Copper or iron			

Surface Unit

Utensil	Temperature		
	1 Min	**2 Min**	**5 Min**
Glass			
Aluminum			
Copper or iron			

Conclusions: Which materials have the highest specific heat?

In which method of heating is radiant energy most important?

In which method of heating does the specific heat of the material appear to have the greater affect on transfer of heat?

Sensory Quality

Notes:

Goal:	To experience sensory evaluation of primary tastes and the effect of color and aroma on flavor using sensory evaluation testing methods.	

Objectives: To recognize the basic tastes and to identify the effect that one has on the others.
To recognize the effects of color on taste.
To use a variety of sensory evaluation tests: specifically the paired comparison, triangle, duo-trio, and the hedonic scale.
To increase sensitivity to taste.

Questions for study: How does one taste affect another?

What characteristics of a food are important to your ability to taste?

The sensory quality of food encompasses many complex factors: appearance, odor, taste, and texture (mouthfeel). The flavor of food is derived from a combination of odors and tastes and is influenced by its temperature and texture. The primary tastes are generally considered to be bitter, salt, sour, sweet, and unami. Substances that contribute to taste must be in solution before they can be detected. Individuals vary in their ability to identify specific tastes.

Procedure: Preparation: Solutions are prepared according to directions in Appendix A.

Experiment: Below are a series of exercises that will give you some experience in tasting. Series of solutions have been made and coded so that you will not know what they are. You will rotate through each series. For each series, pour a 1 t sample into a clean cup, taste, and evaluate according to the testing method indicated. Following each taste, rinse your mouth with water. When you have finished, you can compare your results with the composition of each solution.

❖Series A: Identification of the Primary Tastes

Taste each of the labeled solutions and place the number in the column that corresponds to the taste sensation you received from the solution.

	Bitter	Sour	Salt	Sweet	Unami
Individual					
Correct key #					

Series B: Effect of Acid on Sweetness: Paired Comparison Sensory Test

Place the code under the correct category.

Identification	Less Sweet	More Sweet	No Difference
Individual			
Correct key #			

Conclusion: How did acid affect sweetness?

Describe a paired comparison sensory test.

Series C: Effect of Salt on Sweetness: Triangle Sensory Test
Choose the sample that is different from the other two. Is it sweeter or less sweet?

Identification	Two of the Same	Different Sample	Different Sample: Sweeter/Less Sweet
Individual			
Correct key #			

Conclusion: How did salt affect sweetness?

Describe a triangle sensory test.

Series D: Effect of Sugar on Saltiness: Paired Comparison Sensory Test
Place the code under the correct category.

Identification	Less Salty	More Salty	No Difference
Individual			
Correct key #			

Conclusion: Sugar (decreases/increases) saltiness.

Series E: Effect of Sugar on Sourness (Acidity): Paired Comparison Sensory Test
Place the code under the correct category.

Identification	Less Sour	More Sour	No Difference
Individual			
Correct key #			

Conclusion: Sugar (decreases/increases) sourness.

Series F: Effect of Sugar on Bitterness: Paired Comparison Sensory Test
Place the code under the correct category.

Identification	Less Bitter	More Bitter	No Difference
Individual			
Correct key #			

Conclusion: Sugar (decreases/increases) bitterness.

Series G: Effect of Sugar Structure on Sweetness: Triangle Sensory Test

Select the sample that is different. Is it sweeter/less sweet?

Identification	Two of the Same	Different Sample	Different Sample: Sweeter/Less Sweet
Individual			
Correct key #			

Conclusion: Sucrose is (sweeter/less sweet) than fructose when tasted in solution at room temperature.

Series H: Effect of Above Threshold Levels of Salt on Sweetness: Duo-Trio Test

Choose the sample that is different from the standard. Is it sweeter or less sweet?

Identification	Identical to Standard	Sweeter/Less Sweet
Individual		
Correct key #		

Conclusion: Salt in larger amounts (decreases/increases) sweetness.

Describe the duo-trio sensory test.

Series I: Effect of Processing Method on the Flavor of Lemonade: Consumer Preference Hedonic Scale Sensory Test

Rate the 3 lemonade samples from "dislike extremely" to "like extremely" by checking the appropriate box.

Sample #693

❑	❑	❑	❑	❑	❑	❑	❑	❑
Dislike Extremely	Dislike Very Much	Dislike Moderately	Dislike Slightly	Neither Like nor Dislike	Like Slightly	Like Moderately	Like Very Much	Like Extremely

Sample #054

❑	❑	❑	❑	❑	❑	❑	❑	❑
Dislike Extremely	Dislike Very Much	Dislike Moderately	Dislike Slightly	Neither Like nor Dislike	Like Slightly	Like Moderately	Like Very Much	Like Extremely

Sample #893

❑	❑	❑	❑	❑	❑	❑	❑	❑
Dislike Extremely	Dislike Very Much	Dislike Moderately	Dislike Slightly	Neither Like nor Dislike	Like Slightly	Like Moderately	Like Very much	Like Extremely

Conclusion: How do frozen lemonade, a dried lemonade mix, and lemonade made from fresh lemons compare?

Describe the consumer preference hedonic scale sensory test.

Series J: Effect of Color on Flavor
Identify the flavor of each solution.

Code	Flavor
382	_____
296	_____
432	_____
871	_____

Conclusion: Did color affect your perceived flavor?

Summary
Although the concentration appears to affect the following results, the following perceived interrelationships of tastes are generally observed.

Sweet
- Reduces sourness
- Decreases saltiness
- Decreases bitterness

Sour
- Reduces sweetness
- Increases bitterness

Salt
- Reduces sourness
- Decreases sweetness if used in large amounts, enhances sweetness in small amounts

Bitterness
- Reduces sweetness

Series K: Spatial Sensitivity of the Tongue
Dip a Q-tip in the solution and touch to tip, side, center, and back of tongue. Rinse mouth with water between each touch. Identify the flavor at each location. Did you sense the flavor at each location?

Conclusion: Does the location of tasting on the tongue affect the ability to taste a flavor?

Series L: Effect of Aroma on Flavor
Blindfold a partner. Have the partner hold his or her nose. Place a jelly bean in partner's mouth. Have partner identify the flavor. Release nose and report flavor of jelly bean. Place a second jelly bean in mouth. Have partner identify the flavor of the second jelly bean.

Conclusion: How did the absence of sight and aroma affect the flavor of the jelly bean?

Series M: Effect of Genetic Predisposition on Tasting Phenylthiocarbamide (PTC)
Taste a PTC taste paper. Do you taste anything, and if you do, what is the quality?

Conclusion: About 30% of the Caucasian population does not have the ability to taste this substance.

Series N: Effect of Genetic Predisposition on the Ability to Smell Androstenone
Sniff androstenone. Notice the aroma.

Conclusion: About 50% of the population does not have the ability to smell this substance. Approximately 25% of the smellers rate it as pleasant, and 25% of smellers rate it as musky, urinous.

Series O: Effect of Water Activity on Mouthfeel

    10 Triscuit crackers
    10 Ritz crackers
    5 oz American processed cheese

Place thin slice of cheese on 1/2 of each cracker variety. Place in microwave to melt.

Conclusion: Which cracker stays crisp? Which cracker turns warm and soggy?

    How does water activity affect crispness?

Beverage Solutions

Notes:

COFFEE AND TEA

Goal: To compare preparation methods and quality of teas and coffees.

❖Experiment I: Flavor of Fresh Coffee versus Reheated Coffee

Objective: To taste the increased bitterness in reheated coffee.

Variables:

A Take pH of water. Prepare coffee by drip method using the electric drip coffee maker. Place a filter in the brewing basket and add (10.6 g) 2 T of drip coffee. Attach to coffee maker. Add (355 ml) 12 oz water. Place covered brewing basket and cup/carafe on the base of the beverage maker. Press the "heat" or "on" lever. Dispense coffee. When dripping stops, the coffee is done. Take pH of coffee

B. Take previously prepared cold coffee, made identically to the above method, and reheat this coffee to 85°C. Take pH of coffee. Record data in the following table.

Results: Rate as a paired comparison sensory test for lighter or darker brown; more clear or more cloudy; stimulating aroma or less aroma; and stronger or weaker flavor.

Age of Coffee	Color	Clarity	Aroma	Flavor	pH	
					Water	Coffee
Fresh						
Reheated coffee						

Conclusions: Did one coffee taste more bitter? Which?

Which coffee-making principle would indicate that these two coffees might differ?

❖Experiment II: Flavor of Coffee Made with Fresh Water Brought Just to Boiling versus Water Previously Boiled for an Extended Time

Objective: To taste the difference between coffees with and without natural gases from water present.

Variables:

A. Take pH of water before and after boiling. Prepare coffee by the drip method using a drip coffee maker with a filter. Place (10.6 g) 2 T of drip grind coffee in the filter paper, which has been formed into a cone shape. Place this in the Chemex or similar drip coffee pot. Heat (474 ml) 2 c fresh cold tap water to boiling. Immediately pour (355 ml) 1 1/2 c into hot measure and pour into the filter paper with the coffee. As soon as coffee no longer drips, it is ready to serve.

B. In a second identical coffee maker, prepare coffee as above, but use the previously boiled water provided by the instructor.

Take pH of coffee.

Record data in the table.

Results: Rate as a paired comparison sensory test for lighter or darker brown; more or less clear; more or less aroma; and more or less full flavor.

Water Variation for Coffee	Color	Clarity	Aroma	Flavor	pH of Water Before	After	pH of Coffee
Water brought just to boiling							
Water boiled for an extended time							

Conclusions: What was the difference in coffee flavor?

Which coffee-making principle would indicate that these two coffees might differ?

Why might water that had boiled for some time affect coffee flavor?

How was the pH of the water affected by boiling?

❖Experiment III: Comparison of Various Coffee Types

Objective: To identify types, advantages, and disadvantages of coffee preparation.

Variables:

A. Percolator coffee: Place (21.2 g) 4 T regular grind coffee in the basket of a percolator. Put 3 c cold tap water in the pot. Set on medium strength and plug in.

B. Freeze-dried coffee: Bring to a boil (355 ml) 1 1/2 c fresh cold tap water. Measure out 1 measuring cup of water and add (.8 g) 3/4 t coffee.

C. Instant coffee: Bring to a boil (355 ml) 1 1/2 c fresh cold tap water. Measure out 1 measuring cup of water and add (.6 g) 3/4 t instant coffee.

D. Instant flavored coffee: Bring (355 ml) 1 1/2 c fresh cold tap water to a boil. Measure out 1 measuring cup of water and add (.6 g) 3/4 t flavored coffee.

E. Espresso coffee: Follow directions for espresso coffee maker.

F. Drip coffee: Obtain (118 ml) 1/2 c drip coffee from the unit used in Experiment I.

Take pH of each coffee and record data in the table.

Results: Rate each coffee on a 9-point hedonic scale with 9 = extremely brown, extremely clear, extremely bitter, and extremely full flavored, and 1 = light brown, extremely cloudy, extremely mild, and extremely lacking in flavor.

Type of Coffee	Brownness	Clarity	Bitterness	Strength of Flavor	pH
Percolator					
Freeze dried					
Instant					
Flavored					
Espresso					
Drip					

Conclusions: Do some coffees seem to have more full-bodied flavor than others?

Which?

Drip coffee makers provide a means to retain a temperature below boiling and retain more aromatic compounds than percolators (a). Drip coffee makers have a variety of nonelectric designs (b), and electric designs (c). Espresso drip coffee makers (d) operate on the same principle.

❖Experiment IV: Comparison of Methods of Tea Making

Objective: To taste difference in bitterness and flavor of tea due to brewing temperature and processing.

Procedure: Take pH of water.
Prepare the following variables.
Take pH of final product and record results in table below.

Variables:

A. Steeped: Prepare black tea using loose leaves. Bring to boil about (474 ml) 2 c fresh cold tap water. Rinse two teapots with about (118 ml) 1/2 c boiling water. Put (.75 g) 1/2 t tea leaves into the pots or into tea balls and then into pots. Pour (237 ml) 1 c boiling water over the leaves. Cover the pot and let steep for 3 min. Stir. After brewing 3 min, strain the tea into another previously heated pot immediately or remove the tea ball.

B. Boiled: Bring to a boil about (355 ml) 1 1/2 c fresh cold tap water. Rinse pot with about (118 ml) 1/2 c boiling water. Measure (.75 g) 1/2 t tea leaves into the pan with 1 c boiling water. Boil for 3 min. Stir. After boiling 3 min, strain the tea into the previously heated pot immediately.

C. Instant: Bring to a boil about (355 ml) 1 1/2 c fresh cold tap water. Rinse pot with about (118 ml) 1/2 c boiling water. Measure (.75 g) 1/2 t instant tea and put into the teapot. Pour (237 ml) 1 c boiling water over the instant tea.

Results: Rate color and flavor on a 9-point hedonic scale with 9 = darkest color, most bitter flavor, and most full flavor, and 1 = lightest color, most mild flavor, and least full flavor.

Method	Color	Bitterness	Full Flavor	pH	Comments
Steeped					
Boiled					
Instant					

Conclusions: What principles of tea making are not adhered to in variable B?

How does the instant tea compare with steeped tea? Do you notice a difference in aroma?

Experiment V: Comparison of Types of Tea

Objective: To taste the flavor difference due to fermentation and leaf size and additives in tea.

Using the direction of experiment IV. A., make 1 c each of the following teas and record results in the table.

Procedure: Take pH of water.
Prepare the following variables.
Take pH of final tea and record results in table below.
Variables: black, oolong, green, jasmine, herb tea, spiced tea.

Results: Rank color and aroma on a 9-point hedonic scale with 9 = extremely dark color and extremely strong aroma, and 1 = extremely light color and extremely weak aroma. Identify strength and type of flavor.

Type of Tea	Color	Aroma	Flavor	pH	Comments
Black					
Oolong					
Green					
Jasmine					
Herb					
Spiced					

Conclusions: Which teas were lightest in color? Why?

Which teas were darker in color? Why?

Which teas were most bitter? Why?

Which teas were least bitter?

What other flavor differences did you notice?

Solutions and Ice Crystallization

Notes:

I. Composition of Solutions

A solution consists of two or more substances. The substance that contains the other is the *solvent*. That which dissolves in the solvent is the *solute*.

To dissolve, the orderly nature of a crystal is destroyed. Like molecules become separated from each other. Water is the primary solvent in food products. Water surrounds molecules freed from a crystal very quickly. Water has dipole-ion attractive forces with the solute. Water also forms strong hydrogen bonds. Example below:

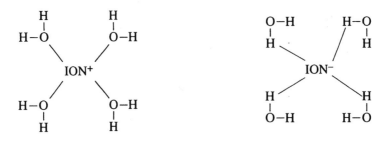

II. Colligative Properties of Solutions

Certain properties of a solution depend on the concentration of the solution. These are called colligative properties. The following are colligative properties.

A. Vapor Pressure

A solute dissolved in a solvent will lower the vapor pressure; that is, the pressure for the solvent to evaporate. An example is the sugar solution. When sugar is added to a solvent such as water, the water is less apt to evaporate. Food with a high sugar concentration keeps more moist because of this lowered vapor pressure.

B. Boiling Point Elevation

A nonvolatile solute added to a solvent will raise the boiling point of the solvent. When salt is added to water, the sodium chloride ionizes to sodium and chloride ions. These ions lower the *vapor pressure*. In addition, the *boiling* temperature is elevated .52°C for each mole of sodium and of chloride.

Sugar in solution raises the boiling point even more than would be expected by the molecular concentration. Hydrogen bonding of the sugar molecule to water is probably the mechanism for the greater rise in boiling point.

Examples of boiling points for sugar in water at specific concentrations are:

70% sucrose	106.5°C
80% sucrose	112.0°C
90.8% sucrose	130.0°C

C. Freezing Point Depression

Increasing concentrations of solute in a solution lowers the freezing point. One gram molecular weight per 1000 g solution of a nonelectrolyte will depress the freezing point 1.86°C. For electrolytes, 1.86°C must be multiplied by the number of ions per molecule. The presence of foreign molecules or ions in solutions delay the crystallization process until a colder temperature is reached.

D. Osmotic Pressure

The osmotic pressure of the solvent rises when particles are dissolved in a solvent.

III. Application of Colligative Properties

Knowing the effects of solution concentration on the above properties can be useful in the preparation of solutions. Examples include:

A. Boiling point of solutions can be used to estimate the concentration of sugar solutions.

B. Concentration of solute in a frozen product can be used to estimate the freezing temperature.

WATER CRYSTALLIZATION: FROZEN DESSERTS

Goal: To observe and taste the effect of formula and procedure on crystal size of frozen desserts.

Objectives: To taste the difference in smoothness due to turning speed.
To taste the effect of stabilizers and egg on crystal size and body of ice cream and other frozen desserts.
To taste the effect on smoothness, body, and mouthfeel of reduced-fat formulas using fat replacers in frozen dessert formulas.
To observe the decreased freezing point due to concentration of sugar in solution.
To identify the differences in formula for ice cream, sherbet, ices, and frozen yogurt.

Frozen desserts are generally sugar solutions that have been reduced in temperature until crystallization is attained. The concentration of sugar affects the colligative property: *freezing point depression*. Since most frozen desserts are sugar solutions, they must attain a temperature below 0°C to form ice crystals. Commercially, electric ice cream freezers reduce the temperature of the freezing coolant. In home freezers, a salt/ice mixture will absorb heat from the ice cream mix at temperatures below 0°. The higher the salt concentration, the more heat it will absorb; thus the faster ice cream will freeze.

Crystal size depends on freezing speed, turning speed, and ingredients that separate and stabilize crystals such as fat, concentrated sugar solution, gums, and fat replacers.

General Directions for Freezing Frozen Desserts

1. Wash equipment in hot soapy water. Rinse well.

2. Place mix into freezer.

3. Measure height of mix on can.

4. Layer ice and salt around dessert mix in a ratio of 8:1 to within 1 in. of the top of freezer. Be careful not to get any ice or salt inside freezer container.

> 4 c ice—bottom
> (72 g) 1/4 c salt
> 2 c ice
> (72 g) 1/4 c salt
> 2 c ice
> (144 g) 1/2 c salt

5. Turn according to directions.

6. As ice melts, add ice and salt in 8:1 ratio to level of mix in freezer.

7. Record temperature when mix is frozen.

8. Remove dasher and pack into bottom of freezer; mark level on can of ice cream; allow to ripen.

9. Compute overrun:

$$\text{Percent overrun} = \frac{\text{height ice cream} - \text{height of mix}}{\text{height of mix}} \times 100$$

I. Experiments: Frozen Desserts Turned Continuously While Freezing

❖A. **Effect of rate of turning ice cream**

Philadelphia or Plain Ice Cream
(474 ml) 2 c thin cream (16–18% fat)   (4 ml) 3/4 t vanilla
(75 g) 3/8 c sugar   (1 g) 1/8 t salt

Procedure: Read general directions above. Mix ingredients, stirring to dissolve sugar. Freeze, using an 8:1 ice and salt mixture. Use one recipe for each variant.
1. Turn at 40 revolutions per min—slow.
2. Turn at 40 revolutions per min for 3 min, then 100 revolutions per min.

❖B. Effect of stabilizer on ice cream

Plain Ice Cream with Stabilizer
(.2 g) Sea Kem* and (.8 g) CMC—7HF (Aquaton)*

(474 m) 2 c thin cream (16–18% fat)	(4 ml) 3/4 t vanilla
(75 g) 3/8 c sugar	(1 g) 1/8 t salt

Procedure: Read general directions on page 23. Mix Sea Kem or CMC with sugar thoroughly, then beat into remaining ingredients. Freeze using 8:1 ice/salt mixture at 40 revolutions per min for 3 min, then 100 revolutions per min.

❖C. Effect of egg yolk in ice cream

Custard Ice Cream

(15 g) 1 egg yolk, slightly beaten	(1 g) 1/8 t salt
(237 ml) 1 c milk, scalded	(474 ml) 2 c thin cream (16-18% fat)
(100 g) 1/2 c sugar	(6 ml) 1 1/2 t vanilla

Procedure: Read general directions on page 23. Beat egg just enough to mix, but not foam. Scald milk, cool slightly. Add sugar, salt, and milk to egg. Cook over hot, not boiling, water, such as a double boiler, stirring constantly until mixture *coats spoon*. Immediately remove from hot water and set in cold water to stop cooking. Cool. If custard curdles slightly, place in cold water and beat with a rotary beater. To cooked custard add cream and vanilla. Freeze, using an 8:1 ice and salt mixture. Turn at 40 revolutions per min for 3 min, then 100 revolutions per min or freeze with electric freezer until frozen.

D. **Effect of fat replacements used in ice cream and frozen desserts**
Fat replacement is a major reformulation project for most food companies in the 1990s. A variety of fat replacers are being used in industry to duplicate the functional qualities of fat in traditional recipes. These qualities include flavor, mouthfeel, increased tenderness, and texture. Formulas for a variety of frozen desserts using fat replacers follow.

1. **Effect of Paselli SA2 in low-fat frozen dessert**

Reduced Fat Plain Ice Cream

(10 g) 1 1/2 T Paselli SA2*	(237 ml) 1 c skim milk
(75 g) 3/8 c sugar	(1 g) 1/8 t salt
(237 ml) 1 c milk (3.25%)	(4 ml) 3/4 t vanilla

Procedure: Read general directions on p. 23. Mix paselli with sugar and warm in the microwave with 1 c milk for 4 min. Stir once. Add skim milk, salt, and vanilla. Freeze using 8:1 ice/salt mixture. Turn at 40 revolutions per min for 3 min, then 100 revolutions per min, or freeze with electric freezer until frozen.

2. **Effect of Paselli SA2 and stabilizer in low-fat frozen dessert**

Reduced Fat Plain Ice Cream

(88 g) 3/8 c + 1 T sugar	(540 ml) 2 1/4 c whole milk (3.25% fat)
(24 g) 1/8 c nonfat dry milk	(48 ml) 1/4 c skim milk
(20 g) 3 T whey powder	(60 g) 3 T corn syrup 42DE*
(10 g) 1 1/2 T Paselli SA2*	(5 ml) 1 t vanilla
(4.0 g) 1 t stabilizer (Kontrol)*	

Procedure: Read general directions on p. 23. Stir sugar, nonfat milk, whey powder, Paselli , and stabilizer together. Add 240 ml milk and heat in microwave on high power for 4 min., stirring once. Mix remaining milk, corn syrup, and vanilla. Add to hot milk mixture. Place in ice cream freezer. Cool. Freeze in electric ice cream freezer.

*Source listed in Appendix B

3. **Effect of N-Lite D on nonfat chocolate frozen dessert**

   Variables:
   a. Nonfat frozen dessert
   b. Control frozen dessert

Nonfat Frozen Dessert
(60 g) 1/4 c + 1 T sugar
(5 g) 2 t N-Lite D*
(8 g) 1 T + 1 t cocoa powder
(2 g) 1/2 t Sherex 302*
(20 g) 1 T corn syrup
(250 ml) 1 c + 1 T skim milk

Control
(60 g) 1/4 c + 1 T sugar
(0 g) N-Lite D
(8 g) 1 T + 1 t cocoa powder
(2 g) 1/2 t Sherex 302*
(20 g) 1 T corn syrup
(250 ml) 1 c + 1 T half & half

Procedure: See general directions on p. 23. Mix dry ingredients together well. Add corn syrup and milk or half & half. Heat to 175°F for 30 seconds and hold 5 min (not boiling). Cool to 40°F in ice. Freeze in electric ice cream freezer.

E. **Effect of formula on crystal size in ice**

Lemon Ice (no stabilizer)
(200 g) 1 c sugar   (474 ml) 2 c water
(75 g) 3/8 c lemon juice (use fresh lemons)

Procedure: See general directions on p. 23. Mix ingredients, stirring until sugar dissolves. Freeze, using an 8:1 ice and salt mixture. Freeze in electric ice cream freezer.

Lemon Ice with Gelatin
(1 g) 1/2 t gelatin   (200 g) 1 c sugar
(474 ml) 2 c water   (88 ml) 6 T lemon juice (use fresh lemons)

Procedure: Read general directions on p. 23. Add 1/2 t gelatin to 1 T cold water; allow to hydrate. Stir remaining water and sugar together; heat to boiling. Stir the hydrated gelatin into the hot syrup. Cool to 30°C. Add lemon juice. Freeze, using an 8:1 ice and salt mixture in an ice cream freezer. Freeze in electric ice cream freezer.

Lemon Ice with Egg Whites
(237 ml) 1 c water   (2 g) 1 t grated lemon rind (1 lemon)
(200 g) 1 c sugar   (11 g) 1/2 c lemon juice (use fresh lemons)
(1 g) 1/8 t salt   (20 g) 1 egg white, frozen pasteurized*

Procedure: Stir water, sugar, and salt over low heat until sugar is dissolved. Boil mixture rapidly for 5 min. Cool. Add rind and juice. Beat egg white to a soft peak. Beat sugar syrup into beaten egg white. Place in freezer and turn until firm using an ice and salt mixture of 8:1. Freeze in electric ice cream freezer.

F. **Effect of Formula on Crystal Size in Sherbet**

Lemon Sherbet
(2 g) 1 t grated lemon rind   (150 g) 3/4 c sugar
(60 ml) 1/4 c lemon juice   (1 g) 1/8 t salt
   from fresh lemons   (474 ml) 2 c milk, chilled

Procedure: Read general directions on p. 23. Mix lemon rind and juice. Add sugar and salt. Stir until sugar is dissolved. Chill. Pour mixture slowly into chilled milk, stirring constantly. Place in freezer and turn until firm, using an ice and salt mixture of 8:1. Freeze in electric ice cream freezer.

*Source indicated in Appendix B.

Orange Cream Sherbet—Use 1/2 recipe

(150 g) 3/4 c sugar

(30 ml) 2 T lemon juice

(237 ml) 1 c orange juice

(119 ml) 1/2 c milk

(119 ml) 1/2 c thin cream (16–18% fat)

(20 g) 1 egg white, frozen pasteurized*

Procedure: Read general directions on p. 23. Set aside 2 T sugar. Dissolve the remaining sugar in the fruit juices. Gradually add milk and cream, stirring constantly. Beat egg white to soft peak. Gradually beat in reserved sugar. Beat to stiff peak. Fold liquid mixture into the egg white. Freeze using an 8:1 ice and salt mixture in an electric ice cream freezer.

G. Effect of Fat Replacer in Frozen Yogurt

Nonfat Frozen Yogurt

(58 g) 1/4 c nonfat dry milk solids

(52 g) 1/4 c cane sugar

(21 g) 1 T corn syrup (36DE)*

(40 g) 2 T + 2 t yogurt

(8 g) N-Lite D*

(3.4 g) Sherex*

(250 ml) 1 c water

Procedure: Read general directions on p. 23. Mix dry ingredients together well. Heat with water to 175°F for 30 seconds and hold (not boiling) for 5 min. Add corn syrup and yogurt. Cool to 40°F in ice and freeze in electric ice cream freezer.

*Source indicated in Appendix B.

H. Frozen desserts

Results: Record data for time and temperature to freeze and percent overrun. Rate texture, flavor, and body on a 9-point hedonic scale with 9 = extremely smooth, extremely desirable flavor, and mouthfeel, to 1 = extremely grainy, extremely undesirable flavor, and extremely undesirable mouthfeel.

Ice Cream	Rate of Freezing	Min to Freeze	Temp. when Frozen	% Overrun	Texture	Flavor	Body
A1. Plain or Philly	40 rpm						
A2.	40 rpm for 3 min then 100						
B. Stabilizer in ice cream	40 rpm for 3 min then 100						
C. Custard ice cream	40 rpm for 3 min then 100						
D. Ice cream 1	100 rpm						
w/ paselli 2							
D2 a. Frozen dessert control	40 rpm for 3 min then 100						
D2 b. Frozen dessert with N Lite D nonfat	40 rpm for 3 min then 100						
E1. Lemon ice no stabilizer	100 rpm						
E2. Lemon ice gelatin	100 rpm						
E3. Lemon ice plus egg white	100 rpm						
F1. Lemon sherbet	100 rpm						
Nonfat Frozen Yogurt	100 rpm						

Conclusions: How does speed of stirring affect crystal size?

Why does turning rate need to be carefully regulated at beginning of freezing?

What ingredients are used to maintain small ice crystals in frozen desserts?

What ingredients may be used as fat substitutes? Why?

How did paselli and N-Lite D affect ice cream mouthfeel?

What are the functions of Sea Kem, carrageenen, or CMC (carboxymethyl cellulose) in frozen dessert formula?

Indicate what ingredient separates crystals in each of the lemon ice variables.

What causes overrun? What ingredients may increase overrun?

How does the formula for frozen yogurt differ from a nonfat frozen dessert?

Is the frozen yogurt product smooth?

II. Experiments: Frozen Desserts Made Without Continuous Stirring

A. Ice Cream

(237 ml) 1 c heavy cream, whipped
(28 g) 1 sq (1 oz) unsweetened chocolate
(158 ml) 2/3 c sweetened condensed milk

(158 ml) 2/3 c water
(98 ml) 1 1/2 t vanilla

Procedure: Whip heavy cream until stiff. Set aside. Melt unsweetened chocolate. Add condensed milk and water; continue to warm to disperse chocolate. Add vanilla. Fold in whipped cream. Pour into ice cube tray. Place in freezer. Stir occasionally from sides and bottom of tray. Allow 2–4 hours for freezing.

B. Strawberry Parfait

(60 g) 3 T egg whites, frozen, pasteurized;*
    beaten stiff
(100 g) 1/2 c sugar

(28 ml) 6 T water
(237 ml) 1 c heavy cream whipped
(237 ml) 1 c crushed fresh strawberries

Procedure: Beat egg whites to a stiff peak. Set aside. Boil sugar and water to soft-ball stage (234°F, 114°C). Pour slowly onto egg whites, and continue beating until room temperature. Beat heavy cream until stiff. Add cream and strawberries to egg white mixture. Pour into ice cube tray and freeze.

*Source indicated in Appendix B.

Results: Rate texture, flavor, and body on a 9-point hedonic scale, with 9 = extremely smooth, extremely desirable flavor, and extremely desirable mouthfeel, to 1 = extremely grainy, extremely undesirable flavor, and extremely undesirable mouthfeel.

Dessert	How Frozen	Body	Texture	Flavor
A. Ice cream	Freeze without continuous stirring			
B. Strawberry parfait	Without stirring			

Conclusions: Compare freezing point depression of ice, ice cream, and sherbet. Why do these differ?

What limited the crystal size in frozen desserts made without continuous stirring?

Sugar Solutions and Crystallization

Notes:

SUGAR SOLUTIONS

Goal: To observe the characteristics and effects of added ingredients on sugar solutions when saturated, supersaturated, and following crystallization.

Objectives: To compare the relationship between sugar concentrations and boiling temperature of a sugar solution.
To observe the degree of crystallization or lack of crystallization resultant from varying sugar concentrations.
To observe the effect of cooking, speed of beating, and added ingredients on crystal size of crystalline candies.
To differentiate between crystalline and noncrystalline candies.
To compare temperature readings in Celsius and Fahrenheit.

Factors that affect consistency and crystallization include not only final cooking temperature (final concentration of sugar) but also added ingredients such as acids that with heat produce more soluble monosaccharides, fats that separate crystals, and gums such as carrageenen.

I. Thermometer Calibration

A. Fill a saucepan 1/2 full of water.

B. Boil water.

C. Center thermometer in water, read the thermometer at eye level, and record the temperature at which water boils.

D. If reading is lower than 100°C, *add* the difference from 100°C to all future thermometer readings of that thermometer. (For example, if thermometer reads 98°C at boiling, always add 2°C to each reading when cooking. If thermometer reads 115°C, assume it to be 117°C.)

E. If reading is higher than 100°C, *subtract* the difference from 100°C from all future thermometer readings. (For example, if thermometer reads 102°C at boiling, always subtract 2°C from each reading when cooking. If thermometer reads 115°C, assume it to be 113°C.)

II. Tests for Stages of Sugar Cookery

Place 300 g sucrose and 175 ml hot water in 500 cc beaker. Place beaker on an asbestos pad and bring to a boil. Using a thermometer suspended from a ring stand, cook the sugar syrup to the various stages listed below. Make sure the bulb of the thermometer is covered with syrup but not touching the bottom of the beaker. Also, readings should be made with the eye at a right angle to the upper level of the mercury in the thermometer. At each stage remove approximately 1/2 teaspoonful and place in 125 ml of fresh cold water. If the sample can be removed from the water, place it on waxed paper and observe the degree of firmness.

Test	Temperature °F	Temperature °C	Temp. (°C) Sample Removed	Description of Sample	Example of Product
Thread	230–236	110–113			
Soft ball	235–240	113–116			
Firm ball	246–250	119–121			
Hard ball	250–265	121–129			
Soft crack	270–290	132–143			
Hard crack	300–310	149–154			
Caramel	320–348	160–177			

Conclusions: Why does boiling cause the temperature to rise?

What does temperature tell you about sugar concentration?

III. Effect of Dry Heat on Sucrose

Heat 150 g sucrose slowly in heavy frying pan. Stir with a wooden spoon. When liquid, pour out a small portion on a buttered sheet of waxed paper. Continue heating slowly until a golden brown color results. Pour 1/2 on the paper. Add a pinch of soda (about 1/16 t) to the remaining portion. Stir and pour out the paper.

Liquid	Temperature	Product Formed	Color	Texture	Flavor
1. Clear	320°F 160°C				
2. Brown	348°F 177°C				
3. Soda added	320°F 160°C				

Conclusions: Does sugar melt?

At what temperature does sugar caramelize?

How and why did baking soda change the characteristics of the melted sugar?

IV. Sugar Solutions: Crystalline Candies

❖A. Fondant

(250 ml) 1 c water

(400 g) 2 c sugar

(.4 g) 1/8 t cream of tartar *OR*

(41 g) 2 T light corn syrup

General Directions: Before beating, rinse plate with cold water. Dry plate. Place thermometer with mercury column up on plate (on wire rack), and tape thermometer in position. Pour candy on plate to cool. Leave undisturbed until desired temperature is reached (don't move or jar!!). Beat with a heavy spoon or heavy mixer.

Procedure: Mix ingredients, stir, and heat to boiling point on high heat. Turn heat down to medium. Cook without stirring to temperature indicated in your variable. Wash crystals from sides of pan as they form, or cover pan a few minutes while cooking to dissolve them. Pour mixture onto a prepared plate as indicated under general directions. Cool to temperature indicated in your variable. When cooled appropriately, stir and work back and forth until mixture is white and creamy. Then knead until smooth.

Variables:

1. **Effect of temperature of beating (use cream of tartar in place of corn syrup)**

Procedure: Read general directions. Cook to soft ball stage: 237°F (114°C). 1 1/2 times recipe or 1/2 recipe for each variable (use cream of tartar). Divide cooked fondant between three plates:
   a. Beat immediately
   b. Cool to 70°C; beat as indicated above
   c. Cool to 40°C; beat as indicated above

2. **Effect of addition of other sugars (use corn syrup in place of cream of tartar)**

Procedure: Read general directions. Prepare 1/2 recipe of A. Fondant (use corn syrup in place of cream of tartar). Cook to soft ball stage: 114°C (237°F). Cool to 104°F (40°C) before beating.

3. **Effect of cream in place of water**

Cream Fondant

(250 ml) 1 c half & half cream

(400 g) 2 c sugar

(.4 g) 1/8 t cream of tartar

Procedure: Read general directions. Mix ingredients and heat on medium heat, stirring constantly until mixture boils. Adjust heat so that it continues to boil but does not scorch. Wash crystals from side of pan. Cook to 114°C. Pour onto plate and cool as indicated in general directions. Cool to 60°. Stir until creamy and knead until smooth.

a   b   c

The hot liquid saturated sugar solution (a) becomes supersaturated when cooled. When the supersaturated solution is disturbed, crystal nucleii form and other crystals build on these (b). The lower the cooling temperature before disturbing (stirring), the more supersaturated the solution and the more crystal nucleii form, resulting in smaller crystals and a smoother mouthfeel (c).

Results: Record cooking temperature, beating temperature, and beating time needed to crystallize. Rate on a 9-point hedonic scale, with 9 = extremely white color and extremely smooth texture, to 1 = extremely grey color and extremely course. Rate consistency on a scale from 9 = extremely firm, to 5 = moldable, and 1 = extremely runny.

Variation	Cooking Temp. °C	Beating Temp. °C	Beating Time	Color	Texture	Consistency	Flavor
A. Fondant							
1 a. Beating temp.	114	114					
b.	114	70					
c.	114	40					
2. Corn syrup	114	40					
3. Cream in place of water (cream of tartar)	114	60					

Conclusions: What are the functions of cream of tartar in a crystalline candy?

Why may cream of tartar be replaced with corn syrup?

How does temperature of beating affect crystal nuclei formation?

What is the effect on crystal size of replacing water with cream? Why?

Why is there a color difference in fondant made with cream of tartar vs. fondant made with corn syrup?

B. Fudge

(75 ml) 1/3 c evaporated milk
(225 g) 1 c + 2 T sugar
(45 ml) 3 T water
(27 g) 1 T + 1 t corn syrup

(1 1/2 g) 1/4 t salt
(35.5 g) 1 1/4 oz baking chocolate (1 sq. = 1 oz)
(19 g) 1 T + 1 t margarine
(2.5 ml) 1/2 t vanilla extract

Procedure: Mix sugar, milk, water, corn syrup, salt, and chocolate. Cook and stir over medium heat until sugar dissolves and chocolate melts. Cook to temperature indicated in experiment below. Add vanilla. Add margarine. Remove from heat. Cool as indicated in experiment below. Beat until candy is creamy and has lost its gloss, then pour quickly into oiled pans, making a 3/4- to 1-in. layer. Cut into 1-in. squares when nearly cold. It may be kneaded and molded if preferred.

Variables:
   ❖1. **Effect of temperature of cooking: Correlation of end point temperature and concentration**

Procedure: 1 1/2 times recipe or 1/2 recipe for each variable. Follow directions for fudge (B) above.
   a. Pour out 1/2 recipe at 110°C; cool to 40°C; beat with heavy mixer.
   b. Pour out 1/2 recipe at 113°C; cool to 40°C; beat with heavy mixer.
   c. Cook 1/2 recipe to 118°; pour out; cool to 40°C; beat with heavy mixer.

2. **Effect of temperature of beating and speed of beating on crystal size**

Procedure: 1 1/2 times recipe or 1/2 recipe for each variable. Follow directions for fudge (B) above. Cook to 113°C. Divide between three bowls.
   a. Beat immediately on low speed.
   b. Cool to 40°C; beat on low speed.
   c. Cool to 40°C; beat on high speed.

3. **Microwave Fudge**
   (200 g) 1 c sugar   (20.5 g) 1 T corn syrup
   (28.2 g) 1/4 c cocoa   (60 g) 1/4 c margarine
   (80 ml) 1/3 c half & half   (7.5 ml) 1 1/2 t vanilla

Procedure: Lightly butter plate. Mix sugar and cocoa in 2 qt Pyrex bowl. Add half & half, corn syrup, and margarine. Cook for time specified below. Remove immediately. Add vanilla, place thermometer into bowl, and record temperature after 1 1/2 min. Pour into mixing bowl of electric counter-top mixer. Beat on high speed until mixture loses its gloss. Pour onto plate.

Variables: One recipe for each variable.
   a. Cook 1 recipe on high 3 min, then cook on medium 5 min.
   b. Cook 1 recipe. Choose time to make best product. Cook on high 3 min, then cook on medium either 4 1/2 or 5 1/2 min.

C. **Divinity:** Effect of protein addition
   (255 g) 1 1/4 c sugar   (1 1/2 g) 1/4 t salt
   (61.5 g) 2 1/2 T light corn syrup   (6.2 g) 2 1/2 T egg white
   (75 ml) 1/2 c water   (2.5 ml) 1/2 t vanilla extract

Procedures: Cook sugar, syrup, water, and salt to hard-ball stage (260°F, 127°C). Using electric counter-top mixer, beat egg whites until stiff peak is reached. Pour slightly cooled sugar solution over egg whites while constantly beating on high speed. Beat until candy holds its shape. Add vanilla. Pour into oiled pans. Cut into squares when cold. Candy may be formed into irregular pieces by dropping it from tip of spoon onto wax paper.

Results: Record end point cooking temperature and beating time and temperature. Rate color from extremely dark to extremely light, texture from extremely course to extremely fine, and consistency from extremely firm to extremely runny.

Variation		Cooking Temp. °C	Beating Temp. °C	Beating Time	Color	Texture	Consistency	Flavor
B. Fudge								
1. Cooking temp.	a							
	b							
	c							
2. Beating temp. and speed	a							
	b							
	c							
3. Microwave	a							
	b							
C. Divinity								

Conclusions: What functions do milk, cream, chocolate, and egg white serve in crystalline candies?

How does temperature of beating affect crystalline nuclei formation?

How are the colligative properties of solutions illustrated in these experiments?

How does cooking temperature affect sugar concentration?

Why may microwave times be difficult to determine when making fudge?

V. Sugar Solution: Noncrystalline Candies
❖A. Vanilla Caramels—Cook to end point temperature of 118°C.

(130 g) 1 c + 2 T sugar
(65 g) 1/3 c brown sugar
(75 ml) 1/3 c light corn syrup
(150 ml) 2/3 c light cream

(14 g) 1 T margarine
(1 g) 3/16 t salt
(5 ml) 1 t vanilla extract

Variables:

1. Effect of fat and protein content of milk products on consistency:
   a. One recipe—use light cream.
   b. One recipe—use evaporated milk in place of cream.

Procedure: Mix all ingredients except vanilla. Place on medium high heat initially and *lower heat as cooking continues.* Stir occasionally at beginning of cooking and constantly toward end of process. Cook to firm-ball stage (118°C). Add vanilla. Turn into oiled pan. Cool. Cut into 3/4-in. squares. Remove from pan. This is a soft, rich, chewy caramel.

2. Effect of gum on consistency: One recipe with carrageenan.

Procedure: Add 1.5 g carrageenan (Sea Gel GP 713*) to 40 g sugar. Disperse in light cream. Heat to 85°C. Add corn syrup and remaining sugar. Blend in blender for 5 seconds. Return to sauce pan and cook to 118°C, stirring occasionally at beginning, and lowering heat and stirring constantly near the end of cooking. Add vanilla, salt, and margarine. Remove from heat. Turn into oiled pan. Cool. Cut into 3/4-in. squares. Remove from pan. This is a soft, rich, chewy caramel.

B. Peanut Brittle

(200 g) 1 c sugar	(19 g) 1 T + 1 t margarine
(155 ml) 2/3 c light corn syrup	(190 g) 1 1/3 c raw (unblanched) peanuts
(75 ml) 1/3 c water	(5 ml) 1 t vanilla extract
(3 g) 1/2 t salt	(7 g) 1 3/4 t baking soda

Procedure: Cook sugar, syrup, water, salt, and margarine to soft-ball stage (234–240°F, 112–116°C). Add unblanched peanuts. Continue cooking slowly until syrup is light brown and meets hard-crack test (306°F, 152°C). Remove from heat. Add vanilla and soda. Mix ingredients well. Pour onto oiled baking sheet, spreading as thin as possible. When mixture is nearly cool, wet hands in cold water, and turn candy over, stretching to desired thinness. Cut into squares or break into pieces.

C. Lollipops

(90 ml or 123 g) 3/8 c light corn syrup	vegetable coloring
(75 ml) 1/3 c water	(5 ml) 1 t flavoring
(100 g) 1/2 c sugar	

Procedure: Cook sugar, syrup, and water to 310°F, 155°C. Stir only until sugar is dissolved. Remove any crystals that form on sides of pan. Cook slowly toward end of process so syrup does not scorch. Cook to extreme hard crack stage (310°F, 155°C). Remove from heat and add coloring and flavoring, stirring only enough to mix.

    Drop mixture from tip of a tablespoon onto a smooth, oiled surface, taking care to make drops round. Press a toothpick or skewer into edge of each before it hardens. Any decorations are pressed on at same time. Candies should be loosened from slab before they are quite cold to prevent cracking.

*Source listed in Appendix B

Variation	Cooking Temp.	Color	Texture	Flavor
A. Vanilla caramels				
1. Light cream				
2. Evaporated milk				
3. Carrageenan				
B. Peanut brittle				
C. Lollipops				

Conclusions: Why do these candies not crystallize?

Why do light cream and evaporated milk cause differing consistencies in caramel?

Aeration of peanut brittle mixture is obtained by what process?

What function does carrageenan serve in caramels?

What does the boiling temperature tell you about concentration of these sugar solutions?

MICROSCOPIC EXAMINATION OF SUGAR CRYSTALLIZATION

Procedure: Place 1 dot (needle-tip size) of candy on slide; with toothpick stir in 1 drop glycerine. Place cover slip on slide and adjust on microscope. Compare number and size of crystals

Results: Draw a diagram of the crystal size in the box beside each variable.

IV. A. Fondant
1a. Beaten hot

1b. Beaten at 70°C

1c. Beaten at 40°C

IV. B. Fudge
1a. Cooked to 100°C

1b. Cooked to 113°C

1c. Cooked to 118°C

IV. C. Divinity

V. C. Lollipop
Do you see crystals?

Fats and Oils

Notes:

FATS, EMULSIONS, AND SALADS

Use of Fats and Oils in Salad Dressings

Goals: To make, recognize, and use temporary and permanent emulsions as salad dressings.
To make salads using a variety of fruits, vegetables, and legumes.

Objectives: To form and reconstitute an emulsion.
To use emulsifying agents and stabilizers in salad dressing emulsions.
To be able to distinguish between the types of salad dressings.
To taste a variety of salad dressings.
To taste low-fat and no-fat salad dressings.
To use ingredient formulations that limit fat in salad dressings.
To identify salad greens.
To gain recognition of quality in salad preparations.

An emulsion is a dispersion of one immiscible liquid in another. Dispersions of water and oil are the most common food emulsions. Emulsions may be either *permanent* or *temporary*. Without emulsifiers or stabilizers the components of emulsions separate quickly. These emulsions are called *temporary*. Emulsifying agents such as lecithin or egg yolk or stabilizers such as starch, powders, or gums will enable the emulsion to remain *permanent*.

The fat content in salad dressings traditionally ranged from 30–75%. The standard of identity for mayonnaise is 65% fat; the standard for mayonnaise-type salad dressing is 30% fat. Other salad dressing emulsions often contain 65–75% fat. With the emphasis on reducing dietary fat, many reduced fat and no-fat salad dressings have been developed. These often contain carbohydrate-based fat replacers. Some of the following experiments utilize these ingredients. Xanthan gum and alginates are examples of gums used as fat replacers, and Thermflo and N-Lite L are examples of starch-based fat replacers.

I.A. Composition of Fats and Oils

Results: From reading the labels of the following fats, compare total fat, saturated fat, polyunsaturated fat, and monounsaturated fat in edible fats and oils. Record data in table below.

	Total Fat g/T	Saturated Fat g/T	Polyunsaturated g/ Tbsp	Monounsaturated Fat g/T	Emulsifier/ Stabilizer	Cal/T
Butter	_____	_____	_____	_____	_____	_____
Margarine*	_____	_____	_____	_____	_____	_____
Marg spread A*	_____	_____	_____	_____	_____	_____
Marg spread B*	_____	_____	_____	_____	_____	_____
Diet margarine	_____	_____	_____	_____	_____	_____
Lard	_____	_____	_____	_____	_____	_____
Canola oil	_____	_____	_____	_____	_____	_____
Olive oil	_____	_____	_____	_____	_____	_____
Soybean oil	_____	_____	_____	_____	_____	_____
Hydro fat A*	_____	_____	_____	_____	_____	_____
Hydro fat B* (Swiftning)	_____	_____	_____	_____	_____	_____
Safflower oil	_____	_____	_____	_____	_____	_____
Peanut oil	_____	_____	_____	_____	_____	_____
Coconut oil	_____	_____	_____	_____	_____	_____
Cottonseed oil	_____	_____	_____	_____	_____	_____
Corn oil	_____	_____	_____	_____	_____	_____
Non-stick coating	_____	_____	_____	_____	_____	_____

*Set this display using one margarine and one hydrogenated fat with vegetable fat, and one margarine and one hydrogenated fat containing beef fat or lard.

Conclusions: Identify the composition and answer the following questions by reading the labels:

Which vegetable oils contain emulsifiers (monoglycerides, diglycerides, polyglycerides)?

Which are hydrogenated fats?

Which fats contain emulsifiers (monoglycerides, diglycerides, polyglycerides)?

Why are emulsifiers added to fats and oils?

Which fats contain the highest percentage of saturated fat?

What fat is contained in butter?

Which fats are contained in margarine?

Do grams of fat per tablespoon differ in butter and margarine?

Which oil is designed for deep fat frying?

What additive traps water and limits hydrolysis in the fat?

Which fat is pork fat?

Which fat has a higher percentage of monounsaturated fat?

What is the composition of a non-stick coating?

I.B. Composition of Mayonnaise and Salad Dressing

Results: From reading the labels of the following salad dressings and mayonnaise, compare total fat, saturated fat, polyunsaturated fat, and monounsaturated fat in edible fats and oils. Record data in table below.

	Total Fat/T	Calories	Serving	1st Ingredient Listed	Emulsifying and Stabilizing Ingredients
Mayonnaise					
Light mayonnaise					
Nonfat mayonnaise dressing					
Salad dressing					
Nonfat dressing					

II. Effect of Stabilizers and Emulsifiers on Emulsions

Variables:

A   No stabilizer.

B. Mix mustard/paprika with sugar. Add to vinegar and shake 25 times.

C. Mix xanthan gum with sugar. Add to vinegar and shake 25 times.

D. Lecithin. Add lecithin to 3 ml oil. Mix thoroughly in small container. Drop oil/lecithin mixture drop by drop into vinegar.

E. Egg yolk. Add egg yolk to vinegar. Shake 25 times.

  1. Label test tubes 1–5.
  2. Pour vinegar into each test tube.
  3. Add stabilizers and emulsifiers as indicated in variable.
  4. Add oil 1 drop at a time and shake thoroughly after each drop until 7 ml have been added.
  5. Continue to add oil 1–2 ml at a time shaking after each addition.
  6. Observe initially, after 3 min, and after 15 min. Record if you observed a separation of water and oil. How large was the oil layer?

Results: Record the degree of separation in the table below.

Variables	Oil (ml)	Vinegar (ml)	Sugar (g)	Stabilizer Emulsifier (g)	Immediate Results	Results in 3 Min	Results After 15 Min
A. No stabilizer	12	4	1	0			
B. Mustard/paprika	12	4	1	0.5			
C. Xanthan gum	12	4	1	0.1			
D. Lecithin	12	4	1	0.5			
E. Egg yolk	12	4	1	2			

Conclusions: Which was a temporary emulsion?

What affect did CMC have on stability?

Did egg yolk or lecithin maintain the emulsion? Why?

III. Salad Dressings
A. Comparison of high and low-fat French dressing.
1. **French Dressing** (72% oil)

(3 g) 1/2 t salt
(.2 g) 1/8 t white pepper
1 speck cayenne
(3 g) 1/2 t tomato paste
(2 g) 1/2 t sugar
(.1 g) 1/16 t garlic powder

(37.5 ml) 3 T salad oil
(15 ml) 1 T vinegar or lemon juice
(0.2 g) 1/8 t paprika
(.3 g) 1/8 t mustard powder
(.3 g) 1/8 t onion powder

Procedure: Mix dry ingredients. Add oil and vinegar or lemon juice alternately, beating until thick. Do this just before serving, as emulsion is temporary.

Alternate Method: Pour ingredients into a bottle or jar. Close tightly, and shake vigorously just before using.

2. **Imitation French Dressing** (6% oil)

(75 ml) 1/3 c water
(8 ml) 1 1/2 T vinegar, white
(4 g) 3/4 t tomato paste
(5 g) 1 T vegetable oil, soybean
(1 g) 1/4 t salt
(6 g) 1 1/2 t sugar
(.5 g) *Keltrol T xanthan gum

(.5 g) monosodium glutamate
(.4 g) garlic powder
(.4 g) *Kelcoloid LVF propylene glycol alginate
(.35 g) *Tween 60 emulsifying agent (ICI)
(.3 g) mustard powder
(.3 g) onion powder
(.1 g) *oleoresin paprika, liquid

Procedure: Blend dry ingredients well. Add dry ingredients to water. Blend in mixer on medium for 15 min. Add emulsifying agent (Tween 60), tomato paste, and paprika. Add oil slowly while beating. Add vinegar and continue mixing 5 min.

3. **Commercial Low-Fat French Dressing**
4. **Commercial French Dressing**

*Source listed in Appendix B.

Results: Compare French dressings by rating on a hedonic scale, with 9 = very thick and extremely good flavor, and 1 = very thin and extremely poor flavor.

Variable	Consistency	Flavor	Fat/T	Cal/T
French dressing (temporary emulsifier)				
Low-fat (emulsified French)				
Commercial low-fat French dressing				
Commercial French dressing				

Conclusions: What products were used as a fat replacer in the low-fat dressing?

Is there a difference in mouthfeel between the two dressings?

B. **Piquant Dressing** (make 1/2 recipe)

(100 g) 1/2 c sugar
(6 g) 1 t salt
(2.4 g) 1 t powdered dry mustard
(2 g) 1 t paprika
(1.5 g) 1/4 t celery salt
(80 ml) 1/3 c catsup or chili sauce

(60 ml) 1/4 c vinegar
(60 ml) 1/4 c lemon juice (about 1 lemon)
10 drops Tabasco sauce
(33 g) 1/4 c grated onion
(178 ml) 3/4 c salad oil

Procedure: Blend dry ingredients. Add remaining ingredients; beat thoroughly. Chill. Shake dressing before serving.

C. **Fruit Dressing** (oil)

(50 g) 1/4 c sugar
(1.3 g) 1/2 T cornstarch
(3 g) 1/2 t salt
(3 g) 1/2 t mustard
(1 g) 1/2 t paprika

(1 g) 1/2 t celery seed
(46.3 g) 3 T vinegar or lemon juice
(1.5 g) 1/2 t grated onion
(89 ml) 6 T oil

Procedure: Mix dry ingredients. Stir in vinegar or lemon juice and bring to a boil. Cool to room temperature. Add oil, a little at a time, beating thoroughly after each addition. Add onion. Mix well before serving.

D. **Bacon Dressing**

(19 g) 1 strip raw bacon, minced
(59 ml) 1/4 c water
(7 1/2 ml) 1 1/2 T vinegar

(12 g) 1 T sugar
pinch of salt
1 speck cayenne

Procedure: Cook bacon slowly until brown. Add remaining ingredients; heat to boiling point. Serve at once on spinach salad, leaf lettuce, dandelion greens, potatoes, or cooked string beans. Chopped hard-cooked eggs or green onions may be added.

Results: Describe appearance as smooth, uniform, separated, or curdled and consistency from extremely thick to extremely thin. Rate palatability from 9 = extremely flavorful to 1 = extremely poor in flavor.

Kind of Dressing	Appearance	Consistency	Palatability
B. Piquant dressing			
C. Fruit dressing (oil)			
D. Bacon dressing			

Conclusions: Define emulsion.

What are the two phases of the emulsion in each dressing?

Name stabilizing agents in each dressing.

IV. Permanent Emulsions—Mayonnaise
❖A. **Mayonnaise**

(1 g) 1/4 t sugar, if desired
1 speck cayenne
(0.7 g) 1/8 t salt
(1 g) 1/8 t mustard, if desired

(8 g) 1/2 T egg yolk, pasteurized, beaten
(2 1/2 ml) 1/2 t vinegar
(7.7 g) 1 1/2 t lemon juice
(118 ml) 1/2 C salad oil

Procedure: Mix dry ingredients. Add to egg yolk. Beat well. Add vinegar and lemon juice gradually while beating. Add oil, drop by drop at first, beating well between each addition. After about 1/2 the oil has been added, remainder may be added more rapidly. Mixture should be thick and smooth when finished.
  If dressing separates, start with another egg yolk (16 g) or (15 ml) 1 T water or vinegar. Add separated mixture a small amount at a time, beating well after each addition. One recipe makes 1/2 c.

Variables:
1. Add oil drop by drop until 50 ml are added, then teaspoon by teaspoon.
2. Add oil teaspoon by teaspoon from beginning until 50 ml is added, then tablespoon by tablespoon.

1. **Russian Dressing**

(32 g) 2 T chili sauce
(30 ml) 2 T whipping cream, whipped

(8 g) 1 T chopped green pepper
(60 g) 1/4 c mayonnaise

Procedure: Add chili sauce, whipped cream, and green pepper to mayonnaise.

2. **Thousand Island Dressing**

(16 g) 1 T chili sauce
(3 g) 1/2 t tomato catsup
(4 g) 1/2 t chopped green pepper
1/2 T chopped pimento

(3.7 g) 1/2 t chopped chives or minced onion
(1.5 g) 1/4 t paprika
(60 g) 1/4 c mayonnaise

Procedure: Add chili sauce, catsup, green pepper, pimento, chives or minced onion, and paprika to mayonnaise.

3. **Whipped Cream Mayonnaise**

(120 g) 1/2 c mayonnaise

(60 ml) 1/4 c whipping cream (whipped)

Procedure: Mix ingredients.

B. Blender Mayonnaise

(50 g) 1 egg, pasteurized   (15 ml) 1 T vinegar
(3 g) 1/2 t salt   (15 ml) 1 T lemon juice or vinegar
(1.2 g) 1/2 t dry mustard   (237 ml) 1 c vegetable oil

Procedure: Put the egg, seasonings, vinegar, lemon juice, and 1/4 c oil into blender container, cover, and process at blend for 15 seconds. Immediately remove feeder cap and pour in the remaining oil in a steady stream. Use rubber spatula if necessary to keep ingredients flowing to process in blades. Yield: About 1 1/4 c.

Results: Describe appearance on a scale from extremely smooth to curdled to extremely separated and consistency from very thick to very thin. Rate palatability from 9 = extremely flavorful to 1 = extremely poor in flavor.

Variation	Appearance	Consistency	Palatability
Mayonnaise variable 1			
Mayonnaise variable 2			
Reconstituted broken mayonnaise			
Russian dressing			
Cream dressing			
Blender mayonnaise			

Conclusions: Name the emulsifying agent in the above mayonnaise.

Name the two phases of the emulsions.

Can a broken mayonnaise be reformed? If so, how?

How do the variables in experiment II compare to:
    a.   Temporary emulsions (salad dressings)?

    b.   Permanent emulsions (salad dressings)?

What stabilizers are used in temporary emulsions?

Name emulsifiers used in emulsions.

Name stabilizers used in emulsions

What principles are illustrated in using emulsifiers and stabilizers to make a salad dressing permanent?

How do Russian, cream, and thousand island dressings differ from mayonnaise?

What conditions cause an emulsion to break?

What techniques are necessary to form an emulsion?

V. Other Examples of Emulsions Stabilized by Egg or Cooked Starch

A. **Hollandaise Sauce:** Served with artichoke

(33 g) 2 egg yolks
(15 ml) 1 T lemon juice
1 speck of cayenne

(113 g) 1/2 c butter or margarine,
    divided into 3 portions

Procedure: Place egg yolks in top of double boiler. Add lemon juice and 1/3 of butter. Cook over hot, not boiling, water, stirring constantly until thickening begins. Add second portion of butter. Allow mixture to thicken again. Then add third portion of butter and seasonings. Serve as soon as thickened. If sauce separates, cream may be beaten into it.

Artichoke: May be dipped into hollandaise sauce.

Procedure: See page 50, in Salads and Vegetables.

B. **Fruit Dressing** (make 1/2 recipe)

(100 g) 1/2 c sugar
1 pinch salt
(100 g) 2 eggs, beaten

(178 ml) 3/4 c hot fruit juice (equal parts
    orange, lemon, and pineapple)
(118 ml) 1/2 c cream, whipped

Procedure: Combine sugar, salt, and eggs. Add fruit juice gradually. Cook in double boiler over hot water, stirring constantly until mixture thickens. Cool. Fold in cream just before serving. Other acid fruit juices may be used.

C. **Cooked Salad Dressing** (flour thickener)

(1.5 g) 1/4 t salt
(1.2 g) 1/2 t mustard
(25 g) 2 T sugar
(7 g) 1 T flour
1 speck cayenne

(16.5 g) 1 egg yolk, slightly beaten
    or (25 g) 1/2 whole egg
(89 ml) 3/8 c milk or water
(30 ml) 2 T mild vinegar
(13 g) 1 T vegetable oil

Procedure: Mix dry ingredients. Add egg yolks to milk. Mix well. Add egg milk mix to dry ingredients gradually, then add vinegar very slowly. Cook, stirring until mixture thickens. Add fat. Cool.

❖D. **Salad Dressing** (starch thickener)

(25 g) 1/2 egg
(12 g) 1 T sugar
(4.5 g) 3/4 t salt
(2.4 g) 1 t dry mustard
(0.2 g) 1/8 t paprika

(30 ml) 2 T vinegar
(90 ml) 6 T vegetable oil
(5.2 g) 2 T cornstarch
(59 ml) 1/4 c cold water
(59 ml) 1/4 c hot water

Procedure: Place egg, sugar, seasoning, vinegar, and oil in a mixing bowl but *do not stir.* Make a paste by mixing cornstarch with the cold water, then stir in hot water. Cook, stirring constantly, until clear. Add hot cornstarch mixture to ingredients in mixing bowl. Beat with rotary beater until well blended. Cool.

❖E. **Comparison of 0% oil vs. 45% oil salad dressings using starch-based fat replacer**
Variables:

1. 0% oil
2. 45% oil

No-Fat Salad Dressing	0% Oil	Control (45% Oil)
Soy oil	0	45 ml
Water	110 ml	67 ml
Vinegar	14 ml	17.1 ml
Sugar	5 g	7 g
Thermflo*	6 g	0
Egg yolk, frozen pasteurized	0	5 g
Purity 420	0	3–4 g
Whey protein	3 g	0
N-Lite L*	2 g	0
Salt	1.3 g	1.3 g
Mustard powder	.5 g	.5 g
Garlic powder	.03 g (2 specks)	.03 g (2 specks)
Onion powder	.02 g (speck)	.02 g (speck)
Paprika	.01 g (speck)	.01 g (speck)

Procedure: Blend all dry ingredients. Add to water and vinegar. Heat to 190°F (88°C) and hold over a double boiler 15 min. Cool to 80°F (27°C). In control, add egg yolk to paste using medium speed of mixer. Add oil to control very slowly, beating constantly in mixer. Beat nonfat dressing for 5 min on medium speed. Beat both 1 min on high speed.

Results: Describe appearance on a scale from extremely smooth to curdled to extremely separated and consistency from very thick to very thin. Rate palatability from 9 = extremely flavorful to 1 = extremely poor in flavor.

Dressing	Appearance	Consistency	Palatability
Hollandaise sauce: Serve with green vegetables, such as artichokes or broccoli			
Fruit dressing (1/2 recipe) (egg thickened)			
Salad dressing with starch filler			
Cooked salad dressing (starch thickened)			
Salad dressing (45% oil)			
Salad dressing (0% oil with fat replacer)			

Conclusions: What is the emulsifying agent in hollandaise sauce?

What may overheating break the hollandaise sauce emulsion?

What products stabilize these emulsions?

How does mouthfeel differ between mayonnaise, salad dressing, and no-fat salad dressing?

What is the major ingredient in no-fat dressings?

What ingredients were used as fat replacers in the no-fat dressing?

*Source of ingredients found in Appendix B.

V. Salads and Vegetables

A. Greens of a wide variety serve as the base for many salads. Identify at least 6 salad greens.

B. Production of salad dressing illustrates physical and chemical properties of emulsions. Production of the salad demands fresh high quality produce as well as artistic skill. Food will not be eaten nor will it be sold if it is not aesthetically pleasing to the eye and to the taste bud. Demonstrate your ability.

C. Recipes

Artichoke
1 fresh artichoke

Procedure: Place 2 c water in saucepan. Bring to boil. Clip off tips of artichoke leaves. Place in boiling water. Simmer 15 min. Serve with mayonnaise or hollandaise sauce.

Avocado and Grapefruit Salad
(113 g) 1/4 avocado (cut in wedges)   (30 g) 2 T lemon juice
(151 g) 1/3 grapefruit (sections)   lettuce leaf

Procedure: Dip avocado in lemon juice. Arrange avocado wedges and grapefruit sections in a lettuce cup. Serve with fruit (oil) dressing.

Grapes-Pineapple Ring-Fluted Salad
(227 g) 1 small bunch grapes   (151 g) 1 kiwi, peeled, sliced
(56 g) 1 ring pineapple   1 carambola, sliced
(113 g) 1/2 of fluted (scored) banana (sliced),
    dipped in lemon juice

Procedure: Arrange on salad greens. Serve with fruit (egg thickened) dressing.

To "Score" a Banana: Hold the peeled banana in the left hand and draw the tines of a fork lengthwise in parallel lines. Slice straight across or at an angle. Each slice will have an attractively notched edge.

Waldorf Salad
(61 g) 1/2 c diced red eating apple, not pared   whipped cream mayonnaise dressing
(30 g) 1/4 c diced celery   lettuce
(16 g) 1–2 T chopped walnut meats

Procedure: Combine apple, celery, and nut meats. Add enough dressing to moisten. Heap onto lettuce.

Crisp Spinach Salad: You can prepare the salad and dressing ahead; mix them together just before serving.
(13 g) 4 oz spinach   (56 g) 2 oz fresh bean sprouts
(56 g) 2 oz water chestnuts, drained and sliced   (12 g) 1/4 hard-cooked egg

Procedure: Trim and discard the tough spinach stems; rinse the leaves well, pat dry, and break into bite-sized pieces. In a large salad bowl combine the spinach, bean sprouts, and water chestnuts. Garnish with hard-cooked egg slices. Serve bacon dressing over spinach salad.

Tossed Vegetable Salad

Procedure: Any convenient variety of coarsely shredded or broken greens, such as head and leaf lettuce, spinach, endive, escarole, cabbage, and watercress, form the base of these salads. To the greens add any other vegetables available. Sliced raw carrots, radishes, and cucumber; tomato wedges; and pepper and onion rings are examples. Chopped chives and parsley may be added for flavor. Chill vegetables. Add salad dressing just before serving.

Potato Salad

(163 g) 1 c diced cooked potato
(50 g) 1 hard-cooked egg, diced
(1.5 g) 1/4 t salt
(.05 g) 1 t minced parsley
(2.5 g) 1 t minced onion

(40 g) 1/3 c diced celery
mayonnaise or cooked dressing
salad greens
radish roses, green pepper, or pimento

Procedure: Place 1 medium sized potato peeled and quartered in 1 c boiling water. Cook covered until tender. Dice. Place 1 egg in cold water to cover. Bring to just under a boil, turn heat to low, let stand 15 min. Remove from water. Dice. Combine all ingredients except mayonnaise or cooked dressing, salad greens, and radish roses or other garnishes. Add enough dressing to moisten. Chill. Arrange on salad greens. Garnish with radish roses, green pepper, or pimento.

Cole Slaw

(120 g) 1 1/2 c shredded cabbage (6 oz)
(14 g) 2 T chopped green pepper

(2.5 g) 1 t minced onion
cooked salad dressing or mayonnaise to moisten

Procedure: Combine ingredients by tossing lightly. Serve at once.

Orange-Onion Salad

5 thin slices Bermuda onion
piquant dressing
lettuce or watercress

6 thin slices (not sections) peeled orange,
(preferably navel orange)

Procedure: If desired, marinate onion slices in piquant dressing 1/2 hour. Drain. Arrange onion and orange slices on lettuce or watercress. Serve with French dressing.

Kidney Bean Salad

(138 g) 3/4 c cooked or canned kidney beans
2 small sweet pickles, chopped

(30 g) 1/4 c diced celery
(30 g) 2 T mayonnaise or cooked salad dressing

Procedure: Combine. Serve on lettuce and garnish with slices of hard-cooked egg.

Egg Salad

(100 g) 2 hard-cooked eggs, chopped
(30 g) 1/4 c finely diced celery
(15 g) 1 T cooked dressing or mayonnaise
(1 ml) 1/4 t Worcestershire sauce
(5 ml) 1 t lemon juice

2 black olives, sliced
salt to taste
pepper to taste
salad greens
salad dressing

Procedure: Combine all ingredients except salad greens and salad dressing. Season to taste. Chill. When ready to serve, place on salad greens. Garnish with salad dressing. Molds may be used for shaping if desired.

Salads

Results: Identify the salad green and describe the compatibility of the salad dressing with the salad.

Salad	Dressing	Salad Green	Comments
Fruit: Avocado—grapefruit	fruit (oil)		
Pineapple—banana—grape—kiwi	fruit (egg)		
Waldorf 1 recipe	cream mayonnaise		
Vegetable: Wilted spinach	bacon		
Fresh tossed	French		
Potato	starch-filled salad dressing		
Cole slaw	cooked		
Head lettuce	Russian		
Broccoli or artichoke	hollandaise		
Fruit and vegetable: Onion and orange	piquant		
High protein: Kidney bean	cooked or mayonnaise		
Egg	cooked or mayonnaise		

FAT AS A FRYING MEDIA

Goal: To recognize and practice principles that maintain high quality fried foods.

Objectives: To categorize fats from high to low smoke points.
                  To list factors that reduce smoke point.
                  To list conditions and formulas that increase fat absorption into a product being deep fat fried.
                  To taste the affect of low vs. high fat absorption when frying.
                  To practice safety when frying with fat.

CAUTION: Be prepared to prevent danger from fat fires. Use a lid, cookie sheet, or tray to smother. Use the fire extinguisher.

In contrast to fats with emulsifiers added that are used in salad dressings, fats used in deep fat frying should maintain a high smoke point. A high smoke point is maintained if at least part of the water released from the food being cooked can be trapped. Using a fat with an antifoam agent such as methyl silicone maintains a higher smoke point, whereas using a fat with monoglycerides and diglycerides reduces the smoke point. When the smoke point is low, the frying temperature must be reduced and more fat will be absorbed into the product. Ingredient formation also affects fat absorption into the product with increased liquid, sugar, fat, and egg in the formulation, increasing fat absorption.

A non-caloric fat replacer is currently approved for use in deep frying snack foods. The compound, olestra, is used in many corn and potato chip products. Since fat may contribute mouthfeel, texture, and flavor to fried foods but is also high in calories and has negative health effects on blood lipids, this new fat replacer may serve both a nutritional and functional purpose. Olestra is a sucrose polyester. The structure consists of a sucrose molecule with 6–8 fatty acids attached to the hydroxyl sites of sucrose. This molecule contains no calories because with 6–8 fatty acids attached to the sucrose, enzymes cannot get to the center to break down the compound while it moves through the digestive tract; thus the compound is excreted.

General Directions: Use a fat with an antifoam agent and no emulsifiers to fill the deep fat fryers 1/3–1/2 full.

I. Smoking Temperature: Demonstration

Heat each selected fat in a small beaker (approximately 1/2 full) over low electric heat. Suspend a thermometer so that the bulb is covered with fat but does not touch the bottom of the beaker. Watch carefully for smoking and record temperature. Observe any changes in the fat after cooling.

Kind of Fat	Smoking Temperature °F	Changed Appearance
Butter		
Lard		
Hydrogenated shortening		
Vegetable oil		

Conclusions: Which fat had the highest smoke temperature?

Which fat had the lowest smoke temperature?

Why do the smoke temperatures differ?

❖II. Effect of Temperature on Fat Absorption

A. Use 1 pkg. refrigerated biscuits

Procedure: Fill deep fryer 1/3–1/2 full of fat. Heat to 325°F. Divide each refrigerated biscuit in half. Roll into a ball. Fry 1/3 of balls at each temperature given below. Fry first batch brown to golden color. Fry remaining 2 batches to same color. Record frying time.

Result: Comment on texture, color, and flavor. Rate fat absorption from 1 = extremely low fat absorption to 9 = extremely high fat absorption.

Temp. °F	Texture	Color	Flavor	Fat Absorption	Time	Internal Doneness
325°						
365°						
390°						

B. Use 4 oz frozen French fries

Variables:
1. Fill deep fat fryer 1/3–1/2 full with frying oil. Cook French fries starting in cold fat.
2. Fill deep fat fryer 1/3–1/2 full with frying oil. Cook French fries in fat at 360°F. Cook to same light brown color.

Results: Comment on texture, color, and flavor and rate of fat absorption from 1 = extremely low fat absorption, to 9 = extremely high fat absorption.

Treatment	Texture	Color	Flavor	Fat Absorption
Begin in cold fat				
Fat at 365°				

Conclusions: How does frying temperature affect fat absorption?

III. Effect of Formulation on Fat Absorption in Cake Donuts

Cake Donuts

(250 g) 2 c Bisquick (baking mix)	(50 g) 1 egg
(30 ml) 2 T milk	(25 g) 2 T sugar

Procedure: Mix above ingredients. Weigh 65-g portions. Make donuts by forming a ball and using a 1/2-in. diameter cutter to cut out center. Deep fat fry at 375°F until golden brown. **Time cooking time.** Deep fat fry all variables at the same temperature and for the same time.

Variable:

A. Make 1/2 recipe

B. Make 1/2 recipe with (25 g) 2 T sugar

C. Make 1/2 recipe with (25 g) 2 T sugar and (15 ml) 1 T oil

Results: Rate on a hedonic scale with 9 = very desirable color and flavor and extremely high fat absorption, and 1 = very undesirable color and flavor and extremely low fat absorption.

Variable	Color	Flavor	Fat Absorption
A.			
B.			
C.			

Conclusions: Which variable was most greasy?

Which variable browned most?

Which variable was most tender?

What ingredients increase fat absorption?

IV. Effect of Breading in Deep Fat Frying
❖A. **Cheese Croquettes**

(13 g) 1 T fat

(22 g) 1 1/2 T flour

(.37 g) 1/16 t salt

(79 ml) 1/3 c milk

(113 g) 1 c grated cheese

Breading

(50 g) 1 egg

(51 g) 1/2 c finely ground bread crumbs

Procedure: Melt fat. Add flour and salt. Stir until smooth. Add milk to make white sauce. Cook until thickened (bring to a boil), stirring occasionally. Add cheese to white sauce. Allow to melt; cool briefly. Shape into 1-in. balls.

Variables:
1. Breaded: Beat 1 egg slightly. Mix with equal amount of cold water. Place 1/2 c finely ground bread crumbs on plate. Roll balls in crumbs, then in egg, and finally in crumbs.
2. Unbreaded: After shaping, croquettes are ready to fry with no breading.

Frying:
1. Heat fat to 385°F (196°C).
2. Fry croquettes until golden brown.
3. Fry unbreaded croquette last.

Results: Using a paired comparison sensory test, identify which holds a more uniform shape, less uniform shape, or no difference; identify which appears to have greater or lesser fat absorption or no difference; and identify which has the more or less appealing flavor.

	Shape	Fat Absorption	Flavor
Breaded			
Not breaded			

Conclusions: Why does breading hold product together?

B. Parsnip Puffs

(422 g) 2 c parsnips, cooked, mashed, seasoned   (76.5 g) 3/4 c fine dry bread crumbs
(50 g) 1 egg beaten   (14.5 ml) 1 T water

Procedure: Temperature: deep fat, 375°F. Frying time: about 3 min.

Cook parsnips in 1/2 their weight in water until tender. Remove core and mash. Season with salt and pepper. Combine parsnips and half the egg.

Shape parsnip mixture into balls. Roll in bread crumbs. Blend remaining egg and the water. Dip balls into egg mixture, then into crumbs. Be sure balls are thoroughly coated with each layer before proceeding to the next.

Fry in deep fat heated to 375°, about 3 min or until brown. Drain on absorbent paper and serve hot.

V. Effect of Fat Replacer, Olestra, on Texture, Flavor, and Mouthfeel of Potato and Corn Chips

Procedure: Prepare samples of commercially fried fat-based and olestra-based corn and potato chips. Label with sample numbers. Evaluate.

Sample #693

❏	❏	❏	❏	❏	❏	❏	❏	❏
Dislike Extremely	Dislike Very Much	Dislike Moderately	Dislike Slightly	Neither Like nor Dislike	Like Slightly	Like Moderately	Like Very Much	Like Extremely

Sample #054

❏	❏	❏	❏	❏	❏	❏	❏	❏
Dislike Extremely	Dislike Very Much	Dislike Moderately	Dislike Slightly	Neither Like nor Dislike	Like Slightly	Like Moderately	Like Very Much	Like Extremely

Sample #796

❏	❏	❏	❏	❏	❏	❏	❏	❏
Dislike Extremely	Dislike Very Much	Dislike Moderately	Dislike Slightly	Neither Like nor Dislike	Like Slightly	Like Moderately	Like Very Much	Like Extremely

Sample #357

❏	❏	❏	❏	❏	❏	❏	❏	❏
Dislike Extremely	Dislike Very Much	Dislike Moderately	Dislike Slightly	Neither Like nor Dislike	Like Slightly	Like Moderately	Like Very Much	Like Extremely

VI. Deep Fat Fried Foods

A. **Apple Fritters**—Use 1/2 recipe.

(155 g) 1 1/3 c flour	(158 ml) 2/3 c milk
(3 g) 1/2 t salt	(50 g) 1 egg
(7.6 g) 2 t baking powder	(13 g) 1 T fat, melted
(4 g) 1 t sugar, if desired	(237 ml) 1 c fruit, vegetable, meat, or grated cheese

Procedure: Sift dry ingredients together. Add milk to egg. Add fat to milk-egg mixture. Combine dry and liquid mixture. Stir only enough to mix ingredients slightly. Stir fruit, vegetable, meat, or cheese into batter. Fry by spoonfuls in deep fat heated to 375°F (191°C). If desired, serve sprinkled with powdered sugar.

Syrup

1/4 c brown sugar   1/4 c water

Procedure: Heat to a boil. Serve with fritters.

B. **Corn Fritters**

Procedure: Use well-drained whole kernel corn for the vegetable and follow directions for apple fritters. May be served with syrup, above.

C. **Potato Chips**

Two potatoes: 1 Idaho, 1 red potato.

Procedure: Heat oil in deep fat fryer to 365°F. Pare one red and one white potato. Using a *vegetable peeler,* slice potato into paper thin slices. Rinse potato slices in cold water. Dry on a towel. Fry in deep fat to light golden brown. Fry each potato for identical times and at identical temperatures and observe browning. (White Idaho potatoes generally have a lower content of sugar and thus do not brown as readily.)

D. **French Fried Onions (Batter Fried)**

(151.5 g) 1 large onion, sliced	(118 ml) 1/2 c milk
(87 g) 3/4 c flour	(6 g) 1 t salt
(50 g) 1 egg	

Procedure: Wash and peel 1 large sweet onion. Use a sharp knife with a long blade. Cut the slices no more than 1/2-in. thick and preferably a little thinner. Separate slices into rings. Dip rings in 1/4 c flour. Make a batter of beaten egg, milk, remaining flour, and salt. Dip floured rings in batter and fry a few at a time in deep fat heated to 375°F. Remove when golden brown. Drain on soft crumbled paper and sprinkle with salt.

E. **French Fried Onions (No Batter)**

(151.5 g) 1 large onion, sliced	(58 g) 1/2 c flour
(118 ml) 1/2 c milk	

Procedure: Wash, peel, and slice onion. Separate slices into rings. Soak in milk 1/2 hr. Shake slices individually in flour. Deep fat fry at 375°F. Remove when golden and drain on paper.

F. **French Fried Egg Plant, Zucchini, and Cauliflower**

(227 g) 1 zucchini or 1/2 egg plant or	(118 ml) 1/2 c milk
(151.5 g) 1/4 cauliflower	(1 1/2 g) 1/4 t salt
(50 g) 1 egg	(58 g) 1/2 c flour, bread crumbs, or cornmeal

Procedure: Cut vegetable into small slices or strips. Mix egg, milk, and salt. Dip vegetable in egg and milk mixture. Divide vegetable in thirds. Coat each third in either flour, cornmeal, or bread crumbs. Fry at 375°F until golden brown. Drain on paper.

Results: Evaluate the fat absorption, doneness, crispiness, and overall quality of the deep fat fried foods.

Food	Comments
A. Fritters (fruit)	
B. Fritters (corn)	
C. Potato chips: red potato white potato	
D. Parsnip puffs	
E. Batter-fried French-fried onion rings	
F. No-batter French-fried onions	
G. Egg plant, zucchini, or cauliflower	

Conclusions: What factors will increase fat absorption in above products?

What factors will increase browning of above products?

What function does breading serve?

VII. Pan-Fried Foods
A. Fried Raw Potatoes

Procedure: Wash and pare potatoes. Cut into desired shape. Rinse pared potatoes in water, wipe dry with a clean towel, and fry at once. Fry in skillet with 1/4-in. fat, cooking only a small quantity at a time. Drain on paper. Sprinkle with salt. Serve at once.

B. French Toast

3 slices of French bread, cut 3/4-in. thick	(4.2 g) 1/2 t sugar
(50 g) 1 egg	(118 ml) 1/2 c milk
(1 1/2 g) 1/4 t salt	(.25 g) 1/8 t cinnamon

Procedure: Combine egg, salt, sugar, and milk. Dip bread in egg mixture. Allow egg moisture to reach center of slice, but avoid over-soaking bread since it tends to break in handling. Spray griddle with non-stick coating before heating. Brown on one side; turn and brown the other side. Add fat necessary to keep from sticking. Serve plain or with syrup, jam, honey, or confectioners' sugar.

Syrup

1/4 c brown sugar	1/4 c water

Procedure: Heat to a boil; serve with French toast.

C. Fried Green Tomatoes

    (227 g) 2 green tomatoes   (35 g) 1/4 c yellow cornmeal
    (25 g) 1/2 egg   (29 g) 1/4 c flour
    (79 ml) 1/3 c milk   (1 1/2 g) 1/4 t salt
                                  (28 g) 2 T margarine

Procedure: Slice green tomatoes. Mix egg and milk. Mix cornmeal, flour, and salt in separate bowl. Dip green tomato slices in milk-egg mixture, then in cornmeal-flour mix. Saute in margarine until golden brown.

Results: Evaluate the fat absorption, doneness, crispiness, and overall quality of the pan-fried foods.

Food	Comments
Raw potatoes, fried	
French toast	
Green tomatoes	

Conclusion: How may you limit fat absorption in frying?

Milk, Cream, and Milk Products

Notes:

MILK AND CREAM

Goal: To observe factors that cause denaturation and/or coagulation of milk protein.

Objectives: To observe the effects of heat, acid, heat and acid, rennin, and carrageenan on milk protein.
                 To observe denaturation, coagulation, and gelation of milk protein.
                 To observe factors that increase volume and stability of whipped milk and cream foams.

Milk is composed of lactose particles in solution, an emulsion of fat in water, and a dispersion of proteins in water. Proteins are larger than those particles that go into solution; thus they fit into the size range defined as a colloid. The surface of the colloid is important to its remaining in dispersion. The surface of the casein protein is negatively charged. This charge keeps particles separated and permanently dispersed. In the following experiments, a change of charge will destabilize the colloidal dispersion. The colloid may also be stabilized by a water layer. Removal of the water layer may destabilize the dispersion. Heat, change of pH, or enzymes may affect the protein dispersion in milk.

I. Effect of Heat on Milk

Use small, heavy aluminum saucepan. Heat but don't boil (118 ml) 1/2 c fresh homogenized milk for 10 min (scald) without stirring. Use variables below.

Results: Using a paired comparison evaluation, describe which variable has the thinner/thicker scum and which variable has more/less residue on the pan.

Variable	Thickness of Scum	Coagulation on Pan	Conclusions
Uncovered pan			
Covered pan			

Conclusions: Scum formation is increased by what conditions?

                  Scum formation is reduced by what conditions?

                  Scum formation is due to what?

II. Effect of Acid on Milk

❖A. **Effect of acid: Acid soured milk**

Take pH of milk. Add (7.5 g) 1/2 T vinegar or lemon juice slowly to (118 ml) 1/2 c milk. Stir. Note thickening and consistency. Take pH after thickening occurs.

B. **Effect of acid and heat: Tomato soup**

Note: Stir well while blending juice and milk. Simmering point means bubbles rise to surface—*don't boil!* "Hot" means heated to drinking temperature (130˚).

    ❖1. **Plain Tomato Soup**
        (118 ml) 1/2 c milk (120–130˚F)   (118 ml) 1/2 c tomato juice (120–130˚F)
        (.75 g) 1/8 t salt

Procedure: Take pH of milk before and after juice is combined.

          a. Gradually add hot juice to hot milk; add salt.
              1. Serve half immediately.
              2. Hold half over boiling water **until curdling takes place.**

b. Gradually add hot milk to hot juice.
1. Serve half immediately.
2. Hold half over boiling water **until curdling takes place.**

2. **Cream of Tomato Soup**

(22 g) 2 t butter   (118 ml) 1/2 c milk (120–130˚F)
(2.5 g) 2 t flour   (1.5 g) 1/4 t salt
(118 ml) 1/2 c tomato juice

Procedure: Take pH of milk before and after juice is combined. Melt butter. Stir in flour. Add tomato juice.
Thicken sauce with tomato juice, flour, and butter by bringing to a boil. Add hot, thickened juice to
hot milk; add salt.
a. Serve half immediately.
b. Hold half over boiling water until curdling takes place.

3. **Commercial Condensed Tomato Soup**
Procedure: Take pH of milk before and after canned soup is combined. Read and record ingredients on the label.
Add equal amounts of milk to canned tomato soup. Heat.
a. Serve half immediately.
b. Hold half over boiling water for 30 min.

C. **Effect of acid and heat: Cottage cheese made from a lactic acid culture**

Small Curd Cheese from Buttermilk
(948 ml) 1 qt pasteurized skim milk   (15 ml) 1 t half & half
(7 ml) 1 1/2 t buttermilk   cheese cloth

Procedure: Take pH of skim milk and of cheese before final preparation.
This portion of preparation needs to be started 2 1/2 days ahead. Add buttermilk to 1 c skim milk.
Hold at 70–75˚ for 16–24 hours to curdle. After holding, use a cool teaspoon to place 1 t curdled milk
in 1 c skim milk. Hold for 12–18 hours to curdle. Warm 2 c milk. Add 2 t curdled milk. Cover and let
stand at 72˚F for 16–24 hours.
Cut curd in to 1/4-in. pieces and let stand 10 min. Transfer to top of double boiler. Heat water in
double boiler to 72˚F. Raise temperature of milk to 100˚F in 30–40 min, raise temp. **very, very** slowly.
Stir curd gently every 4–5 min. Heat to 115˚ in 10–15 min more. Hold for 20–30 min at 115˚F. Heat
to 120–125˚F if curd doesn't firm. Pour over a cheese cloth in a colander. Immerse curd in water to
rinse. Drain. You may salt and add cream to curd.
(Adapted from USDA Home & Garden Bulletin No. 129.)

D. **Effect of acid and heat: Yogurt**
Yogurt
(474 ml) 1 pt skim milk   (5 g) .17 oz yogurt culture

Procedure: Heat milk to 82˚C (180˚F) and cool to 48˚C (118˚F). Mix in the yogurt culture. Incubate at 40–46˚C
(105–115˚F) until milk has curdled (about 4 hours). Take pH at beginning and after each hour.
Record. Place yogurt in refrigerator.

Results: Evaluate soup by rating viscosity as very thin, thin, slightly thick, thick, and very thick. Evaluate curdling as slightly curdled, curdled moderately, and very curdled. Describe size of curds in cottage cheese and firmness of gel in yogurt.

Variable		pH	Comments	Holding Time Required for Curdling
Plain tomato soup	Served immediately			
	Held 30 min			
Cream of tomato soup	Served immediately			
	Held 30 min			
Commercially condensed tomato soup				
Cottage cheese				
Yogurt				

Conclusions: Curds are composed of what component?

What conditions will destabilize the colloidal dispersion in milk?

How can acid, heat, and milk be combined to avoid curdling?

Describe what conditions cause curd formation in cottage cheese.

Describe what conditions cause curd formation in yogurt.

❖III. Effect of Rennin on Milk

Variables:

A. Add rennin to milk at 98°F. Let stand at room temperature.

B. Add rennin to milk at 43°F. Let set at refrigerator temperature.

C. Add rennin to milk at 212°F (100°C). Let set at room temperature.

D. Add rennin to reconstituted nonfat dry milk at 98°F. Let set at room temperature.

(118 ml) 1/2 c milk	(.6 ml) 1/8 t vanilla
1/4 rennin tablet	fg salt
(5 ml) 1 t cold water	(6 g) 1/2 T sugar

Procedure: Convert temperatures to Celsius before beginning experiment and record in the following table. Warm the milk in a double boiler to temperature indicated in variable, except leave milk for variable B cold. Dissolve the rennin tablet in cold water. Add rennin and remaining ingredients to the milk. Mix. Pour quickly into custard cup. Let stand at temperature indicated in the variable for 1 hour. Compare gel formation.

Results: Describe gel formation as very firm gel, firm gel, moderately firm gel, soft gel, very soft gel, and no gel.

Methods	Comments
A. Milk: 98°F (°C)	
B. Milk: 43°F (°C)	
C. Milk: 212°F (°C)	
D. Milk: Reconstituted dry 98°F (°C)	

Conclusions: What is rennin?

How does rennin destabilize the protein dispersion in milk and cause gelation?

At which temperature is rennin most active?

❖IV. Effect of Carrageenan on Milk Gelation

Chocolate Flan

(50 g) 1/4 c sugar   1 g carrageenan (Sea Gel)*
(500 ml) 2 1/8 c milk   (14 g) 1/2 sq. chocolate

Procedure: Mix carrageenan with sugar. Stir sugar mix into 500 ml cold milk in a saucepan. Heat to a boil in approximately 5–7 min while constantly stirring. Add chocolate. Pour into desired molds. Cool in refrigerator or at room temperature.

Conclusions: How does carrageenan in milk cause gelation?

What commercial products use carrageenan to thicken milk?

*Source listed in Appendix B

V. Comparison of Milk Products

Read the label for each product. Taste each product. Note color, flavor, and mouthfeel.

Kind	Market Unit	Cost	Cost/Qt Reconstituted	% Fat	Comments
Homogenized					
Skim—fortified					
2% fortified					
Half & half					
Acidophilus milk					
Buttermilk					
Whipping cream					
Evaporated					
Milnot					
Sweetened condensed					
Nonfat dry milk solids					
Coffee whitener					

Conclusions: What is the percent fat of each milk?

Which products have water evaporated to reduce water content and increase percent solids?

Which products contain vegetable oils replaced for butter fat?

VI. Effect of Butter-Fat, Temperature, pH, and Stabilizer on Whipped Toppings

Whip 125 ml for each variable, using small bowls and electric beaters for the entire series. Chill bowls and beaters for 10°C variable. Stop beating as soon as foam will stand in peaks. Measure total volume. To determine drainage, place 100 ml of the whipped product in a funnel (wire mesh over hole). Place funnel over a 100 ml graduate; allow to drain 30 min. Measure drainings (5 ml = 1 t).

Results: Record the ml of volume produced from each foam and the ml of drainage to assess stability, and evaluate the flavor and mouthfeel of each foam on a hedonic scale with 9 = like extremely, 5 = neither like nor dislike, and 1 = dislike extremely.

Variable	Time for Whipping Min. Sec	Volume (ml)	Cost per Cup Whipped	Drainage in 30 Min (ml)	Flavor	Mouthfeel
1 Whipping cream (30–35% fat) 10°C						
2 Whipping cream 20°C						
3 Coffee cream (18% fat) 10°C						
4 Coffee cream + 1/2 t lemon juice 10°C						
5 Coffee cream (18% fat) + 3 g gelearin GP 359						
6 Milnot—10°C or colder						
7 Evaporated milk— chilled until partially frozen						
8 Nonfat dry milk solids (1/4 c water + 1/4 c solids) room temperature						
9 Nonfat dry milk solids (1/4 c fruit juice + 1/4 c solids) room temperature						
10 Dry, packaged whipped topping (whip according to package label)						
11 Frozen whipped topping—don't whip; measure 100 ml and drain						

*Source of ingredients listed in Appendix B.

Conclusions: Why do cold temperatures produce more stable whipped toppings in foams using fat?

Besides fat, what other products may stabilize a milk foam?

What component in cream forms a foam?

Which foams produce the greatest volume?

What forms the foam in dry packaged or frozen whipped toppings?

Which foams are least expensive?

Cocoa

Notes:

Goal: To prepare and taste cocoa products made with a variety of products and methods.

Objectives: To compare cocoa beverages prepared from chocolate, breakfast cocoa, and Dutch processed cocoa. To observe settling time following the use of differing preparation methods and differing cooking procedures.

Cocoa or hot chocolate combines the principles of both milk products and starches. Cocoa contains starch; thus it must be heated to thicken unless a pregelatinized product is used. Since hot chocolate and hot cocoa are made with milk, the principles for heating milk must also be adhered to.

I. Effect of Type of Cocoa and Formula on Flavor and Settling

A. Hot Chocolate

(7 g) 1/4 sq unsweetened chocolate   (44 ml) 3 T hot water
(12 g) 1 T sugar   (206 ml) 7/8 c milk, scalded
fg salt

Procedure: Place chocolate, sugar, salt, and water in saucepan. Slowly bring to a boil, stirring constantly. Add milk, beat for 5 min. Do not boil. Beat with rotary beater just before serving. Flavor improves if mixture is allowed to stand 1/2 hour or more over hot water. A few drops of vanilla may be added just before serving. Garnish with whipped cream or marshmallow if desired.

B. Cocoa (Breakfast)

(14 g) 1 T cocoa   (44 ml) 3 T water
(12 g) 1 T sugar   (206 ml) 7/8 c milk, scalded
1/16 t salt

Procedure: Mix cocoa, sugar, and salt. Add water. Slowly bring to a boil, stirring constantly. Add milk; beat with rotary beater just before serving.

C. Cocoa Processed with Alkali
Procedure: Use an alkali-processed cocoa in above recipe.

D. Creamy Cocoa.
Procedure: Prepare as for Cocoa (B.), but mix 1/2 T flour or 1 t cornstarch with sugar, salt, and cocoa. This makes a thicker beverage that does not separate readily.

Results: Rate the uniformity of the chocolate drinks on a hedonic scale with 9 = extremely uniform throughout to 1 = extremely settled. Rate the color from extremely brown to brown-red to red, and the body from extremely thick to extremely thin. Comment on appearance and palatability.

Variable	Appearance	Uniformity (Settling Out)	Color	Body	Palatability
A. Unsweetened cocoa					
B. Cocoa (breakfast)					
C. Cocoa processed with alkali					
D. Creamy cocoa					

Conclusions: Which cocoa appears to have oil droplets floating? Why?

Which cocoa appears to be thickest? Why?

Which cocoa had the least settling? Why?

II. Effect of Cooking and Not Cooking the Cocoa, Sugar, and Water Mixture

Procedure: Prepare hot cocoa (as in I.B.).

Results: Rate the uniformity of the chocolate drinks on a hedonic scale with 9 = extremely uniform throughout to 1 = extremely settled. Rate the color from extremely brown to brown-red to red, and the body from extremely thick to extremely thin. Comment on appearance and palatability.

Variable	Appearance	Uniformity (Settling Out)	Color	Body	Palatability
A. Cocoa, sugar, salt, and water cooked before adding milk as directed					
B. Mix cocoa, sugar, and salt with hot water and add to hot milk without further cooking					

Conclusions: Why is cocoa cooked to boiling?

Why is cocoa mixed with water rather than milk when cooked to boiling?

How would you expect the flavor and viscosity to change when cocoa is brought to a boil with water rather than mixed and not brought to boil?

III. Effect of Various Milks on Hot Cocoa

Variables:

A. Follow recipe and procedure in I. B.

B. Follow recipe in I.B. with this procedure: Mix cocoa, sugar, salt, and water. Bring to boil, stirring briskly. Mix 1 c water with (118 ml) 1/3 c dry milk solids. Add milk to cocoa mixture slowly. Continue cooking 5 min. *Do not boil.*

C. Follow recipe in I.B. and procedure III.B.

D. Make cocoa as in III.B., but add 1 T non-dairy creamer to sugar-cocoa mixture.

Results: Rate the uniformity of the chocolate drinks on a hedonic scale with 9 = extremely uniform throughout to 1 = extremely settled. Rate the color from extremely brown to brown-red to red, and the body from extremely thick to extremely thin. Comment on appearance and palatability.

Variable	Appearance	Uniformity (Settling Out)	Color	Body	Palatability
A. Homogenized breakfast cocoa					
B. Reconstituted dry skim milk—regular strength dry					
C. Dry skim milk/double strength dry milk					
D. Reconstituted dry skim milk with dairy creamer					

Conclusions: Why is the flavor of nonfat dry milk different from homogenized milk when used in cocoa?

Cheese

Notes:

Goal: To identify, prepare, and taste a variety of cheeses.

Objectives: To observe the differences in flavor and consistency of products made from natural vs. processed cheese.
To identify a variety of natural cheeses.
To cook cheese products utilizing protection from severe heat (e.g., cooking in double boiler or insulating in pans of water).

CHEESE PREPARATION

 Cheese, like milk, contains protein. The proteins in cheese may become tough and stringy and may separate from other ingredients if handled improperly. During cooking, cheese products should be *insulated* from extreme heat. Placing cheese dishes in a pan of water in the oven will avoid extreme heat toughening the edges. A double boiler will prevent sauces from becoming too hot.

NATURAL VS. PROCESSED CHEESE IN PREPARATION

Natural and processed cheese have different flavors and textures upon cooking. Which flavor is more appealing is personal choice, but a wide variety of distinctive flavors may be found when using natural cheese.

The texture of natural cheese in a cooked product is usually less smooth and uniformly blended than processed cheese. Sometimes a slightly curdled appearance will be noticed in a natural cheese. This appearance is alleviated by the use of emulsifiers in processed cheese, but the distinctive flavor of natural cheese may outweigh this texture improvement in processed cheese.

In your products, note texture and flavor differences.

A. Classification of Natural and Processed Cheese

Identify a variety of natural cheeses below.

Results: From the variety of cheeses displayed, identify which cheeses fit into each category.

	Unripened	**Mold Ripened**	**Bacteria Ripened**
Soft			
Semi-soft			
Semi-hard			
Hard			

Illustrated here are a few of the wide variety of natural cheeses available: (a) cojack, (b) gouda, (c) brie, (d) feta, (e) ricotta, and (f) cottage. Processed cheese (g) and processed cheese food may appear alike as sliced. Other process cheese food (i) is spreadable, as are some process cheese spreads (j).

B. Cheddar Cheese

Results: Evaluate the flavor, from 9 = most cheese flavor to 1 = least cheese flavor, and texture from 9 = most smooth to 1 = least smooth. From the label, find the fat grams per oz.

Type	Flavor	Texture	Moisture	Fat/Oz	Cost/Lb
Natural					
Process					
Process cheese food					
Process cheese spread					

III. Effect of Natural vs. Processed Cheese in Cheese Dishes

One lb cheese = 4 c grated cheese.

For each cheese dish, compare one recipe using natural cheddar cheese with one using processed American cheese and one using low-fat cheese.

Variables: Natural cheese
Processed cheese
Low-fat cheese

A. Baked Cheese Souffle

(14 g) 1 T margarine
(7.3 g) 1 T flour
(79 ml) 1/3 c milk
(.7 g) 1/8 t salt

(28 g) 1/4 c cheese, grated
(16.6 g) 1 egg yolk, beaten
(33.4 g) 1 egg white, beaten to stiff peak

Procedure: Melt margarine. Add flour. Stir. Add salt and milk; heat to boil. Stir occasionally. Reduce heat to low, cover, and cook 5 min without stirring. Add grated cheese. Add 1/2 of mixture to beaten yolks. Add yolk mixture back to cheese sauce. Fold in egg whites gently. Pour into 10-oz oven-safe casserole. Set in pan of water and bake at 350°F until knife comes out clean (30–45 min).

B. Microwave Cheese Souffle

(28 g) 2 T margarine
(16.5 g) 2 T finely chopped onions
(14. 5 g) 2 T all purpose flour
(118 ml) 1/2 c half & half cream
(33.4 g) 1 egg white
(16.6 g) 1 egg yolk

(56.5 g) 1/2 c grated cheddar
(.6 g) 1/4 t dry mustard
(1.5 g) 1/4 t salt
(.2 g) 1/10 t pepper
(.3 g) 1/18 t cream of tartar

Procedure: In a 16-oz microwave-safe casserole combine margarine and onion and cook on high 1 min. Stir in flour. Add half & half cream and cook on high 45 seconds. Stir. Cook 45 seconds longer until thick. Add cheese, mustard, salt, pepper, and egg yolks. Stir. Beat egg whites with cream of tartar until stiff. Fold into egg yolk mixture gently. Cook on defrost for 6 min. Rotate and cook 4 min longer or until top is dry.

C. Baked Cheese Fondue

(79 ml) 1/ 3 c milk, scalded
(34 g) 1/3 c soft, stale bread crumbs
(37.5 g) 1/3 c diced cheese
(.75 g) 1/8 t salt

1 speck cayenne
(16.6 g) 1 egg yolk, beaten thick
(33.4 g) 1 egg white, beaten stiff

Procedure: Mix scalded milk, crumbs, cheese, salt, and cayenne. Add beaten egg yolks. Fold in stiff egg whites. Pour into ungreased 10-oz baking dish. Set in pan of hot water. Bake at 350°F until firm and a sharp-pointed knife comes our clean, approximately 30 min.

D. Cheese Strata

4 slices thin, buttered bread
(85 g) 3/4 c grated cheese
(100 g) 2 eggs, slightly beaten

(237 ml) 1 c milk
(1 1/2 g) 1/4 t salt
pepper

Procedure: Place 1/2 of the bread on the bottom of an oiled 10-oz baking dish. Add cheese; cover with remainder of bread. Mix eggs, milk, salt, and pepper. Pour over bread and cheese. Set in pan of hot water and bake at 375°F for about 30 min or until firm. Ham or sausage may also be layered with the bread and cheese in this product.

❖E. Cheese Rarebit

Make one recipe for natural and processed cheese and one for low-fat cheese.

(5 g) 1 t butter or margarine
(79 ml) 1/3 c milk or light cream
(141 g) 5 oz sharp cheddar cheese, grated
(9.3 g) 1 1/2 T eggs, slightly beaten

(1 ml) 1/4 t Worcestershire sauce
(.5 g) 1/4 t paprika
(.8 g) 1/8 t salt
(.2 g) 1/16 t dry mustard
toast

Procedure: Heat butter or margarine and milk or cream over simmering water in top of double boiler. Add cheese slowly, stirring constantly until cheese is melted and mixture is smooth. Pour slowly into eggs, stirring constantly. Return mixture to double boiler. Add seasonings. Stirring constantly, cook 2–3 min longer to cook egg. Serve promptly over hot toast.

F. Macaroni and Cheese

1. Prepared from recipe

(56 g) 1 c cooked macaroni (2 oz, uncooked)
(56.5 g) 1/2 c grated cheese

1 c medium white sauce (below)
buttered crumbs

Procedure: Place alternate layers of macaroni, cheese, and white sauce in oiled baking dish. If preferred, cheese may be added to hot white sauce and stirred until melted to give a smoother mixture. Cover top with buttered crumbs. Bake at 375°F until sauce bubbles and crumbs brown.

Medium White Sauce
(28 g) 2 T margarine
(14.5 g) 2 T flour

(3 g) 1/2 t salt
(237 ml) 1 c milk

Procedure: Melt margarine. Stir in flour and salt. Stir in milk. Bring to boil. Cook on low heat 5 min. Makes 1 c.

2. Prepared from dry boxed mix

Procedure: Prepare according to box directions. Compare consistency, flavor, and cost with home-prepared sauce.

G. Cheesy-Mushroom Soup

(42 g) 3 T butter or margarine
(75.5 g) 1/2 small onion, chopped
(113.5 g) 1/4 lb fresh mushrooms, sliced
(14. 5 g) 2 T flour
(1.2 g) 1/2 t dry mustard
(.3 g) 1/8 t white pepper

(3.68 g) 1 beef bouillon cube
(237 ml) 1 c hot water
(237 ml) 1 c milk
(99 g) 3 1/2 oz cheddar cheese, shredded
1/2 lg. carrot, shredded
(1.5 g) 1 1/2 T minced parsley

Procedure: Cook onion and mushrooms in butter until onions are limp and liquid is gone. Stir together flour, mustard, and pepper. Dissolve bouillon in hot water. Add flour mixture to mushrooms. Add bouillon mixture. Bring to boil, stirring until thick. Cook 5 min. Remove from heat. Add milk. Bring to simmer. Remove from heat. Add cheese, carrot, and parsley. Warm until cheese melts.

IV. Additional Cheese Dishes

A. Swiss Cheese Dipped Fondue

1/2 clove garlic
(84 g) 3 oz Swiss cheese
(28 g) 1 oz Gruyere cheese
(.9 g) 1 t cornstarch

(79 ml) 1/3 c homogenized milk or
(60 ml) 1/4 c sauterne + (5.14 g) 1 t lemon juice
(.125 g) 1/16 t pepper
(.125 g) 1/16 t nutmeg

Procedure: Rub inside of fondue pan or sauce pan with garlic clove. Discard. Combine Swiss cheese and Gruyere cheese, shredded with cornstarch. Pour milk or sauterne and lemon juice into pan. Warm until bubbles start to form and rise. Add cheese very slowly. Stir vigorously and constantly. Keep heat on low medium. Do not boil. When cheese has melted, add a dash of nutmeg and pepper.

If fondue becomes too thick, add warmed liquid. Spear bread cube with fondue fork, piercing crust last. Dip bread into fondue and swirl to coat bread. The swirling is important to keep fondue in motion. Makes 2 servings.

Suggested dippers: French bread, boiled potatoes, shrimp, chicken, artichokes, or mushrooms.

B. Effect of cottage cheese, consistency, and flavor on cheese cake

1. Cheese cake using cottage cheese with graham cracker crust

Blender Cottage Cheese Cake with Cottage Cheese

(79 ml) 1/3 c low-fat sour cream
(50 g) 1 egg, separated
(2.5 ml) 1/2 t vanilla extract
(5.14 g) 1 t lemon juice

(25 g) 2 T sugar
(.75 g) 1/8 t salt
(150 g) 1/3 lb creamed cottage cheese
(10 g) 1 T + 1 t sifted flour
(168 g) 6 oz can reduced-calorie cherry pie filling

Procedure: Combine all ingredients except egg white and 1 T sugar in blender. Blend 1 min. Beat egg white with remaining sugar until stiff. Gently fold cheese mixture into egg whites. Pour over 2–5-in. graham cracker crusts. Bake at 325° for 30 min until cake is firm. Chill before removing from pan. Top with cherry pie filling before serving.

Crust

(64 g) 3/4 c graham cracker crumbs
(about 10 crackers)

(25 g) 2 T sugar
(28 g) 2 T butter or margarine, melted

Procedure: Roll graham crackers to fine crumbs in plastic or cellophane bag or between two sheets of waxed paper. Combine cracker crumbs, sugar, and melted margarine in bowl. Blend with fork or pastry blender. Pour crumbs into 5-in. pie plate and press evenly and firmly around sides and bottom of plate using back of large spoon or second pie plate. Chill crust or bake at 375°F for 8 min.

C. Effect of low-fat sour cream and fat-free cream cheese on cheese cake

Cream cheese contains 100 calories and 10 g fat per oz (28 g), whereas fat-free cream cheese contains 25 calories and 0 g fat per oz (28 g).

❖1. Cheese cake variables
  a. Use fat-free cream cheese and low-fat sour cream
  b. Use full-fat cream cheese and sour cream

Cherry Cheesecake

(227 g) 1 (8 oz) pkg. cream cheese, softened
(50 g) 1/4 c sugar
(2.5 ml) 1/2 t vanilla
(50 g) 1 egg

(60 g) 1/4 c sour cream
1 graham cracker crust
(168 g) 6 oz can reduced-calorie cherry pie filling

Procedure: Mix cream cheese, sugar, and vanilla with electric mixer for 10 min. Add egg; mix until blended. Add sour cream. Make graham cracker crusts according to directions in B.1 above. Pour cream cheese mixture into 2–5-in. graham cracker crust. Bake at 325°F for 30 min or until center is almost set. Cool. Refrigerate. Top with pie filling before serving. Makes 4 servings.

Evaluation

Results: Evaluate the cheese consistency from 9 = extremely smooth to 1 = extremely curdled. Evaluate tenderness from 9 = extremely tender/not stringy to 1 = extremely tough and/or stringy. Evaluate the flavor from 9 = extremely strong cheese flavor to 1 = extremely mild cheese flavor.

	Smoothness	Consistency	Tenderness	Flavor
Cheese souffle a. Natural cheese				
b. Processed cheese				
c. Microwave baked (natural cheese)				
d. Microwave baked (processed cheese)				
Cheese fondue a. Natural cheese				
b. Processed cheese				
c. Low-fat cheese				
d. Swiss cheese dip fondue				
Cheese strata a. Natural cheese				
b Processed cheese				
c. Low-fat cheese				
Cheese rarebit a. Natural cheese				
b. Processed cheese				
c. Low-fat cheese				
Macaroni and cheese (1/2 recipe) a. Natural cheese				
b. Processed cheese				
Cheesy-mushroom soup				
Cheesecake a. Cottage cheese				
b. Full-fat cream cheese				
c. Fat-free cream cheese				

Conclusions: Did natural or processed cheese contribute the strongest flavor to the product?

Which cheese provided the smoothest product, especially in the cheese rarebit?

How did the low-fat cheddar cheese compare in flavor and texture to the others?

How successful is microwave baking for a souffle?

How did the low-fat cream cheese compare to regular fat in cheesecake?

Characteristics and Mode of Serving Commonly Used Cheese

Cheese	Characteristics	Mode of Serving
American	Hard; smooth; light yellow to orange; milk. Made of cow's milk (whole) Cheddar type.	As such; in sandwiches, in cooked foods.
Apple	Hard; sharp flavor; apple-shaped. Made of cow's milk (whole). Smoked.	As such.
Asiago	Hard; granular texture; piquant flavor (sharp in old cheese). Made of cow's milk (whole).	As such; as seasoning (grated) when old.
Blue	Semi-hard; white with blue mold, flavor similar to Roquefort. Made of cow's milk (whole).	As such (dessert); on crackers; in cooked foods; in salads.
Brick	Semi-hard; smooth; flavor between Limburger and cheddar. Made of cow's milk (whole).	As such; in sandwiches; with salads.
Brie	Soft; flavor resembles Camembert. Made of cow's milk (whole).	As such (dessert).
Caciocavalio	Hard; sharp flavor; 10-pin shape. Made of cow's milk (whole or partly defatted).	As such; a seasoning (grated).
Camembert	Soft; full flavor, often ammoniacal. Made of cow's milk (whole).	As such (dessert).
Cheddar	Hard; smooth; light yellow to orange; mild. Made of cow's milk (whole or partly defatted).	As such; in sandwiches; in cooked foods.
Cottage	Soft, white; mildly sour flavor. Unripened; usually made of cow's milk (defatted). Cream may be added to finished product.	As such; in salads; in cooked foods.
Cream	Soft, smooth; buttery; mild, slightly sour flavor. Unripened; made of cream and cow's milk (whole).	As such; in sandwiches; with salads; on crackers.
Edam	Hard; rubbery; cheddar flavor, but nut-like; "cannon-ball" shape. Made of cow's milk (partly defatted).	As such; on crackers.
Gammelost	Hard; golden brown; strong flavor; pungent. Made of cow's milk (defatted, soured).	As such.
Gjetost	Hard; very dark brown; sweetish flavor. Made of goat's milk (whole).	As such; on crackers.
Gorgonzola	Semi-hard; marbled with blue mold; spicy flavor. Made of cow's milk (whole).	As such (dessert; with salads).

Cheese	Characteristics	Mode of Serving
Gouda	Semi-hard; flavor like Edam. Made of partly defatted milk.	As such; on crackers.
Gruyere	Hard with gas holes; nut-like, salty flavor. Made of cow's milk (usually partly defatted).	As such (dessert).
Jack	Semi-hard; smooth; milk; made of cow's milk (whole).	As such; in sandwiches.
Limburger	Soft; full flavor; highly aromatic. Made of cow's milk (whole or partly defatted).	In sandwiches; on crackers.
Muenster	Semi-hard; flavor between brick and Limburger Usually made of a mixture of cow's and goat's milk (whole).	As such; in sandwiches.
Neufchatel	Soft; creamy; white; mild flavor. Unripened. Made of cow's milk (whole).	As such; in sandwiches; on crackers; in salads.
Parmesan	Hard; granular texture; sharp flavor. Made of cow's milk (partly defatted).	As such; as seasoning.
Port du Salut	Semi-hard; rubbery texture, flavor between Limburger and cheddar. Made of whole, slightly acid cow's milk.	As such (dessert).
Primost	Soft; light brown; mild flavor. Unripened; made from whey.	As such.
Provolone	Hard; sharp flavor; usually pear shaped. Made of cow's milk (whole). Smoked.	As such.
Roquefort	Semi-hard; white with blue mold; sweet, piquant flavor. Made of sheep's milk (whole).	As such (dessert); on crackers; with salads.
Sapsago	Hard; green color; flavored with clover leaves; small; cone-shaped. Made of cow's milk (defatted and soured), buttermilk, and whey.	As such; as seasoning (grated).
Stilton	Semi-hard; white with blue mold; spicy flavor. Made of cow's milk (whole with added cream).	As such (dessert); in cooked foods; with salads.
Swiss	Hard with gas holes; nut-like, sweet flavor. Made of cow's milk (partly defatted).	As such; in sandwiches; with salads.

Eggs

Notes:

Goal: To observe denaturation and coagulation of egg protein in a variety of egg products.

Objectives: To observe and list quality characteristics of fresh eggs
To observe the quality of appropriately hard-cooked, poached, and scrambled eggs.
To observe the effects of overcooking egg protein.
To observe and describe the effect of salt, vinegar, liquid, sugar, and temperature on coagulation of egg protein.
To taste quality egg-based products.

PROTEINS

Protein is an important component of both the white and the yolk, but the types of protein differ between white and yolk. Proteins of eggs are of colloidal size. The proteins are also bonded together into a specifically shaped molecule. Heat, acid, and beating can change the shape of the molecule. This process is denaturation. With heat, the denatured proteins may interact forming new bonds. The newly bonded proteins aggregate and form a gel (a process called coagulation). This process is observed in baking or poaching eggs alone and is also observed in custards.

SAFETY

Because Salmonella (a pathogenic microorganism) has been detected in fresh uncooked eggs, current recommendations suggest using pasteurized eggs for any uncooked product. Cooked eggs should reach a temperature of 160°F or be held at 140°F or above for 3 1/2 min. When a knife comes out clean from a baked custard or quiche, it has reached this temperature.

❖I. Observation of Quality
Observe the egg through the light of a candler and after breaking out onto a plate.

Eggs	Description—Broken Out
Held at room temperature for 2 weeks	
Held in the refrigerator for 2 weeks	

Conclusions: How do the air cells compare in size?

Compare the thickness of the whites.

Which yolk stands up best?

❖II.   Hard-Cooked Eggs
Variables:
A. Cover 2 eggs with water in sauce pan (water level should be at least 1 in. above eggs); heat water just to simmering. Turn heat to lowest setting. Cover and let stand 15 min. Cool 1 egg immediately and 1 egg slowly in hot water.

B. Cover 2 eggs with water in sauce pan (water level should be at least 1 in. above eggs); heat until water boils. Cover and boil 15 min. Cool 1 egg immediately and 1 egg slowly in hot water.

Results: Evaluate tenderness of the white and yolk from 9 = extremely tender to 1 = extremely tough, and evaluate the yolk surface, indicating the color as yellow orange, yellow, slightly green, moderately green, green.

Variable	Temperature °C °F	Time in Min	Results White	Yolk
A. Water simmering for 15 min. 1. Cool 1 egg slowly in hot water				
2. Cool 1 egg quickly in cold water				
B. Water boiling for 15 min. 1. Cool 1 egg slowly in hot water				
2. Cool 1 egg quickly in cold water				

Conclusions: On which yolk do you see more green iron sulfide? Why?

Write the chemical reaction.

What are the best instructions for hard cooking eggs?

How does boiling effect tenderness of egg protein?

III. Baked or Shirred Eggs: Effect of Insulating Ingredients

(12.5 g) 2 T soft bread crumbs   (15 ml) 1 T half & half cream
(50 g) 1 egg   Salt and pepper to taste

Procedure: A. Cover bottom of individual oiled custard cup with 1/2 of the crumbs. Break egg, slip onto crumbs. Season, cover with remaining crumbs, and add cream. Set in pan of hot water. Bake at 350°F until white is firm, approximately 20 min.
B. Bake second egg in custard cup with no crumbs or cream. Bake same time as for variable A.

Results: Using a paired comparison evaluation, indicate which has the better appearance, which has the better flavor, and which is more tender.

Variable	Appearance	Flavor	Tenderness
A. Use cream and top with soft bread crumbs. Bake as above.			
B. No insulation, no crumbs, no pan of water. 1 egg. Bake as above.			

Conclusions: Why is protecting the white from extreme heat important?

IV. Poached Egg: Effect of Salt and Acid

Fill oiled shallow pan with water to depth sufficient to cover eggs completely, about 1 1/2 in. Salt or white vinegar may be added according to variable. Heat water to boiling. Break an egg carefully into a cup; slide gently into water. Water may be stirred before first egg is added. If the egg is added at the right moment, the swirl of water will tend to keep it in compact form. Reduce heat to temperature below boiling point and cook until white is completely set and yolks begin to thicken (3–5 min.). Remove eggs individually with a perforated skimmer. It is easier to obtain an even shape if eggs are cooked in oiled muffin rings or in a special egg poacher suspended over hot water.

Variables:

A. Plain water: Follow directions above.

B. Water and salt: Add (4 g) 3/4 t salt to water.

C. Water and vinegar: Add (3 ml) 1/2 t vinegar to water.

Results: Describe appearance, flavor, and tenderness.

Variable	Appearance	Flavor	Tenderness
A. Plain water			
B. Water with salt			
C. Water with vinegar			

Conclusions: Why should salt or vinegar keep the egg in a more compact form?

Compare calories from fat from poached eggs vs. fried eggs.

Why is water held below boiling while cooking the eggs?

V. Fried Eggs

Procedure I: Heat frying pan with 1 T or more of fat. Bacon or ham drippings may be used. Break eggs in saucer. Slip in pan, 1 at a time, and cook slowly until white is completely set and yolk begins to thicken. Lift fat with spoon and pour over egg until a film forms over yolk, or, if preferred, turn eggs once while cooking. Season to taste. Fat should not be hot enough to brown egg or it will be tough. Cooking time approximately 8 min.

Procedure II: Use skillet with tight-fitting lid. Spray non-stick coating on skillet. Heat. Break egg into saucer. Slip into pan. Cook until white is completely set and yolk begins to thicken. Then add 1 T water. Cover tightly and turn off heat. The steam from the water will finish cooking the eggs and will produce a fine film over the yolks. Lift eggs out with pancake turner onto heated plates and serve at once.

Results: Using a paired comparison evaluation, indicate which has the better appearance, which has the better flavor, and which is more tender.

Variable	Appearance	Flavor	Tenderness
Method 1: Dip fat over egg			
Method 2: Add water and cover			

Conclusions: How will egg quality affect final appearance?

Why does egg white protein cover the yolk?

VI. Scrambled Eggs: Effect of Liquid, Beating, and Cooking Method

(6.5 g) 1/2 T fat   (.5 g) 1/16 t salt
(50 g) 1 egg   pepper to taste
(15 ml) 1 T milk

Variables:

A. Place fat in frying pan; heat gently. Beat eggs until whites and yolks are mixed. Beat in milk and seasonings.
Pour into heated pan. Cook slowly, stirring, until eggs are cooked and of creamy consistency.

B. Omit milk from formula and proceed as directed in A.

C. Omit beating whites and yolks together, thus leaving portions of white and yolk, and proceed as directed in A.

D. Place fat in top of double boiler; place water in bottom of double boiler and heat. Beat eggs until whites and yolks
are mixed. Beat in milk and seasonings. Pour into heated pan. Cook, stirring occasionally until eggs are firm.

E. Follow formula and directions in A, but use low-cholesterol egg product.

F. Follow formula and directions in A, but use product with 1/2-yolk-to-white ratio.

G. Microwave scrambled eggs as below.

Microwave Scrambled Eggs

(14 g) 1/2 T margarine   (15 ml) 1 T milk
(100 g) 2 eggs   salt as desired

Procedure: Place margarine in 10 oz Pyrex casserole. Cook on high for 20 seconds or until melted. Beat eggs and
milk well. Add to margarine and cook on high for 45 seconds. Stir outer edges to center. Cook on
high 45 seconds more until almost set but still moist.

Results: Rate the appearance from extremely uniform to extremely separated. Rate the flavor and tenderness
with 9 = extremely flavorful and extremely tender, to 1 = extremely poor flavor and extremely tough.

Variables	Appearance	Flavor	Tenderness
A. Milk added, cook in frying pan			
B. Same as A except no liquid added			
C. Same as A except egg is not beaten			
D. Same as A except cook in double boiler			
E. Same as A except use low-cholesterol egg product			
F. Egg Wells (1/2 yolk, white mix)			
G. Microwave scrambled eggs			

Conclusions: How is the liquid involved in coagulation?

Why do white and yolk coagulate separately if not beaten well?

What advantages are there in cooking eggs in a double boiler or steam-jacketed kettle, especially for large quantity?

How does the low-cholesterol product compare in flavor and texture?

What are the advantages and disadvantages of using the microwave to cook eggs?

What safety precautions need to be considered with microwave cooking of eggs?

VII. Egg Coagulation and Gelation in Custard: Effect of Formula Changes

Objective: To assess the changes in characteristics of baked and stirred custards due to formula variation and due to cooking procedure.

Formula: Custard

Variables:

	A. Basic Formula	B. Egg Yolk Only	C. Double Egg	D. Extra Sugar
Milk	(237 ml) 1 c	(237 ml) 1 c	(237 ml) 1 c	(237 ml) 1 c
Eggs	(48 g) 3 T	(48 g) 3 T	(96 g) 6 T	(48 g) 3 T
Sugar	(25 g) 2 T	(25 g) 2 T	(25 g) 2 T	(50 g) 1/4 c
Salt	(.75 g) 1/8 t	(.75 g) 1/8 t	(.75 g) 1/8 t	(.75 g) 1/8 t.
Vanilla	(1.25 ml) 1/4 t	(1.25 ml) 1/4 t	(1.25 ml) 1/4 t	(1.25 ml) 1/4 t
Equal	_____	_____	_____	_____

	E. Aspartame	F. Egg Beaters
Milk	(237 ml) 1 c	(237 ml) 1 c
Eggs	(48 g) 3 T	_____
Sugar	_____	(25 g) 2 T
Salt	(.75 g) 1/8 t	(.75 g) 1/8 t
Vanilla	(1.25 ml) 1/4 t	(1.25 ml) 1/4 t
Equal	(6 g) 6 pkts.	_____
Egg Beaters	_____	(48 g) 3 T

Procedure for A–G above

1. Beat eggs to mix well, but not to foam. Add milk, salt, and sugar.
2. **Baked Custard:** Place 1/3 c mixture into small custard cup. Add (1/2 ml) 1/8 t of vanilla. Save remaining vanilla for soft custard. Place baking dish in a pan of hot water. Bake at 350°F until tip of a small, pointed knife inserted near center of custard comes out clean (approximately 25 min).
3. **Soft Custard (Stirred Custard):** Use remainder of above mixture. Cook over hot, *not boiling,* water, stirring constantly until mixture coats spoon. Record temperature. Remove quickly from heat and set in cold water. Flavor with remaining vanilla or aspartame.

Caramel Custard

Procedure: Heat (50 g) 1/4 c sugar in a small skillet over medium heat, stirring constantly. When sugar has melted and caramelized to a deep golden brown color, pour around the sides of 2 metal molds (be careful). Prepare one recipe for baked custard (A) and divide between the molds. Bake as described for the control baked custard. Allow baked custard to cool about 10 min, then invert carefully into shallow serving dishes.

Results: Rate flavor and appearance on a 9-point hedonic scale with 9 = most desirable flavor and appearance and 1 = least desirable flavor and appearance. Evaluate viscosity with 9 = extremely thick, to 5 = neither thick nor thin, to 1 = extremely thin. Rate syneresis on a scale with 9 = extreme syneresis to 1 = no syneresis. Record coagulation temperature of the stirred custard.

Baked Custard Variables	Flavor	Appearance	Syneresis	Doneness
A. Basic				
B. Egg yolk				
C. Double egg				
D. Extra sugar				
E. Aspartame				
F. Egg Beaters				

Stirred Custard Variables	Flavor	Appearance	Temperature of Coagulation	Viscosity
A. Basic				
B. Egg yolk				
C. Double egg				
D. Extra sugar				
E. Aspartame				
F. Egg Beaters				

VIII. Baked Custard: Effect of Baking Method
Directions may differ for other oven brands. Make one recipe of basic formula (A) for each variable.

A. Custard: Convection/Microwave/Bake
    Bake 2 custards (100 g in each cup) in Thermodore: convection/microwave/bake.
    1. Place 2 custard cups in bottom portion of 2-piece metal broil pan.
    2. Pour 3 c hot tap water into broil pan around custard cups.
    3. Bake in non-preheated oven: Press convection *ON*. Set microwave on *low* for *8 min.* or until knife inserted comes out clean. Let stand in hot water 3 min. if not completely done.

B. Custard: Convection (Thermodore)
    Bake 2 custards (100 g in each custard cup)
    1. Place 2 custard cups in bottom portion of 2-piece metal broiler pan. Pour 3 c very hot tap water into broil pan around custard cups.
    2. Bake in a non-preheated oven at 300°F with convection *ON* for 29 min. or until knife inserted in center comes out clean.

C. Custard: Baked same time and temperature as convection.
    1. Place 2 custard cups in bottom portion of 2-piece metal broil pan. Pour 3 c very hot tap water into broil pan around custard cups.
    2. Bake in conventional oven at 300°F for 29 min.

IX. Quiche au Fromage

1 9-in. frozen pastry shell	(3 g) 1/2 t salt
(76 g) 4 slices lean bacon cut in 1/4-in. pieces	pinch white pepper
(133.2 g) 2 eggs + 2 extra egg yolks	(85 g) 3/4 c grated Swiss cheese
(355 ml) 1 1/2 c milk	(11.5 g) 2 T grated Parmesan cheese

Procedure: Bake pastry shell according to package directions; cool. Cook bacon; drain. Beat eggs, milk, and seasoning together. Stir in cheese. Place cooled pastry shell on baking sheet. Scatter bacon on the bottom of the pastry shell and carefully ladle cheese-egg custard into it. Bake at 375°F in upper third of oven for 25 min or until custard has puffed and browned and a knife inserted in the center comes out clean. Serve hot or warm.

Results: Rate flavor and appearance on a 9-point hedonic scale with 9 = most desirable flavor and appearance and 1 = least desirable flavor and appearance.

Baked Variables	Flavor	Appearance	Time to Bake	Doneness
A. Convection/microwave				
B. Convection				
C. Convection				
Quiche au fromage				

Conclusions: How is coagulation temperature affected by: increased egg concentration, egg yolk replacing whole egg, and increased or decreased sugar concentration?

How may the change in coagulation temperatures by added ingredients such as sugar be applied to coagulation of cakes?

How do flavor, consistency, and gelation compare with use of Egg Beaters or Egg Wells?

What test determines doneness of cooked and baked custard?

What functional properties of a colloid did you see in these experiments?

What causes syneresis?

How do ovens compare in producing a quality product?

Compare syneresis, browning, and doneness in convection vs. convection microwave ovens.

X. Eggs in Omelets

Plain French Omelet

(50 g) 1 egg
(15 ml) 1 T milk
(.75 g) 1/8 t salt

1 speck pepper
(4 g) 1 t fat or non-stick spray

Procedure: Add seasoning to egg and milk. Beat. Heat a frying pan containing enough fat to cover the bottom or spray with a non-stick spray. Pour in omelet mixture. Spread evenly over pan and cook slowly 2–5 min or until delicately browned underneath. Do not stir. Lift edges to allow uncooked egg to flow to bottom.

Mexican Omelet

(57 g) 1/2 c shredded sharp processed
  American cheese
dash paprika
(59 ml) 1/4 c light cream
(100 g) 2 eggs

1 peeled green chile, diced (canned)
(5 g) 1 t margarine or butter
pepper to taste
salt to taste

Procedure: In top of double boiler, melt cheese with paprika and cream over hot, not boiling water. In mixing bowl, beat eggs lightly with a fork; add diced green chile, salt, and pepper. Heat 8-in. skillet; add 1 t butter. Tilt pan to grease sides. Pour in omelet mixture, leaving heat moderately high. Rapidly stir through top of uncooked egg. Keep omelet an even depth. Stir the uncooked egg out to edges. Lift edges, allowing uncooked egg to flow to bottom. Omelet cooks in 2–3 min. When egg is set, remove pan from heat. Spoon part of cheese mixture across center of omelet; flip sides over, envelope-style, to hold in cheese. Roll omelet onto plate and top with remaining cheese mixture.

Vegetable Omelet

(38 g) 2 slices bacon, diced
(70 g) 1/2 c zucchini, chopped
(142 g) 1/2 10-oz package frozen OR
  (100 g) 1/2 c cooked and drained spinach
(16.5 g) 2 T chopped onion

(1 1/2 g) 1/4 t salt
dash pepper
dash oregano
(150 g) 3 eggs
(5.5 g) 1 T Parmesan cheese

Procedure: Cook bacon; drain or use vegetable oil for strictly vegetarian omelet. Add zucchini, spinach, and onion. Stir well; cook about 5 min. Season with salt, pepper, and oregano. Beat eggs until fluffy; add Parmesan cheese. Pour vegetable mixture into eggs; mix well. Return mixture to frying pan; cover and cook over low heat until slightly browned on bottom, about 5 min. Place in oven at 350° for about 10 min. Loosen omelet; slide onto warm platter. Serves 2.

Results: Describe flavor and tenderness of omelets.

Variable	Results
Plain omelet (French)	
Mexican omelet	
Vegetable omelet	

Conclusion: Compare procedure for cooking scrambled eggs with procedures for omelets.

What food groups may omelets contain?

EGG WHITE FOAMS

Goal: To observe egg white protein denaturation and stabilization when beaten and its function in food products.

Objective: To determine the effect of beating and added ingredients on the stability and volume of egg white foams.
To use egg white foams in making quality omelets, souffles, and meringues.

❖I. Effect of Stage of Beating on Volume and Stability of Egg White Foams

Procedure: Use a small glass bowl for beating 1 egg white, (30 ml) 2 T. While beating, move the beater around so that the mass is beaten evenly. Measure volume. To determine drainage, place in a funnel (square of wire over hole). Place funnel over a 100 ml graduated cylinder; allow to drain for 45 min. Record drainage in ml.

Results: Record original beaten volume and drainage after 45 minutes.

Variables—Stage of Beating	Beaten White— Original Volume (ml)	Drainage After 45 Min. (ml)	Comments: Changes in Appearance, Etc.
1. Foamy—mass is white, but the bubbles are still large and the mixture is frothy.			
2. Soft peak—air cells are smaller; flows slowly in bowl; very shiny and moist; tips formed when the beater is removed fold over, forming rounded peaks.			
3. Stiff peak—air cells very small; white; still glossy, smooth, and moist. Forms points when the beater is removed.			
4. Dry—very white; dull; dry (flakes break off during beating); curds appear in the mixture; breaks when the beater is lifted and is rigid or almost brittle.			

Stages of beating egg white foam: (a) foamy, (b) soft peak, (c) stiff peak, and (d) dry.

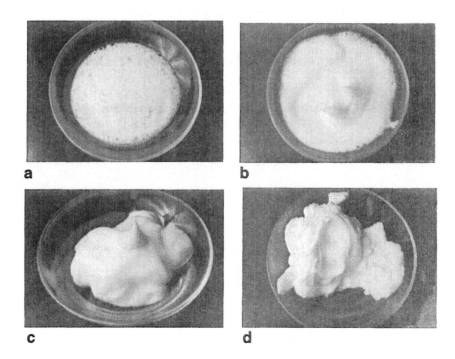

a

b

c

d

Conclusions: Which stage of beating gives the greatest volume and stability?

What are results of over-beating to the dry stage?

❖II. Effect of Added Ingredients on Egg White Foam

Procedure: Use procedure under I. Add one of the ingredients listed below after egg white is beaten to the foamy stage; continue beating until the stiff stage is reached.

Variable	Beaten White—Original Volume (ml)	Drainage After 45 Min. (ml)	Comments: Changes in Appearance, Etc.
1. (15 ml) 1 T water			
2. (15 ml) 1 T tomato juice			
3. (1 g) 1/8 t cream of tartar			
4. (5 ml) 1 t lemon juice and (29 g) 2 t water			
5. (.5 g) 1/2 t egg yolk			
6. (2 g) 1/2 t fat (use hydrogenated fat)			
7. (25 g) 2 T sugar			
8. (.7 g) 1/8 t salt			

Conclusions: Which of the above additions increase volume?

Which of the above additions increase stability?

Which of the above additions hinder foam formation or stability?

❖III. Effect of Sugar and Baking Temperature on Soft Meringues

Variables:

A. (12 g) 1 T sugar, bake at 350°

B. (25 g) 2 T sugar, bake at 350°

C. (50 g) 4 T sugar, bake at 350°

D. (25 g) 2 T sugar, bake at 450°

E. (25 g) 2 T sugar, bake at 250°

Formula:

(33.4 g) 1 frozen (thawed) pasteurized egg white   (25 g) 2 T sugar
(.4 g) 1/16 t salt   (.6 ml) 1/8 t vanilla
(.2 g) 1/16 t cream of tartar

Procedure: Beat egg whites with salt and cream of tartar. After the foam forms soft peaks, add sugar gradually according to variable. Continue beating until stiff but not dry. Add vanilla. Spread meringue on 6-in. circle drawn on brown paper laid on baking sheet. Bake until delicately brown.

Results: Using a 9-point hedonic scale, rate the tenderness with 9 = extremely tender to 1 = extremely tough. Evaluate color from extremely brow to moderately brown to light brown to extremely white. Rate volume with 9 = very large volume to 1 = very small volume.

Variable			Results			
Amount of Sugar	Baking Temp. (F)	Baking Time (Min)	Color	Tenderness	Volume	Other
A. (12 g) 1 T	350°	15				
B. (25 g) 2 T	350°	15				
C. (50 g) 4 T	350°	15				
D. (25 g) 2 T	450°	5				
E. (25 g) 2 T	250°	25				

Conclusions: List characteristics of soft meringues.

Which temperature is both safe and gives a quality product?

Which proportion of sugar to egg white gives stability and a golden color?

Soft meringues are often used on cream pies. (Photo: Courtesy of the American Egg Board.).

IV. Egg White Foams in Hard Meringues

(133.6 g) 4 frozen thawed egg whites (1/2 c)   (2.5 ml) 1/2 t vanilla
(1.5 g) 1/4 t salt   (200 g) 1 c sugar
(.8 g) 1/4 t cream of tartar

Procedure: Beat egg whites to foam. Add cream of tartar and vanilla. Beat to soft peak; add sugar and salt gradually. Continue beating until stiff and whites loose their gloss. Cover baking sheets with brown paper. Make into shells 3–4-in. in diameter with a spoon or pastry bag. Bake 1 hour at 250°F. Remove from paper or pan while hot to avoid breaking. Meringues may be stored in refrigerator 24 hours for ease in cutting and eating.

Results: Describe the color, tenderness, and crispness of the meringue.

Variable	Desirable Characteristics of Hard Meringue
A. Half recipe beaten until stiff	
B. Half recipe beating until dry and gloss lost	

Conclusions: How does the proportion of sugar to egg white differ for soft and hard meringue?

Why does a hard meringue become dry and yet remain white?

a   b

Egg whites (a) are beaten to the dry stage for hard meringues, then baked at a very low temperature. Hard meringues (b) are used in a variety of desserts. (Photo: Courtesy of the American Egg Board.)

V. Effect of Liquid on Egg White Foam in Puffy Omelet
Variables:

(50 g) 1 egg   1 speck pepper
(15 ml) 1 T liquid (as in variable below)   non-stick coating or vegetable oil
(.7 g) 1/8 t salt

Procedure: Separate egg. Add seasoning to yolk and beat. Add liquid (other than milk or cream) to egg white and beat until stiff. Fold egg yolk into egg white. Heat a frying pan containing enough fat to cover the bottom or spray with a non-stick coating. Pour in omelet mixture. Spread evenly over pan and cook slowly 2–5 min or until delicately browned underneath. Bake at 350°F (moderate oven) until top is firm and dry, but not brown (10–15 min). Loosen omelet with spatula, fold, and turn onto hot platter. A larger omelet may need a longer cooking time in the oven.

Results: Rate the tenderness and volume on a scale with 9 = extremely tender and extremely large volume to 1 = extremely tough and extremely small volume.

Variable (Type of Liquid)	Tenderness	Volume
A. Water		
B. (5 ml) 1 t lemon juice and (10 ml) 2 t water in place of water		
C. (15 ml) 1 T tomato juice in place of water		
D. Milk in place of water. Mix milk with yolk rather than white and proceed as directed.		

Conclusion: How does acid added to liquid affect omelet volume?

How may baking temperature and time affect volume and tenderness?

VI. Egg White Foam in Souffle
Souffle

(4 g) 2 t margarine
(7.3 g) 1 T flour
(.8 g) 1/8 t salt
(79 ml) 1/3 c milk

(80 ml) 1/3 c prepared food: chopped apricots, chopped spinach, grated carrots, or prunes
(16.6 g) 1 egg yolk, beaten
(33.4 g) 1 egg white, stiffly beaten

Procedure: Melt fat. Add flour and salt and stir until smooth. Add liquid and cook until thick to make white sauce. (Bring to boil, turn heat to low and cook 3 min.)

Add prepared food to hot white sauce. Stir in egg yolks. Remove from heat and fold in egg whites. Pour into ungreased 10 oz casserole. Set in pan of hot water and bake at 350°F until firm and, when inserted, a sharp-pointed knife comes out clean (30–40 min). Serve immediately.

A. **Variety**
1. Carrot, grated
2. Apricot, chopped
3. Fresh spinach, minced
4. Prune, cooked, diced, or pureed
5. For *chocolate souffle,* add (14 g) 1/2 square chocolate, (38 g) 3 T sugar, and (2.5 ml) 1/2 t vanilla to hot white sauce. Omit prepared food.
6. For *cheese souffle,* add (21 g) 3 T grated cheese and (.3 g) 1/8 t paprika to white sauce

B. **Effect of baking method**
Make 3 recipes. Use cheese souffle recipe for each variable. Place in ovens so that all variables will finish at approximately the same time.

Variables:
1. Bake in conventional oven at 350°F for 30 min or until knife comes out clean.
2. Bake in Thermodore convection oven. Bake in non-preheated oven at 350°F with convection *on* for 25 min or until knife comes out clean.
3. Bake in Thermodore combination convection/microwave. Bake in non-preheated oven. (Other oven brands will require separate directions.)
   a. Press oven heat *on*. Set temperature to 350°F. Press convection on. Set microwave to medium low and move latch to microwave position. Set microwave time to 2 1/2 min.
   b. Continue to bake with convection on and no microwave for 5–6 min until a knife comes out clean.

Souffles

Results: Describe the appearance, texture, consistency, and palatability of each souffle.

Variable	Appearance	Texture and Consistency	Palatability
Carrot			
Apricot			
Spinach			
Prune			
Chocolate souffle			
Cheese souffle—conventional oven			
Cheese souffle—convection oven			
Cheese souffle—convection microwave			

Conclusions: How does temperature of egg coagulation affect volume of souffles?

How does stability of egg white foam affect volume of souffles?

Why is souffle baked in a pan insulated with water?

Compare each baking method for:
   time

   volume

   browning

   moistness

Why is it important to not overcook the white sauce?

Meat

Notes:

MEAT AND POULTRY

Goal: To identify types and cuts of meat and to practice cooking methods.

Objectives: To relate cuts of meat and amount of connective tissue to optimum cooking method for best flavor and tenderness.
To become proficient with cooking methods that use no added moisture: broiling, pan broiling, frying, and roasting.
To identify cuts that adapt best to broiling or to frying.
To observe results of the use of enzymatic tenderizers on less tender cuts of meat.
To compare flavor, appearance, and tenderness of cooking with and without added moisture or in steam.
To observe the moisture retention and flavor of ground beef roasts with soy protein.

The flesh foods of red meat, fish, and poultry contain water as a primary component, but protein is important in determining tenderness, juiciness, color, and flavor. Both the muscle tissue proteins and the connective tissue proteins (especially collagen) affect the tenderness and juiciness. The primal section partially determines size of muscle fiber and amount of collagen. As meat cooking temperatures reach 74–80°C (165–176°F), water loss from muscle fibers accelerates, resulting in a drier meat. Also, muscle fibers become less tender when reaching 65–75°C (149–167°F). The connective tissue collagen is converted to gelatin when meat is held at a temperature above 65°C (149°F) for an extended time in the presence of moisture; thus the amount of collagen will determine the best cooking temperature and the length of time needed to tenderize.

Cuts of meat that contain low amounts of collagen are generally most tender and juicy when dry heat methods are used to cook to temperatures up to 73°C (160°F). The rib, short loin, sirloin of beef, and loin and leg of pork may be cooked by dry heat methods. Dry heat methods include broiling, pan broiling, roasting, and frying. Cuts of meat containing higher amounts of collagen may be tenderized by an extended cooking time with moist heat and temperatures held above 65°C (149°F). Beef chuck, round, flank, and pork shoulder are some of the cuts with more collagen. Moist heat methods include braising, stewing, and using slow cookers or pressure cookers.

Most poultry that is young is tender and can be cooked by dry heat.

I. Primal and Retail Carcass Identification

Identify the primal and retail cuts of the carcass on lines A and B. Indicate appropriate cooking methods for the retail cuts on line C.

Lamb

Lamb Chart
A. Primal cuts
B. Retail cuts
C. Cooking methods

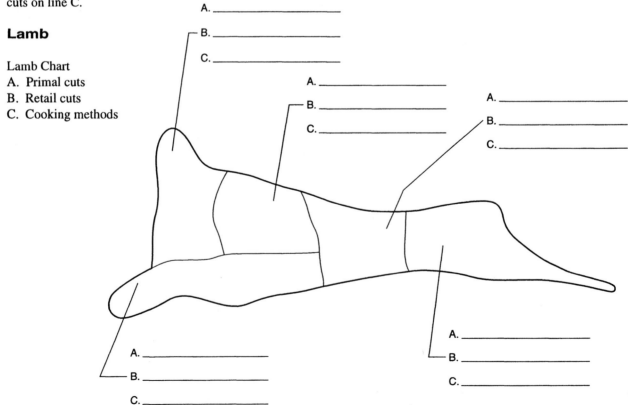

A. _____

B. _____

C. _____

A. _____

B. _____

C. _____

A. _____

B. _____

C. _____

A. _____

B. _____

C. _____

A. _____

B. _____

C. _____

Beef

Identify the primal and retail cuts of the carcass on lines A and B. Indicate appropriate cooking methods for the retail cuts on line C.

Beef Chart

A.   Primal cuts
B.   Retail cuts
C.   Cooking methods

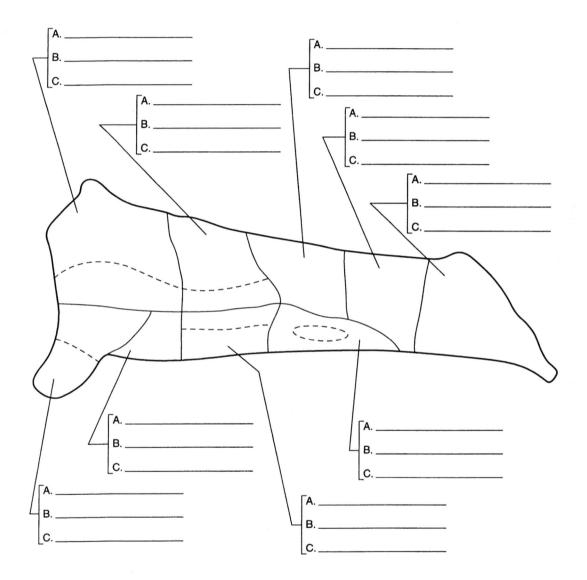

Pork

Identify the primal and retail cuts of the carcass on lines A and B. Indicate appropriate cooking methods for the retail cuts on line C.

Pork Cuts

A. Primal cuts
B. Retail cuts
C. Cooking methods

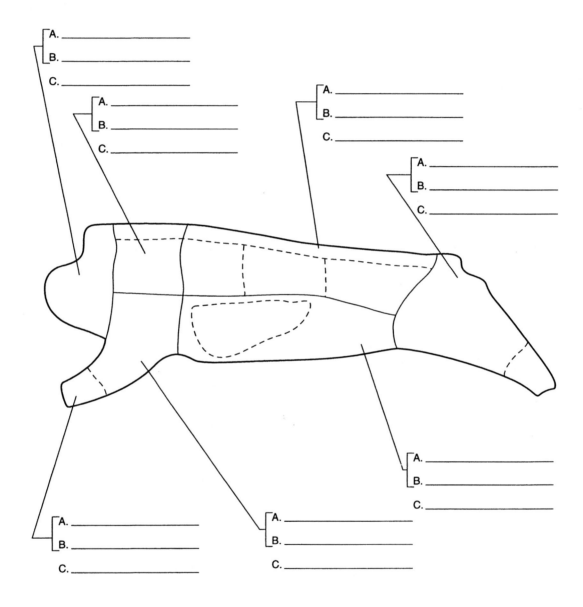

A. _____
B. _____
C. _____

A. _____
B. _____
C. _____

A. _____
B. _____
C. _____

A. _____
B. _____
C. _____

A. _____
B. _____
C. _____

A. _____
B. _____
C. _____

A. _____
B. _____
C. _____

II. Comparison of Muscle Fiber, Collagen, and Elastin

Place 1/2 c *lean* less-tender meat (trim off visible fat) in a heavy blender with 3/4 c water. Run on high speed 1/2 min. Place in a strainer and stir. Remove portion from the strainer and rinse by stirring into 1/2 c water. Drain in the strainer again. Some of the muscle fiber proteins go through the strainer with the water; much of the collagen remains in the strainer. Obtain a piece of elastin. To determine effect of heat, cook the 3 samples (muscle fiber, collagen, and elastin) for 45 min. Use 3 small beakers on the same heat source. Add about the same amount of water to the collagen and elastin that is on the muscle fiber. Keep at the simmering point.

Variable	Effect of Heat
Muscle fiber	
Collagen	
Elastin	

Conclusions: Which cuts contain the most collagen?

How does cooking affect collagen?

How does cooking affect elastin?

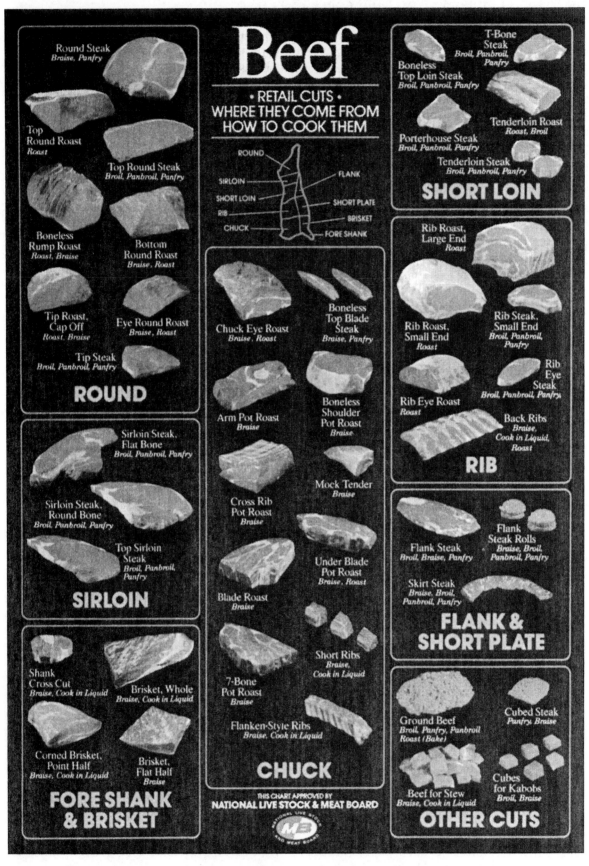

(Photo: Courtesy of the National Cattlemen's Beef Association)

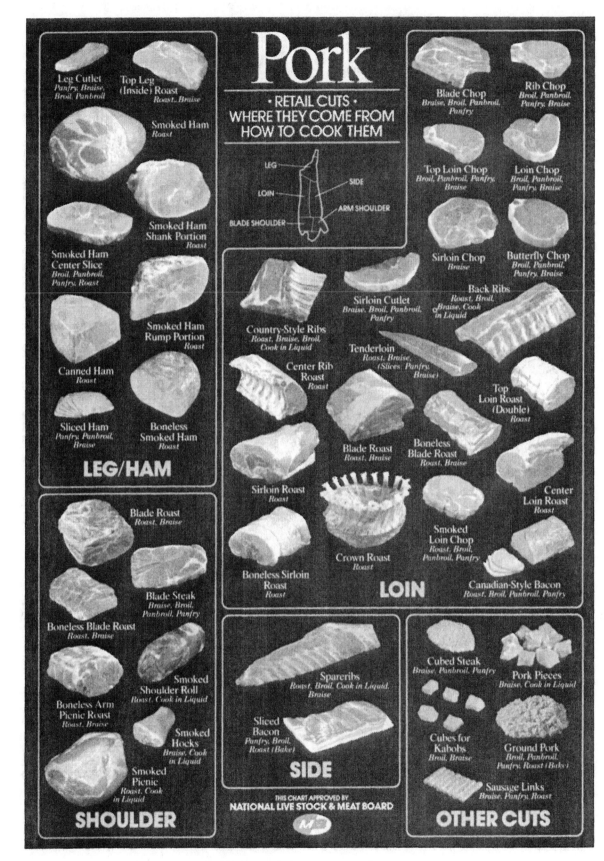

(Photo: Courtesy of the National Cattlemen's Beef Association)

(Photo: Courtesy of the National Cattlemen's Beef Association)

Dry Heat Cooking

SAFETY: End point cooking temperature recommendations to assure safety of fresh meat include the following.

	Food Handlers		
	Retail		**Consumers**
Patties	157°F		160°F
Roast beef	145°F		145°F
Poultry	165°F		180°F Whole
			150°F Parts
Pork	150°F		160°F

I. Effect of Pan-Broiling Tender Cuts

A. Ham and Lamb Chops

Procedure: Weigh before and after cooking.

Steaks or chops less than 1-in. thick may be prepared satisfactorily by pan-broiling. Place meat in a heavy skillet or on a griddle that may or may not be preheated. Cook meat slowly and turn occasionally with tongs. Pour off fat as it accumulates in pan. In pan-broiling, no fat or water is added. Pan is uncovered. Meat will toughen if broiling continues after the medium to well-done stage (160°–170°F).

B. Hamburger

Procedure: Weigh before and after cooking.

Pan-broil 4 oz of hamburger. Place patty in skillet. Cook slowly. Pour off fat as it accumulates. Do not add water or cover. Cook to 160°F until gray and juices run clear. Pan broil remaining 4 oz hamburger on higher heat; turn and press frequently.

Variables:
1. Cook on low heat.
2. Cook on high heat.

Results: Rate on a 9-point hedonic scale with 9 = most tender, most juicy, or most flavorful imaginable, and 1 = least tender, least juicy, or least flavorful imaginable.

Meat	Color	Tenderness	Juiciness	Flavor	Weight		Shrinkage*
					Before	**After**	**% Loss**
(228 g) pork ham slice 8 oz							
Turkey ham slice							
Lamb chops (2)							
❖(114 g) hamburger 4 oz low heat							
❖(114 g) hamburger 4 oz high heat							

* % Shrinkage = $\dfrac{\text{Weight before cooking} - \text{weight after cooking}}{\text{weight before cooking}} \times 100$

Conclusions: Do ham and lamb loin chops maintain tenderness when broiled?

Are these cuts from a tender primal section?

Which method of cooking hamburger gave the greater yield?

Describe pan broiling.

II. Effect of Oven Broiling on Tender and Less-Tender Cuts

A. Rib steak
Procedure: Weigh before and after cooking.

Turn the oven regulator to broil. The broiler may or may not be preheated. The temperature is regulated by the distance the meat is placed from the source of the pan. The top surface of the meat should be 2–3 in. from the heat. The closer the meat is placed to the heat, the more likely the surface becomes browned while the interior remains less well done. Broil until top side is brown or until meat is approximately half done. Season top side, turn with tongs, and brown the other side.

B. Chuck steak with and without tenderizer
Procedure: Weigh before and after cooking.

Fork an enzymatic meat tenderizer into 1 chuck steak, according to tenderizer directions. Place both chuck steaks on broiler and broil according to directions for A. Weigh and calculate shrinkage.

Results: Rate on a 9-point hedonic scale with 9 = most tender, most juicy, or most flavorful imaginable, and 1 = lease tender, least juicy, or least flavorful imaginable.

| Meat | Color | | Tenderness | Juiciness | Weight | | Shrinkage* | Flavor |
	Exterior	Interior			Before	After		
❖Rib steak 5/8-in. thick								
❖Chuck steak without tenderizer, 8 oz								
❖(228 g) chuck steak with tenderizer, 8 oz								

* % Shrinkage = $\dfrac{\text{Weight before cooking} - \text{weight after cooking}}{\text{weight before cooking}} \times 100$

Conclusions: How do rib steak and chuck steak without tenderizer compare in tenderness?

What is the active component of a meat tenderizer?

How effective was the tenderizer in tenderizing chuck steaks?

What is the action of the tenderizer?

III. Effect of Pan Frying

A. Liver and bacon

Fry 2 slices of bacon in a heavy skillet and reserve 1 t fat from bacon for frying the liver. Fry liver until just brown and tender. It can easily be overcooked, which toughens it.

Brown on both sides. Cook uncovered at moderate temperature until meat is done, turn occasionally. In panfrying the meat is cooked without added water.

Results: Rate on a 9-point hedonic scale with 9 = most tender, most juicy, or most flavorful imaginable, and 1 = least tender, least juicy, or least flavorful imaginable.

| Meat | Color | | Tenderness | Juiciness | Shrinkage* | Flavor | Time |
	Exterior	Interior					
Beef or calf liver and bacon (114 g) 4 oz							
Beef or calf liver (cooked extra 5 min)							
Pork liver and bacon (114 g) 4 oz							

* % Shrinkage = $\dfrac{\text{Weight before cooking} - \text{weight after cooking}}{\text{weight before cooking}} \times 100$

Conclusions: Does liver become more tender with further cooking? Why or why not?

Describe the difference in flavor between beef and pork liver.

❖IV. Use of Soy Protein in a Ground Beef Roast

Variable A: Control Meatloaf

(3.1 g) 1 t beaten egg
(6.4 g) 1 t bread crumbs
(8.3 g) 1 t diced onion
(14.2 g) 1 t tomato sauce

(1 1/2 g) 1/4 t salt
dash pepper
(140 g.) 5 oz ground beef
(32 g) 2 T barbecue sauce

Procedure: Stir together beaten egg, bread crumbs, diced onion, tomato sauce, salt, and pepper. Add ground beef; mix well. Shape into a small loaf. Spread top with barbecue sauce. Bake at 176°C (350°F) for approximately 30 min. Weigh before and after roasting.

Variable B: Meatloaf with soy protein

(28 ml) 1/8 c water
(20 g) soy protein
(8 g) 1 T diced onion
(120 g) 4 oz ground beef
(15 ml) 1 T beaten egg

(6 g) 1 T bread crumbs
(16 g) 1 T tomato sauce
(1 g) 1/4 t salt
dash of pepper
(32 g) 2 T barbecue sauce

Procedure: Hydrate soy protein using water and soy protein. Allow to stand 15 min. Meanwhile, mix onion, ground beef with beaten egg, bread crumbs, tomato sauce, salt, and pepper. Add 30 g hydrated soy protein. Shape A and B loaves identically. Spread top with barbecue sauce. Weigh loaves. Bake variable A and B identically at 176°C (350°F) for approximately 30 min. Weigh before and after roasting.

V. Effect of Cooking Method on Meatloaf

Use formula and procedure for mixing as in problem IV.A. Shape into loaf. Spread with barbecue sauce. Weigh meatloaf before and after baking in the dish and out of the dish. Bake as per variable below.

Oven instructions may vary for other brands of ovens.

Variable:

A. **Microwave**

Place meatloaf in 10-oz casserole dish with barbecue sauce on top. Cook on high power for 4 min.

B. **Microwave/convection**

Place meatloaf in 10-oz casserole dish with barbecue sauce on top. Cook with combination convection/microwave; combination 2 in G.E. microwave as follows.
1. Press combination *cook*.
2. Press *2*.
3. Press *10*.
4. Press *start*.

C. **Combination microwave/convection/bake:** Bake for 5 min as follows:
1. Set Thermodore oven to *350°F.*
2. Press convection to *on.*
3. Set microwave on medium high for *5* min.
4. Slide latch to microwave position.

Results: Rate on a 9-point hedonic scale, with 9 = most tender, most juicy, or most flavorful imaginable, and 1 = least tender, least juicy, or least flavorful imaginable.

Variable	Weight (g) Before Cooking	After	% Weight Loss*	Amount of Drippings (ml)	Roast Time	Cost/ Loaf	Flavor, Color, and Juiciness
Conventional meatloaf							
Meatloaf with soy protein							
Meatloaf made in microwave							
Microwave convection							
Microwave convection bake							

* % Shrinkage = $\dfrac{\text{Weight before cooking} - \text{weight after cooking}}{\text{weight before cooking}} \times 100$

Conclusions: What advantages result from adding soy protein to meat?

What disadvantage do you see in the use of soy protein?

How does soy protein affect the yield of the meatloaf?

Which method of baking was quickest?

Which method of baking produced the greatest yield?

Which method of baking gave the best product?

Observe the surface of each loaf. How do they differ?

❖VI. Effect of Methods on Quality of Fried Chicken

Fried Chicken

4 chicken legs
(30 g) 1/4 c flour
(3 g) 1/2 t salt

(.2 g) 1/8 t pepper
(.1 g) 1/2 t paprika

Procedure: Roll chicken legs in a mixture of flour, salt, pepper, and paprika. Weigh before and after cooking to calculate shrinkage.

Variables

1. Oven fried: Place one leg in pan with (14 g) 1 T oil or spray with non-stick coating. Place in oven at 325°F for 30–45 min until tender.

2. Braised: Place one leg in skillet with (14 g) 1 T oil. Brown. Add 2 T water. Cover and cook on low for 30 min or until tender.

3. Microwave fried: Place 2 legs in Pyrex casserole dish, thicker portions to outside. Cover with waxed paper. Cook 4–7 min on high until fork tender. Turn after 4 min.

Results: Rate on a 9-point hedonic scale with 9 = most tender, most juicy, or most flavorful imaginable, and 1 = least tender, least juicy, or least flavorful imaginable.

| | Color | | Tenderness | Juiciness | Shrinkage* | Flavor |
	Exterior	Interior				
Oven fried broiler leg						
Braised broiler leg						
Microwave-fried broiler leg						

* % Shrinkage $= \dfrac{\text{Weight before cooking} - \text{weight after cooking}}{\text{weight before cooking}} \times 100$

Conclusions: Which method browns most uniformly?

Which is most tender?

VII. Stir-Fried Chicken and Vegetables

(4 g) 1 t granular chicken bouillon
(2.6 g) 1 1/2 t cornstarch
(237 ml) 1 c water
(15 ml) 1 t soy sauce
(.5 g) 1/4 t ginger

1 chicken breast
(113.5 g) 1 small onion
(84 g) 3 oz mushrooms, fresh, sliced
(84 g) 3 oz pea pods, fresh, stemmed
2 T oil

Procedure: Mix bouillon, cornstarch, cold water, soy sauce, and ginger. Set aside. Cut chicken into thin 1/4-in. strips. Stir fry onion, mushrooms, and peapods. Remove from pan. Stir fry chicken in oil. Lift chicken to sides of pan. Add back stir fry vegetable mixture. Add bouillon mixture; heat to thicken.

Results: Rate on a 9-point hedonic scale with 9 = most tender, most juicy, or most flavorful imaginable, and 1 = least tender, least juicy, or least flavorful imaginable.

	Tenderness	Juiciness	Flavor
Stir-fried chicken			

Conclusions: Why is chicken tender when stir fried?

What food safety precautions are necessary with this product?

Moist Heat Cooking

Goal: To use moist heat cooking methods to make less tender meat cuts quality products.

Objectives: To observe the effect on tenderness and yield of low and high heat.
     To observe the effect on tenderness of mechanically breaking muscle fibers.
     To observe the effect of coating on juiciness and tenderness.
     To practice moist heat cooking methods.
     To taste less frequently used cuts of meat.

❖I. Effect of Cooking Temperature on Flank Steak Bavarian Style

Flank Steak Bavarian

1 flank steak   (15 ml) 1 T lemon juice
(65 g) 1/4 c chili sauce

Procedure: Weigh steak with sauce before and after cooking. Divide flank steak. Spread each piece with chili sauce and lemon juice. Cook covered in a baking dish. Place variable A in oven 1 hour before placing B in the oven.

Variables:
A. Bake at 275°F for 2 hours.
B. Bake at 400°F for 1 hour.

Results: Rate on a 9-point hedonic scale with 9 = most tender, most juicy, or most flavorful imaginable, and 1 = least tender, least juicy, or least flavorful imaginable.

Variable	Time	Tenderness	Juiciness	Flavor	Weight Before	After	% Loss*
A. Oven 275°F	2 hours						
B. Oven 400°F	1 hour						

* % Shrinkage = (Weight before cooking – weight after cooking / weight before cooking) x 100

Conclusions: How does the higher temperature affect tenderness?

How does the higher temperature affect yield?

II. Effect of Pounding on Tenderness

❖A. Braised Beef Round

Procedure: Braising is a moist heat method of cooking used to help tenderize less tender cuts of meat. Divide one piece of round.

Variables: 1. Pound and flour one piece. Weigh.
     2. Do not treat second piece. Weigh.
      Place both pieces in skillet and brown in (14 g) 1 T fat. Place both pieces in same covered casserole dish with (60 ml) 1/4 c water. Bake covered at 325°F for 1 hour and 15 min or more. Weigh each piece.

Results: Rate on a 9-point hedonic scale with 9 = most tender, most juicy, or most flavorful imaginable, and 1 = least tender, least juicy, or least flavorful imaginable.

Variables	Time	Oven Temp.	Tenderness	Juiciness	Flavor	Weight Before	After	% Loss*
1. Pounded and floured	1 hour + 15 min	325°F						
2. No treatment	1 hour + 15 min	325°F						

* % Shrinkage = $\dfrac{\text{Weight before cooking} - \text{weight after cooking}}{\text{weight before cooking}}$ x 100

❖B. **Microwave Beef Round Rolls**

(113.5 g) 4 oz beef round (sliced thin, 3/8–1/2 in.)   (118 ml) 1/2 c water
(.7 g) 1/8 t salt   (25.5 g) 1/4 c soft bread crumbs
(.1 g) 1/16 t pepper   (3 g) 1 T egg
(28.3 g) 1 oz sausage, hot   (14 g) 1 T butter
(4 g) 1/2 T chopped onions   (56 g) 1/2 small onion, sliced
(1.8 g) 1/2 t beef broth granules   (7.5 g) 1 T flour

Procedure: Pound meat to 1/4-in. thickness. Salt and pepper. Cook chopped onion and sausage on high 1 min until no longer pink. Stir in bread crumbs and egg. Spoon sausage mixture into steak. Roll and fasten with toothpicks. Combine butter and sliced onion. Cook on high 2 min. Add flour. Dissolve 1/2 beef bouillon cube into 1/2 c water. Add to sliced onion mixture. Cook on high 2 min or until thick. Place thickened mixture over meat rolls. Cook covered 2 min on high, 3 min on medium. Turn and cook 5 min more on medium. Let stand 5 min.

Results: Rate on a 9-point hedonic scale with 9 = most tender, most juicy, or most flavorful imaginable, and 1 = least tender, least juicy, or least flavorful imaginable.

Variable	Tenderness	Juiciness	Flavor
Microwave beef round rolls			

Conclusions: How does pounding influence tenderness?

Will less tender cuts be acceptable cooked in a microwave?

What factors influence this?

III. Effect of Breading on Pork Chops

Breaded Pork Chops

2 shoulder blade pork chops   (50 g) 1/4 c dried bread crumbs
(31 g) 1/4 c flour   (28 g) 2 T fat
(50 g) 1 egg   (60 ml) 1/4 c water
(15 ml) 1 T water

Breaded Procedure: Weigh chop, then flour. Mix water and egg. Dip chop in egg mixture; roll in bread crumbs. Weigh. Brown in fat in skillet. Add 1/4 c water and cook 30 min. Weigh.

Unbreaded Procedure: Weigh chop. Braise without treatment. Place pork chop in skillet with fat to brown. Add 1/4 c water, cover, and cook 30 min. Weigh.

Results: Using a paired comparison sensory test, indicate which is the most tender and most juicy, and record the shrinkage.

Variable	Tenderness	Juiciness	Shrinkage*	Flavor
A. Breaded				
B. Unbreaded				

* % Shrinkage = Weight before cooking – weight after cooking x 100
                      weight before cooking

Conclusions: Did breading affect shrinkage, juiciness, or tenderness? Why?

Would you expect pork shoulder to be tender with dry heat?

Would you expect pork shoulder to be tender with moist heat?

IV. Moist Heat Cooking Methods

A. Beef Swiss Steak (Braised)

(227 g) 8 oz chuck arm roast   (150 g) 1 onion
(14 g) 2 T flour   (119 g) 1/2 c canned tomatoes
(30 ml) 2 T oil   (118 ml) 1/2 c water

Procedure: Pound a chuck arm roast thoroughly with flour (on each side). Brown on each side in a small amount of oil. Place onion, sliced canned tomatoes, and water on roast. Braise for 2 hours at 325°F in a covered pan in the oven or cook covered on top of the range.

Results: Rate on a 9-point hedonic scale with 9 = most tender, most juicy, or most flavorful imaginable, and 1 = least tender, least juicy, or least flavorful imaginable.

Color	Tenderness	Juiciness	Shrinkage*	Flavor
Exterior				
Interior				

* % Shrinkage = Weight before cooking – weight after cooking x 100
                      weight before cooking

Conclusions: Is chuck roast a tender cut?

Does moist heat tenderize the chuck roast?

B. **Stew**: Cooking in liquid

(113.5 g) 4 oz meat cubes (lamb)	(.5 g) 1/4 t pepper
(14.5 g) 2 T flour	(150 g) 1 onion, quartered
(25.5 g) 2 T oil	(302 g) 2 potatoes, small cubed
(3 g) 1/2 t salt	(150 g) 2 carrots cut in 1/2-in. small pieces
water to cover	

Procedure: Dredge cubes of meat in flour; brown in 1-2 T vegetable oil. Season with salt and pepper; add onion. Add hot water to cover. Simmer covered for 30 min or longer. If substituting beef, stew for 1 1/2 hours. Add potatoes and carrots. Simmer until meat and vegetables are fork tender.

Results: Rate on a 9-point hedonic scale with 9 = most tender, most juicy, or most flavorful imaginable, and 1 = least tender, least juicy, or least flavorful imaginable.

Variable	Color	Tenderness	Juiciness	Flavor
Lamb stew				

Conclusions: What primal cuts of beef, pork, or lamb would provide meat suitable for stewing?

C. **Pressure cooking**

   Tongue: Serve with horseradish sauce.

1/4–1/2 tongue	(474 ml) 2 c water

Procedure: Place tongue in pressure cooker with water. Cook 60 min at 10 lbs. Cool pan 5 min with lid on. Then place covered pan under water faucet until cool. Remove lid. Pare skin from tongue. Serve sliced with horseradish sauce.

   Horseradish Sauce

(30 g) 2 T heavy sweet or sour cream	1 t prepared horseradish
soft bread crumbs	

Procedure: Whip cream. Fold in horseradish with sufficient bread crumbs to give it body.

Results: Rate on a 9-point hedonic scale with 9 = most tender, most juicy, or most flavorful imaginable, and 1 = least tender, least juicy, or least flavorful imaginable.

Variable	Appearance	Tenderness	Juiciness	Flavor
Tongue				

Conclusions: Why is tongue cooked in moist heat?

How does pressure cooking affect time to tenderize?

D. **Parboiling with pressure**
   1. **Stuffed Heart**

Procedure: Place heart in pressure cooker with (355 ml) 1 1/2 c water. Cook 50 min at 10 lb pressure. Cool for 5 min with lid on. Then place covered pressure cooker under water faucet until cool. Remove lid. Place cooked heart in baking dish over bread stuffing. Pour 1/2 c broth over heart. Bake for 25–30 min at 350°F.

Bread Stuffing

(79 ml) 1/3 c boiling water, stock, or (hot milk)
(102 g) 1 c 1/2-in. cubed dry bread
(7.5 g) 1 T chopped celery
(13 g) 1 T fat
(1.5 g) 1/4 t salt

dash pepper
(.1 g) 1/8 t sage
(2.5 g) 1 t finely chopped onion
(.4 g) 1 t finely chopped parsley
(3.1 g) 1 T egg, slightly beaten

Procedure: Add seasoning to bread and mix. Melt fat in hot liquid, add bread, and mix lightly. Add egg. Place under the piece of heart.

Results: Rate on a 9-point hedonic scale with 9 = most tender, most juicy, or most flavorful imaginable, and 1 = least tender, least juicy, or least flavorful imaginable.

Variable	Appearance	Tenderness	Juiciness	Flavor
Stuffed heart				

Conclusions: Which cuts of meat may appropriately be pressure cooked or parboiled?

What connective tissue does moist heat tenderize?

❖V. Comparison of Dry and Moist Heat Cooking of Chuck Roast

Procedure: Use two identical cubes of chuck roast—approximately a 3 1/2 x 2-in. cube. *Weigh* before and after treatment.

A. Place 1 cube on rack in roasting pan in oven at 135˚C (275˚F) until it reaches an internal temperature of 71˚C (160˚F).

B. Place 1 cube in cooking bag in roasting pan in oven at 135˚C (275˚F) until it reaches an internal temperature of 71˚C (160˚F).

or

Place 1 cube in 135˚C (275˚F) oven in roasting pan with 100 ml water, cover with lid, and bake to an internal temperature of 71˚C (160˚F).

Results: Rate on a 9-point hedonic scale with 9 = most tender, most juicy, or most flavorful imaginable, and 1 = least tender, least juicy, or least flavorful imaginable.

Variable	Weight Before	After	% Yield*	Amount of Dripping	Roast Time	Color	Tenderness	Flavor
Dry roasted 275˚F								
Moist heat 300˚F								

*% Yield = (Final Weight ÷ Initial Wt.) x 100

Conclusions: Can a less tender *roast* such as a chuck roast be cooked by either dry heat or with added moisture? Why?

What differences are expected?

FISH

Goal: To become aware of the many market forms of seafood and to relate fish composition to the variety of cooking methods available.

Objectives: To recognize market forms of fish.
To recognize characteristics of fish doneness when cooked.
To taste a variety of seafood.
To prepare seafood in a variety of ways.

I. Market Forms

Whole or round—as they come from the water.

Drawn—only the entrails removed. Scales not removed.

Dressed—scaled and eviscerated, usually with the head, tail, and fins removed. The smaller sizes are ready for cooking as purchased (pan dressed). The larger sizes of dressed fish may be baked as purchased but frequently are cut into steaks or serving-size portions.

Steaks—cross section slices of the larger sizes of dressed fish.

Single Fillet—sides of the fish, cut lengthwise away from the backbone.

Butterfly Fillet—the two sides of the fish corresponding to two single fillets held together by uncut flesh and the skin.

Sticks—pieces of fish cut lengthwise or crosswise from fillets or steaks into portions of uniform width and length.

II. Quantity to Purchase

Steaks, fillets, or sticks—1/3 lb per person

Dress—1/2 lb per person

Whole—1 lb per person

III. Storing of Fresh Fish

Fish, like many other food products, will spoil easily if not handled with care. Fish is preferably stored on ice in a refrigerator in a moisture-proof covering or container. Fish should be stored for only 1 day in a refrigerator without ice.

Store on ice if stored more than 1 day.

IV. Cooking Fish: Recipes

Fish contains short muscle fibers and very little collagen. The connective tissues disintegrate easily, allowing fish to *flake* when tender. Thus fish can be prepared by methods used for tender cuts of meat.

To introduce variety, it is often prepared by methods used for less tender cuts.

A. Poached Haddock Steak

(113.5 g) 4 oz haddock steak (75.5 g) 1/2 onion, sliced
(46.3 g) 3 T lemon juice water
  salt and pepper

Procedure: Tie fish in cheesecloth; place in kettle. Add quantity of boiling water required to *just* cover the fish. Add 3 T lemon juice or vinegar and several slices of onion. Simmer 6–20 min per pound, depending upon thickness, or until done. Meat should "flake" easily when tested with tip of knife or fork. Drain; serve hot or cold with lemon wedges, cream, hollandaise, or tartar sauce. Season with salt and pepper

B. Baked Finnan Haddie or Smoked Cod in Cream

(113. 5 g) 1/4 lb finnan haddie or smoked cod (120 ml) 1/2 c thin cream
(14 g) 1 T melted butter

Procedure: Wipe finnan haddie with a damp cloth. Cut into serving-size pieces. Spray non-stick coating on baking pan or 1-qt casserole. Place fish in pan and cover with cream. Bake at 350°F for 30–40 min until cream is absorbed and fish becomes brown. Pour melted butter over fish just before serving.

C. **Lobster a la Newberg**

(28 g) 2 T butter or margarine
(3.5 g) 1/2 T flour
(1.5 g) 1/4 t salt
(59 ml) 1/4 c milk
(.1 g) 1/16 t pepper

fg cayenne
(59 ml) 1/4 c half & half cream
(16.6 g) 1 beaten egg yolk
(2.5 g) 1/2 t lemon juice
(5 oz) 1 c lobster or lobster tail meat

Procedure: Cook lobster tail by either broiling until meat is opaque rather than translucent or by simmering 5–6 min. Set aside. Melt fat, add flour, and stir until smooth. Add seasonings and cream. Cook until smooth and thick. Mix yolk with milk and add gradually. Cook 2–3 min. Add lemon juice. Add cooked lobster meat.

❖D. **Halibut**

2 halibut steaks
(34 g) 2 T ketchup
(15.4 g) 1 T lemon juice
(.6 g) 1/4 t prepared mustard

(15 ml) 1 T vegetable oil
(2 ml) 1/2 t Worcestershire sauce
(.5 g) 1/8 t garlic salt

1. **Microwave Baked**

Procedure: Place 1-in. halibut steak on microwaveable platter. Combine remaining ingredients to make a sauce. Brush fish with sauce. Cook in microwave on power 7 for 1 1/2 min. Brush with sauce. Cook in microwave on power 7 for 2 1/2 min until fish flakes with fork.

2. **Convection Oven Baked**

Procedure: Place steak on pan. Brush with sauce. Bake on convection at 325°F for 30 min.

❖E. **Broiled Salmon Steak**

1 salmon steak
salt
pepper

(.4 g) 1/4 t chopped parsley
(2.5 g) 1/2 t butter

Procedure: Sprinkle steak with salt and pepper. Place on well-oiled, preheated broiler. Cook until fish starts to flake, about 5 min. Turn and broil until fish flakes. Season with salt, pepper, and butter combined with parsley.

F. **Baked Stuffed Trout**

Procedure: Clean trout; stuff; skewer the opening. Dredge with salt, pepper, and flour. Spray a non-stick coating on bottom of baking dish. Place stuffed fish on it. An oven dish on which fish may be served is ideal. If not available, place fish on piece of cheesecloth for baking so it may be moved without breaking. Bake at 400°F, allowing 10–15 min per pound. Baste with melted margarine. A little water may be added if needed.

Fish Stuffing

(51 g) 1/2 c soft bread cubes
(28 g) 2 T melted margarine
(.8 g) 1/8 t salt
(.1 g) 1/8 t sage
(.1 g) 1/8 t thyme

(.3 g) 1/8 t pepper
(.6 g) 1/2 t minced onion
(.02 g) 1/2 t minced parsley (speck)
(7.7 g) 1/2 T lemon juice
(16 g) 1 1/2 T chopped dill pickle

Procedure: Mix. Stuff into fish.

G. Pan-Fried Perch Fillets

(113.5 g) 4 oz perch fillets
(29 g) 1/4 c flour *or* (35 g) 1/4 c corn meal
   or (25.5 g) fine bread crumbs

salt and pepper
(30 ml) 2 T vegetable oil

Procedure: Sprinkle fillets with salt and pepper; roll in flour, cornmeal, or fine bread crumbs. Season with a shake of salt and pepper. Fry in a small amount of fat.

H. Steamed Sole Fillets

(113.5 g) 4 oz sole fillets

(5 g) 1 t salt
(15 ml) 1 T vinegar or lemon juice

Procedure: Place water in bottom of steamer. Bring water to a boil. Add 1 t salt, 1 t vinegar or lemon juice. Wrap fish in cheese cloth. Place fish in top of steamer. Cook until fish flakes: 5–8 min per pound of fish. Overcooking destroys flavor and toughens.

I. Shrimp, Boiled

(113.5 g) 4 oz shrimp
1 bay leaf

(1 g) 1/2 t caraway seeds

Procedure: Drop shrimp, fresh or frozen, into salted boiling water. Add spices, such as bay leaf, caraway seed, or commercially prepared mixed spices. Simmer 5–8 min. Remove from water and cool. Break shells on underside and remove. Make a slit down center back and remove dark sand vein. One lb of green (fresh) shrimp will yield approximately 1 c cooked after shells are removed.

J. Scalloped Oysters

(28 g) 2 T margarine
(7.5 g) 1 T celery, chopped fine
(8 g) 1 T onion, chopped fine
(10.28 g) 2 t lemon juice

(3 ml) 1 t Worcestershire sauce
20 Ritz crackers, broken
(113.5 g) 4 oz oysters
(118 ml) 1/2 c light cream

Procedure: Melt margarine. Saute celery and onion in margarine. Add lemon juice, Worcestershire sauce, and crackers. Layer cracker mixture with oysters in a casserole dish. Pour light cream over. Bake at 350° for 25–30 min.

K. Sauteed Scallops

Procedure: Clean and dry scallops. Saute in 2 T margarine or butter in skillet until cooked through (2–5 min). Season with garlic or other spices and herbs.

❖L. Seafood Salad

(113.5 g) 4 oz frozen crab or shrimp-flavored surimi
(7.5 g) 1 T chopped celery
(20 g) 2 T chopped black olives
(1.5 g) 1/4 t salt

(5 g) 1 t lemon juice
(14 g) 1 T mayonnaise
1 lettuce cup

Procedure: Break surimi into small pieces or flakes. Add remaining ingredients. Serve in lettuce cup.

Score Sheet for Fish

Results: Select the words that best describe the product.

	Appearance	Texture	Palatability
	Outside: Soft Crispy Dry Moist Color: white, brown, etc. *Inside:* Dry Moist	Flaky Solid Compact Crumbly Tenderness Tender Hard Tough	Delicate Flavor Strong, Fishy Taste or Odor Stale Well Seasoned Salty Flat Carelessly Served Neatly Served
A. Poached haddock			
B. Baked finnan haddie			
C. Lobster newberg			
D. Halibut— microwaved baked			
oven baked			
E. Salmon steak—broiled			
F. Baked—stuffed trout			
G. Pan-fried perch			
H. Steamed sole			
I. Boiled shrimp			
J. Scalloped oysters			
K. Sauteed scallops			
L. Seafood salad			

Conclusions: How do muscle fibers of fish differ from those in red meats?

Compare amount of collagen in meat to that in fish.

How do muscle fibers and connective tissue allow fish to be cooked by either moist or dry heat?

How does the fat content in meat compare to that in fish?

How do you determine doneness of fin fish?

What affect does overcooking have on fish?

What is surimi and how is it processed?

Sauces for Fish

Choose a sauce to complement the flavor of the fish:

Fat fish—tart sauce

Lean fish—rich sauce

Cucumber Sauce

1 medium cucumber

(15 ml) 1 T vinegar

(3 g) 1/2 t salt

(.2 g) 1/8 t pepper

fg cayenne

(1.2 g) 1/2 t minced onion

Procedure: Pare cucumber. Chop finely. Add remaining ingredients. Serve with fried fish.

Egg Sauce

(28 g) 2 T margarine

(14.5 g) 2 T flour

(237 ml) 1 c milk

(2 ml) 1/2 t Worcestershire sauce

(1 g) 1 T minced parsley

(2.5 ml) 1/2 t onion juice

(50 g) 1 hard-cooked egg, diced

Procedure: Melt margarine, add flour, then add milk. Bring to a boil. Heat for 5 min. Add remaining ingredients to hot white sauce. Blend well. Serve over steamed or poached fish or codfish balls.

Cocktail Sauce

(51 g) 3 T tomato catsup

(15 ml) 1 T lemon juice

4 drops Tabasco sauce

(3 ml) 1 t Worcestershire sauce

(10 g) 2 t grated horseradish

(1.5 g) 1/4 t salt

(2.5 g) 1 t minced onion (if desired)

(1 g) 1/2 t minced green pepper (if desired)

(15 g) 2 t chopped celery

Procedure: Mix and serve with shellfish.

Lemon Butter

(56 g) 4 T butter

(15 ml) 1 T lemon juice

Procedure: Melt butter; add lemon juice. Serve with fish.

Tarter Sauce

(12 g) 1 T pickle relish

(59 g) 4 T mayonnaise

Procedure: Add pickle relish to mayonnaise. Serve with fish.

Garnish Suggestions

Beets, (pickled)—cooked whole—sliced

Carrots—sticks—slices

Celery—sticks—curls

Cucumbers—slices—curls

Green Peppers—rings

Sauces—many varieties

Hard-cooked eggs—slices—wedges- deviled—grated

Lemons—slices—wedges (plain or dipped in parsley)

Paprika—sprinkled sparingly

Parsley sprigs—chopped

Radishes—roses

Tomatoes—slices, quarters

GELATIN

Goal: To observe functional characteristics of a gelatin colloidal dispersion.

Objectives: To identify the temperature for best hydration of gelatin.
To observe the effects of proteolytic enzymes on gelatin.
To observe the functional properties of gelatin including thickening, stabilization, gelation, and foam formation.

Gelatin is a protein made from the collagen of animals. Gelatin will hydrate in water, forming a colloidal dispersion that has many functional attributes in foods. Gelatin will increase the viscosity of a liquid and will foam and form a gel. It can be used to stabilize many other food components.

I. Effect of Temperature of Liquid

A. Procedure: Add (237 ml) 1 c boiling water to (42 g) 1/2 package (1 1/2 oz) flavored gelatin dessert mix. Refrigerate. Record the temperature of thickening.

B. Procedure: Add (237 ml) 1 c water at 65°C to (42 g) 1/2 package (1 1/2 oz) flavored gelatin dessert mix. Refrigerate. Record the temperature of thickening.

Results: Rate on a 9-point hedonic scale with 9 = most stiff, most rubbery, or most cloudy imaginable, and 1 = least stiff, least rubbery, or least cloudy imaginable.

Variable	Temperature of Thickening	Stiffness	Texture	Clarity
A. Hydrated at 100°C				
B. Hydrated at 65°C				

Conclusions: Which thickened at the lowest temperatures?

Why?

II. Effect of Flavor Source

A. Lemon Gelatin

(4.5 g) 1/2 T gelatin   (79 ml) 1/3 c cold water
(29 ml) 2 T cold water   (46.3 g) 3 T lemon juice (fresh lemons)
(90 ml) 3/8 c boiling water   (67 g) 1/3 c sugar

Procedure: Soften gelatin in 2 T cold water. Disperse softened gelatin in boiling water. Add remaining ingredients, and stir until sugar dissolves. Pour into molds and chill.

B. Lemon Gelatin Using Lemon Gelatin Dessert Mix

(237 ml) 1 c boiling water   (42 g) 1/2 package (1 1/2 oz) lemon-flavored gelatin dessert mix

Procedure: Add water to gelatin dessert mix. Stir until clear. Pour into molds and chill.

Results: Rate on a 9-point hedonic scale with 9 = most stiff, most rubbery, or most cloudy imaginable, and 1 = least stiff, least rubbery, or least cloudy imaginable.

Variable	Temperature of Thickening	Stiffness	Texture	Clarity
A. Lemon gelatin				
B. Lemon gelatin dessert powder				

Conclusions: How do unflavored gelatin and gelatin dessert powder differ?

How is unflavored gelatin dispersed in water different from flavored dessert mix? Why?

III. Effect of Proteolytic Enzyme

(42 g) 1/2 package (1.5 oz) strawberry   (237 ml) 1 c boiling water
 gelatin dessert mix

Procedure: Mix dessert mix with water. Divide into 2 equal parts; chill each part until partially thickened.

Variables:
A. Stir (45 g) 1/4 c finely chopped fresh or frozen pineapple into one portion. Chill.
B. Stir (45 g) 1/4 c finely chopped canned pineapple into other portion. Chill.

Results: Rate on a 9-point hedonic scale with 9 = most stiff or most rubbery imaginable, and 1 = least stiff or least rubbery imaginable.

Variable	Stiffness	Texture
A. Fresh or frozen pineapple		
B. Canned pineapple		

Conclusions: Why did one of the above fail to gel?

IV. Effect of Whipping on Gelatin Foam Formation
❖A. **Whipped Gelatin**

(42 g) 1/2 pkg. (1 1/2 oz) cherry gelatin   (118.5 ml) 1/2 c boiling water
                                                     (118.5 ml) 1/2 c cold water or 5 ice cubes

Procedure: Combine cherry gelatin dessert mix with boiling water. Add cold water *or* ice cubes. Chill in ice water in refrigerator until mixture begins to congeal, then whip with a rotary beater until light and frothy. Mold if desired.

B. **Lemon Sponge**

(6 g) 3/4 T gelatin   (61.75 g) 1/4 c lemon juice
(78 g) 3/8 c sugar   (46 g) 3 T egg whites, pasteurized, frozen
(177 ml) 3/4 c boiling water

Procedure: Mix gelatin and sugar thoroughly in a small sauce pan. Gradually add the boiling water, stirring constantly until gelatin is dispersed. Add lemon juice and chill until slightly thicker than egg white. Add unbeaten egg white and beat until mixture begins to hold its shape. To speed up thickening, place mixture over ice water while beating. Chill.

V. Marshmallows

(7 g) 1 envelope unflavored gelatin   (59 ml) 1/4 c water
(88.85 ml) 1/4 c + 2 T water   (2.5 ml) 1/2 t vanilla
(200 g) 1 c sugar   (122 g) 1 c confectioners sugar

Procedure: Soak gelatin in 1/4 c + 2 T water. Cook sugar and remaining water on low heat until sugar is dissolved. Continue cooking to soft-ball stage (237°F or 114°C). Add soaked gelatin. Pour into mixer bowl.

Beat in large heavy duty mixer at high speed until mixture becomes thick and of a soft marshmallow consistency, about 15 min. Add vanilla. Oil or spray a non-stick coating on an 8 x 8-in. pan. Dust bottom of pan with powdered sugar. Pour in marshmallow, smoothing off top with spoon or knife, and sprinkle top with powdered sugar. Let stand in cool place (not refrigerated) until well set, about 1 hour. Cut.

VI. Effect of Gelatin as a Stabilizer

A. Strawberry Bavarian Cream

(9 g) 1 T gelatin, softened in 1/4 c cold water   (180 ml) 3/4 c whipped cream
(29 ml) 2 T boiling water   (75 g) 3/8 c sugar (use less if frozen fruit is used)
(153 g) 3/4 c crushed strawberries

Procedure: Disperse softened gelatin in boiling water. Add sugar and stir until dissolved. Add fruit. Cool in ice in refrigerator. When mixture begins to stiffen, beat until light, then fold in whipped cream.

B. Spanish Cream (use 1/2 of this recipe)

(9 g) 1 T gelatin   (37 g) 3 T sugar
(59 ml) 1/4 c cold milk   (.3 g) 1/16 t salt
(48 g) 3 T egg yolks, slightly beaten   (2.5 ml) 1/2 t vanilla
(296 ml) 1 1/4 c milk, scalded   (46 g) 3 T egg whites, pasteurized, frozen, beaten stiff

Procedure: Soften gelatin in small quantity of cold milk. In the top of a double boiler, combine egg yolk, remaining milk, sugar, and salt. Cook in top of double boiler until mixture coats a spoon to make a soft custard. Disperse softened gelatin in hot custard. Cool, flavor, and as it begins to thicken fold in egg whites. Mold. Chill.

C. Perfection Salad (use 1/2 of this recipe)

(1.5 g) 1/2 t unflavored gelatin   (20 g) 1/4 c finely shredded cabbage
(25 g) 2 T sugar   (60.5 g) 1/2 c chopped celery
(1 1/2 g) 1/4 t salt   (7 g) 1/2 pimento, cut in small pieces or
(59 ml) 1/4 c water, divided   (8 g) 1 T chopped sweet red or green pepper
(8 ml) 1/2 T lemon juice

Procedure: Mix gelatin, sugar and salt thoroughly in a small saucepan. Add 1/2 of water. Place over low heat, stirring constantly until gelatin is dissolved. Remove from heat and stir in remaining 1/2 of water and lemon juice. Chill mixture to unbeaten egg white consistency. Fold in shredded cabbage, celery, and pimento or pepper. Mold. Chill.

D. Frozen Fruit Salad

(324 g) 1 1/2 c mixed, diced fruit (oranges,   (79 g) 1/3 c mayonnaise
    bananas, canned pineapple)   (3 g) 1 t gelatin
(118 ml) 1/2 c whipping cream   (43.5 ml) 1 1/2 T cold water

Procedure: Soften gelatin in cold water and disperse over hot water in a double boiler. Add gelatin to mayonnaise. Whip cream. Mix cream, mayonnaise, and fruit. Freeze in refrigerator tray.

Results: Rate on a 9-point hedonic scale with 9 = most stiff, most rubbery, most cloudy, or most flavorful imaginable, and 1 = least stiff, least rubbery, least cloudy, or least flavorful imaginable.

Product	Texture	Stiffness	Flavor	Function of Gelatin
IV. A. Whipped gelatin				
B. Lemon sponge				
V. Marshmallows				
VI. A. Bavarian cream				
B. Spanish cream				
C. Perfection salad				
D. Frozen fruit salad				

Conclusions: Name three functions of gelatin.

What kind of chemical bonds are formed by gelatin?

What functions does gelatin serve in each of the above products?

At what stage of thickening is gelatin whipped?

At what stage of thickening are fruits and vegetables added? Why?

Starches and Cereals

Notes:

CEREALS

Goal: To observe starch gelatinization and the effect of liquid and cooking on cereals.

Objectives: To compare quantity and cost of 28.35 g (1 oz) portions of cereals. Approximately 1 oz = 100 calories.
To know methods of combining cereal and liquid.
To compare the difference in final product when water or milk is used as liquid.
To observe the results of excess stirring.
To observe the increase in volume after cooking of the various types of cereals, rice, and macaroni, spaghetti, and noodle products.

Cereals including corn, wheat, rice, oats, barley, and rye consist of three components—the bran covering, the germ, and the endosperm.

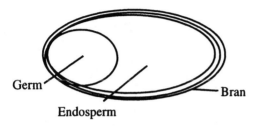

Whole grains contain all three components, but many cereals have the bran and germ removed. Cereals may also be ground or cut to decrease cooking time. Enzymes and disodium phosphate are sometimes added to decrease cooking time. Cooking causes a 2–6 times volume increase, depending upon the amount of water, consistency of final product, and the size of cereal particle used.

I. Observation of 100-Calorie Portions of Cereals

Observe the display of 100 calorie portions of the 10 cereals displayed below. What volumetric and weight measure = 100 calories?

Cereal	Vol.	Weight	Market Unit (Box)	Cost	Cost per Oz

II. Preparation of Cracked, Flaked or Rolled, and Granular Cereals

Add 1/4 t salt per 200 ml of liquid.

Procedure:

1. Add cereal slowly to rapidly boiling salted water. Stir whole or flaked cereal with fork *only as much as necessary*. Cook over direct heat until cereal has absorbed the water and becomes quite thick. Measure volume.

2. Stir the cereal into simmering salted water. Continue stirring until boiling point is reached. Continue cooking the required time, stirring occasionally. Measure volume.

3. In a 16 oz microwaveable bowl, mix 50 ml cereal plus water and 1/8–1/4 t salt. Microwave on high 2 min. Stir. Microwave on high 1 1/2–2 1/2 min. Stir. Measure volume.

4. Add 120 ml boiling water to 1 package instant oatmeal. Stir. Measure volume **or** add 150 ml water to 1 package instant oatmeal and microwave 1 1/2 min.

Results: Record final cooked volume. Rank flavor, appearance, consistency on a 9-point scale with 9 = most desirable, 1 = least desirable.

Cereal (Use 50 ml Cereal)	Liquid	Amount of Liquid	Procedure	Time: Min. Cooked	Cooked Volume	Comments: Flavor	Appearance	Consistency
Whole								
Buck wheat (kasha)	water	300 ml		14				
❖Bulgur wheat	water	200 ml	1	15				
Instant barley	water	150 ml	1	12				
Cracked, buckwheat, roasted (kasha)		150 ml	1	12				
❖Cracked wheat	water	150 ml	1	18				
Quick hominy grits	water	200 ml	1	6				
Flaked or rolled				5				
Regular oats A.	water	100 ml	2*					
❖Regular oats B.	water	100 ml	3	5				
Regular oats C.	water	100 ml	2	5				
❖Quick oats	water	100 ml	1	1				
❖Instant oatmeal	water	100 ml	4	0– 1 1/2				

*Stir entire time

Procedure:

Add 1/4 t salt per 200 ml of liquid.

1. Add cereal slowly to rapidly boiling salted water. Stir whole or flaked cereal with fork *only as much as necessary.* Cook over direct heat until cereal has absorbed the water and becomes quite thick. Measure volume.

2. Stir cold salted water into cereal. Heat gradually to boiling without stirring. Continue cooking the required time. Measure volume.

3. Stir the cereal into simmering salted water. Continue stirring until boiling point is reached. Continue cooking the required time, stirring occasionally. Measure volume.

4. In a 16-oz microwaveable bowl, mix 50 ml cereal plus water and 1/8–1/4 t salt. Microwave on high 2 min. Stir. Microwave on high 1 1/2–2 1/2 min. Stir. Measure volume.

Results: Record time cooked and final cooked volume. Rate on a 9-point hedonic scale with 9 = best flavor, most pleasant appearance, and smoothest consistency imaginable, and 1 = least flavorful, least attractive, least smooth consistency imaginable.

Cereal (Use 50 ml Cereal)	Liquid	Amount of Liquid	Procedure	Time: Min. Cooked	Cooked Volume	Comments:		
						Flavor	Appearance	Consistency
❖Granular cream A.	water	300 ml	1 or 3	10				
of B.	milk	300 ml	1 or 3	10				
wheat C.	water	180 ml	4	10				
Instant cream of wheat	water	250 ml	1	30 sec.				
Yellow cornmeal A.	water	300 ml	1	10				
B.	water	300 ml	1*	10				
White cornmeal	water	300 ml	1	10				

*Add cereal all at once.

Conclusions: How does the replacement of milk for water affect flavor, consistency, and nutrition of cream of wheat?

What procedure for adding granular cereal to water is necessary to prevent lumping?

III. Preparation of Rice: Whole Kernel
Kinds of Rice

Rough rice—unhulled rice kernels

Brown rice—husk removed; contains bran, germ, and endosperm

White or polished rice—endosperm of rice grain only

1. Short grain
2. Medium grain   } classification according to variety
3. Long grain

Converted rice—treated with hot water or steam under pressure before milling, causing some water-soluble nutrients from the bran and germ to go into the endosperm.

Precooked rice—rice that has been cooked, rinsed, and dried. It needs little further cooking.

Wild rice—not a true rice but the seed of a grass. Only the husk is removed. It grows wild in shallow lakes and marshes along the Great Lakes and the Mississippi. Its distinctive flavor has earned it the reputation of being a delicacy prized particularly as a stuffing for game.

Equivalents

Rice: 2 1/3–2 2/3 c = 1 lb (brown, polished, converted, and wild)

Precooked rice: 1 c = 3 1/2 oz

Procedure for Cooking Rice:

Measure 50 ml rice for each variable.

Polished—Bring 100 ml water to boil with 1/4 t salt. Add 50 ml rice. Simmer 20 min covered. Let stand 5 min.

Brown:

    Instant—Bring 50 ml water to boil with 1/8 t salt. Add 50 ml rice. Simmer covered for 5 min. Let stand 5 min.

    Natural—Bring 125 ml water to boil with 1/4 t salt. Add 50 ml rice. Simmer 40 min.

Converted—Bring 125 ml water to boil with 1/4 t salt. Add 50 ml rice. Simmer 20 min covered. Let stand 5 min.

Minute rice—Measure 50 ml water to boil with 1/4 t salt. Add 50 ml rice. Cover. Remove from heat. Let stand 5 min.

Wild—Bring 125 ml water to boil with 1/4 t salt. Add 50 ml rice. Simmer 1 hour.

Flavored—See instructions on box.

Basmati Rice—Bring 120 ml water to boil with 1/4 t salt. Add 50 ml rice. Simmer 15 min. Let stand 5 min.

Results: Record cooking time and final cooked volume. Describe consistency and flavor.

Rice	Cooking Time (Min)	Uncooked Volume (ml)	Cooked Volume (ml)	% Increase in Volume	Cost per 50 ml Cooked	Comments
A. Polished		50 ml				
B. Brown		50 ml				
C. Converted		50 ml				
D. Minute		50 ml				
E. Wild		50 ml				
F. Flavored rice		50 ml				
G. Basmati rice		50 ml				

Results: **Triangle Test.** Prepare two samples of minute rice and one sample of polished rice for sampling. Label: 091, 763, 472. Identify the rice that is different. Which rice has the most desirable texture?

Conclusions: Which rice has the greatest volume increase? How many times did it increase from original?

How does the texture of minute rice differ from the texture of polished rice?

IV. Pasta Products: Macaroni, Spaghetti, and Noodles

Boiled Macaroni, Spaghetti, and Noodles

The pasta products and couscous are made from a coarsely ground flour from durum wheat called semolina.

75 ml macaroni, spaghetti, or noodles   (5 g) 1 t salt
1 liter water

Procedure: Bring water to boil in deep kettle. Break macaroni, spaghetti, or noodles into pieces as desired. Drop gradually into boiling water. Cook uncovered at fast boil, stirring occasionally with fork to prevent sticking. Cook just until tender (9–12 min for pastas; 5–7 min for noodles and couscous). Drain immediately in colander or sieve.

Couscous
(25 ml) 1/3 c couscous   (15 g) 1/4 t salt
(118 ml) 1/2 c water   (7 g) 1/2 T margarine, if desired

Procedure: Bring water, salt, and margarine to a boil. Stir in couscous. Cover. Remove from heat; let stand 5 min.

Results: Record cooked volume and cooking time. Describe the texture as soft, sticky, firm, rubbery, etc.

	Uncooked Volume (ml)	Cooked Volume (ml)	Time for Cooking (Min)	Comments
❖A. Macaroni 75 ml = 36 g	75 ml			
B. Spaghetti 75 ml = 30 g	75 ml			
C. Noodles A 75 ml = 23 g	75 ml			
D. Noodles B cooked 10 min. or longer	75 ml			
❖E. Couscous 25 ml	25 ml			

Conclusions: Why would you expect macaroni and spaghetti to stick together when cooked?

Extra cooking changed the noodles in what ways?

V. Use of Cereal, Rice, Macaroni, Spaghetti, and Noodles in Combination Dishes

Barley Soup
(90 g) 1 1/2 c vegetables (1 carrot, 1/2 onion,   (300 ml) 1 1/4 c broth
    1/2 turnip, 1 rib celery)   100 ml (96 g) cooked instant barley

Procedure: Cook 35 ml barley in 100 ml boiling water; stir until dispersed. Turn down heat. Cook until water is absorbed (about 12 min). Mix vegetables and broth with barley. Heat.

Corn Meal Mush, Fried

(75 g) 5/8 c (100 ml) white corn meal
(600 ml) 2 1/2 c water
(29 g) 1/2 t salt

(14 g) 1 T butter or margarine
(35 ml) 2 T maple flavored syrup

Procedure: Stir cornmeal into salted boiling water. Stir with fork to disperse. Turn down heat. Cook until water is absorbed. Stir occasionally. Place in refrigerator tray in refrigerator freezer for 30 min or longer. Remove; slice in 1/2-in. slices. Saute in butter. Serve with syrup.

Chinese Fried Rice (use 1/2 recipe)

(60 ml) 1/4 c cooking oil
(500 g) 3 c (700 ml) cooked white rice (1 day old)
4 minced scallions
(22 ml) 1 1/2 T soy sauce

(4.5 g) 3/4 t salt
(50 g) 1/3 c finely diced celery
(150 g) 3 eggs

Procedure: The rice for this recipe must be fluffy and at least 1 day old. Heat oil in heavy skillet. Toss in cooked rice and fry until hot and golden. Add scallions, salt, and celery. When these ingredients are well mixed, hollow center of the rice. Break eggs into the hollow and scramble until coagulated. Then stir them into the rice mixture. Sprinkle with soy sauce.

Curried Rice

(470 ml) 2 c hot water
(139 g) 3/4 c polished or converted rice
(120 g) 1/2 c canned tomatoes
(4.5 g) 3/4 t salt

(35 g) 1/4 c finely diced onion
(25 g) 1/4 c sliced green peppers
(28 g) 2 T melted butter
(2 g) 3/4 t curry powder

Procedure: Preheat oven to 350°F. Pour hot water over polished or converted rice. Place the rice where it will remain hot but will not cook for about 45 min. Add remaining ingredients to the rice. Bake these ingredients in a baking dish for 1 1/2 hours or until done. Stir them from time to time. Gradually the rice will absorb the liquid. Remove the dish from the oven while the rice is still moist.

Baked Noodle Ring

(90 g) 1 1/4 c noodles
(33.2 g) 2 egg yolks
(15 g) 3/4 T melted butter
(1 1/2 g) 1/4 t salt
(100 ml) 1/3 c + 1 1/2 T milk

(.3 g) 1/8 t paprika
(.3 g) 1/8 t nutmeg
(55 g) 1/2 c grated cheese or (118 g) 1/2 c cottage
　　cheese
(66.8 g) 2 egg whites
(100 g) 2/3 c cooked green vegetables

Procedure: Preheat oven to 176°C (350°F). Cook noodles. Drain. Beat egg yolks with butter, seasoning, and cheese. Combine with noodles. Beat egg whites until stiff. Fold lightly into noodles. Pour noodle mixture into a buttered 7-in. ring mold and set in a pan of hot water in the oven until done: about 45 min. Invert the contents of the mold on hot plate. Ring may be filled with creamed spinach, peas, chicken a la king, etc.

Rice Custard Pudding

(25 g) 2 T sugar
(3 g) 1/2 t salt
(50 g) 1 egg beaten
(14 g) 1/2 T butter or margarine

(237 ml) 1 c milk, scalded
(170 g) 1 c steamed rice
(36.5 g) 1/4 c raisins

Procedure: Mix sugar and salt with egg. Melt fat in hot milk, and add slowly to egg mixture. Add rice and raisins. Pour into oiled baking dish. Place dish in a pan of water and bake in a 350°F oven.

Couscous with Chickpeas and Vegetables

(5 ml) 1 t vegetable oil
(56 g) 1/2 small onion
(237 ml) 1 c chicken broth
(2 g) 1/2 t salt
(.25 g) 1/8 t pepper
(75 g) 1 carrot
(.5 g) 1/2 t ground cumin
(.1 g) 1/8 t ground cinnamon

(75 g) 1/2 small turnip
(75 g) 1/2 red bell pepper, sliced thin
(50 g) 1/2 zucchini, quartered and sliced into thin slices
(210 g) 7 1/2 oz canned chickpeas (garbanzos), drained and rinsed
(140 g) 7/8 c (5 oz) couscous
(10 g) 1 T fresh parsley

Procedure: Heat oil in saucepan, saute onion 2 min; add broth, salt, and pepper. Bring to boil. Add carrot, cumin, and cinnamon; cover and cook over medium heat 2 min. Add turnip and bell pepper, and cook 1 min more. Add zucchini, chickpeas, couscous, and parsley. Stir, cover, and remove from heat and steam 5 min.

Rice Pudding

(36 g) 3 T uncooked rice
(474 ml) 2 c milk
(38 g) 3 T sugar

(1.5 g) 1/4 t salt
(1 g) 1/2 t lemon rind, grated
(18.25 g) 2 T raisins

Procedure: Wash rice, mix with remaining ingredients, and pour into an oiled baking dish. Cook in microwave 10 min on high. Bake at 250°F (slow oven) about 2 hours, stirring occasionally during first hour of cooking.

Indian Pudding

(237 ml) 1 c milk, scalded
(8.75 g) 1 T yellow cornmeal
(57.5 g) 1 1/2 T molasses

(25 g) 2 T sugar
(1.5 g) 1/4 t salt
(.5 g) 1/4 t ginger

Procedure: Pour milk slowly on cornmeal, and cook in double boiler 20 min. Add remaining ingredients. Pour into oiled baking dish. Bake in microwave 6 min on high; bake at 300°F (slow oven) for 1–2 hours.

Results: Identify the cereal used and describe the function of the cereal.

Recipe	Cereal, Rice, Etc.	Function of Cereal
Barley soup		
Fried mush		
Chinese fried rice		
Curried rice		
Baked noodle ring		
Rice custard pudding		
Couscous with chickpeas and vegetables		
Rice pudding		
Indian pudding		

Conclusions: What function do cereals and rice and pasta products serve in the above dishes?

STARCHY SAUCES AND DESSERTS

Goal: To prepare and observe the results of a variety of starch-based thickening agents in food products.

Objectives: To compare thickening power of a variety of starches.
To compare freeze thaw stability of a variety of starches.
To observe the effect of sugar and acid on starch viscosity.
To use modified starches used in the food industry and compare characteristics with traditional starches.
To use starch as a thickener for a variety of food products.

Starches are a major functional component of many foods. The endosperm of cereals (wheat, corn, rice, oats, barley, and rye) is a major source of starch. In addition, roots such as cassava (tapioca starch) and tubers such as potatoes are major sources. Starch granules swell when heated with water with the water migrating into the granule. This process, called gelatinization, increases the viscosity of the starch. Maximum viscosity occurs at different temperatures depending upon the starch, but wheat and cornstarch both require temperatures of around 90°C (194°F) for maximum viscosity. Most natural starches have two fractions: *amylose* and *amylopectin*. Some starches are genetically modified to change the proportion of amylose and amlopectin. Waxy starches have been modified to contain nearly 100% amylopectin. Amylose is primarily responsible for *gel* strength in a cooled starch paste; thus those starches with no amylose do not form gels at commonly used concentrations. Chemical or physical modification of starch has produced products with unique characteristics for cold water swelling, stability in acid, or stability to freezing (an example is polar gel). Over a period of time a starch gel will *retrograde,* a process of reforming hydrogen bonds, becoming rubbery, and losing water. Some of the chemical modifications of starch available to industry minimize this process.

❖I. Comparative Thickening Power of Thickening Agents

Procedure: Mix (237 ml) 1 c water with (15 g) 2 T thickening agent. Heat until thickened. Turn down heat to low and allow to cook for 5 min. Stir *only* occasionally. Flour and cornstarch must reach a near boiling temperature for thickening to occur. Freeze 1/2 of each product to thaw and evaluate later.

Results: Rate transparency from 9 = most transparent to 1 = most opaque, 9 = thickest to 1 = thinnest.

Thickening Agent	Pasting Temp.	Thickness	Transparency of Cooked Mixture	Consistency Following Freezing and Thawing	Comments
Cornstarch					
Flour					
*Light browned flour					
*Dark browned flour					
Tapioca					
**Polar gel 18W					
Potato starch					
Waxy cornstarch					

*To brown flour, spread a thin layer in a flat pan and bake at 400–450°F. Stir often so flour browns evenly.
**Source listed in Appendix B.

Conclusions: Which starches are most translucent?

Which starches paste at 95–100°C?

Which starches have the smoothest consistency?

Which starches have the greatest freeze-thaw stability?

Why does a starch paste made with polar gel thicken but not gel?

When cooked, flour (a) and cornstarch (b) form a gel. Flour will be less translucent and slightly softer because flour contains proteins as well as starch. Waxy cornstarch (c) is modified to contained only any lopectin and is less likely to gel. Polar gel (d) is a chemically modified starch that thicken but does not form a firm gel.

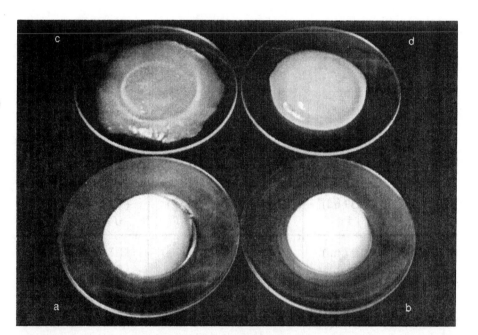

Upon freezing unmodified cornstarch (a) becomes more brittle than immediately upon cooling (b). Syneresis occurs with time.

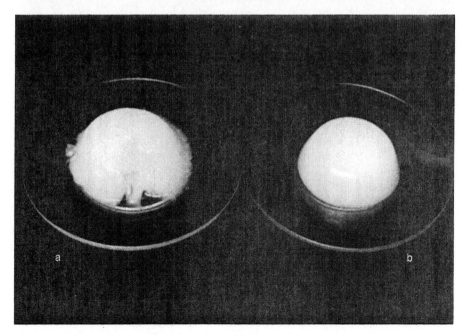

❖II. Comparative Thickness of White Sauces

A. Effect of amount of flour on thickness

White Sauce Procedures:

1. Melt fat; add starch or flour and stir until smooth. Add cold liquid while stirring. Heat until thickening occurs. Cornstarch and flour will reach near boiling temperature before thickening occurs. Stir *only* occasionally. Add salt. After thickening, turn heat to low and continue cooking for 5 min to obtain a non-starchy flavor.

2. Follow directions in method 1, except stir constantly during entire cooking period.

3. Mix starch with sugar. Add to fat and liquid. Heat, stirring occasionally until thickened. Turn heat to low and continue cooking 5 more min to obtain a non-starchy flavor.

Results: Rate viscosity with 9 = extremely thick, 5 = neither thick nor thin, and 1 = extremely thin.

White Sauce	Amount of Milk	Flour	Fat	Salt	Mix Method	Description	Use
Very thin	(237 ml) 1 c	(3.5 g) 1/2 T	(6.5 g) 1/2 T	(1.5 g) 1/4 t	1		
Thin	(237 ml) 1 c	(7.5 g) 1 T	(13 g) 1 T	(1.5 g) 1/4 t	1		
Medium	(237 ml) 1 c	(14.5 g) 2 T	(25.5 g) 2 T	(1.5 g) 1/4 t	1		
Thick	(237 ml) 1 c	(22–29 g) 3–4 T	(39 g) 3 T	(1.5 g) 1/4 t	1		
Very thick	(237 ml) 1 c	(29–36 g) 4–5 T	(52 g) 4 T	(1.5 g) 1/4 t	1		
Medium	(237 ml) 1 c	(14.5 g) 2 T	(25.5 g) 2 T	(1.5 g) 1/4 t	2		

Conclusions: For what purpose is each thickness of sauce used?

Why is flour blended with fat before heating with liquid?

How does method 2 above affect final consistency?

❖B. Effect of reduced fat on white sauce

	Control	Low Fat
Water	110 ml	120 ml
Chicken broth	55 ml	55 ml
Nonfat dry milk solids	15 g	15 g
Corn oil margarine, melted	10.6 g	—
Polar gel 15*	8.3 g	8.3 g
Amalean I Starch*	—	.9 g
Salt	.4	.4

Control Procedure: Melt fat. Mix water and chicken broth. Add 1/3 of water/broth to melted fat. Combine all dry ingredients and blend thoroughly. Add dry ingredients to chicken broth fat mixture and blend until smooth. Add remaining water/chicken broth mixture. Heat to 190°F; hold 3–5 min. Stir constantly.

Reduced Fat Procedure: Combine water and chicken broth. Combine all dry ingredients and blend thoroughly. Add dry ingredients to water/chicken broth mixture and blend until smooth. Heat to 190°F and hold 3–5 min. Stir constantly.

Results: On a hedonic scale, rate clarity as 9 = extremely transparent to 1 = extremely opaque, and consistency as 9 = extremely thick to 1 = extremely thin. Comment on which had the best mouthfeel.

Variable	Clarity	Consistency	Flavor
Control			
Reduced fat			

❖III. Effect of Added Substances on Thickening

A. Effect of sugar (use 1 recipe for each variable)
Variables
1. Control (2 T sugar)
2. No sugar
3. Triple sugar (6 T)

Cornstarch Pudding (Blanc Mange)

(2.6 g) 1 T cornstarch (237 ml) 1 c milk
(.75 g) 1/8 t salt (2.5 ml) 1/2 t vanilla
(25 g) 2 T sugar

Conventional Method
Procedure: Mix cornstarch, salt, and sugar. Add milk gradually while stirring and cook, stirring occasionally until thickened. Cover and cook about 5 min longer on low, stirring occasionally. Cool slightly, flavor, chill, and serve.

Results: Rate thickness on a 9-point hedonic scale with 9 = extremely thick and 1 = extremely thin. Rate clarity with 9 = extremely clear and 1 = extremely opaque.

Variable	Thickness	Clarity	Appearance	Comments
1. Control blanc mange				
2. No sugar				
3. Triple sugar				

Conclusions: How do increased and decreased sugar concentration influence consistency?

❖B. Effect of acid on thickening

Variables
1. Lemon added after cooking. Use regular cornstarch.
2. Lemon added before cooking. Use regular cornstarch.
3. Lemon juice added before cooking. Use modified cornstarch: Polar gel 18W*.
4. Lemon juice added before cooking. Use modified cornstarch: Polar gel 10W*.

Lemon Pie Filling

(2.6 g) 1 T and (1.7 g) 2 t cornstarch   (16.6 g) 1 egg yolk, slightly beaten
(75 g) 6 T sugar   1 lemon rind, grated
1 pinch salt   (14 g) 1/2 T butter
(177 ml) 3/4 c boiling water   (30 g) 2 T lemon juice

Procedure: Mix egg yolk in bowl; set aside. In sauce pan mix cornstarch, sugar, and salt well. Add hot water gradually while stirring. Add lemon juice as indicated in variable. Cook over direct heat until thickened, stirring as needed to prevent lumping. Mix starch mixture *into* egg yolk slowly. Add fat and rind; place back in saucepan and heat 5 min.

Results: On a hedonic scale, rate thickness as 9 = extremely thick to 1 = extremely thin, and lemon flavor as 9 = extremely strong lemon flavor and 1 = extremely mild lemon flavor.

Variable	Thickness	Flavor	Comments
1. Add lemon after cooking (cornstarch: unmodified)			
2. Add lemon before cooking (cornstarch unmodified)			
3. Modified cornstarch polar gel 18W*			
4. Modified cornstarch polar gel 10W*			

Conclusions: How has consistency and flavor changed when lemon juice was added before cooking?

What differences in consistency were noticed with the modified starches?

*Polar gel 10W is designed to be used with acid; polar gel 18W is not for acidic products. Did your results coincide with this?

IV. Effect of Starch Modification and Phosphate Setting Agents on Viscosity and Gelling of Instant Chocolate Cornstarch Pudding

Instant Chocolate Pudding

(15.3 g) 1/4 c + 2 T INSTANT Starch*   (1.2 g) 1/4 t disodium phosphate*
(47.0 g) 1/4 c sugar, baker's special   (0.8 g) 1/8 t vegetable oil
(24.6 g) 1/8 c dextrose   (0.5 g) 1/16 t salt
(7.5 g) 1 T cocoa, dutched (dezaan)   (0.5 g) 1/1/6 t Myvacet 9-45 (Eastman Kodak)*
(2.4 g) 1/2 t tetrasodium pyrophosphate*   (350 ml) 1 1/2 c cold milk

*Source listed in Appendix B.

Variables

A. Commercial instant chocolate pudding (1/2 pkg.). Follow package directions.
B. Use Ultra-Tex 2 for instant starch in formula above.
C. Use Instant Pure-Flo F-1 Starch for instant starch in formula above.
D. Use H50-Modified Waxy Cornstarch for instant starch in formula above.
E. Use H50-Modified waxy cornstarch with *NO* phosphate salts for instant starch in formula above.

Procedure: Pre-blend Myvacet 9-45 and vegetable oil with a portion of the sugar, then dry-blend all ingredients thoroughly. Add dry mix to 350 ml cold milk. Mix 2 min on medium speed of mixer. Freeze 1/2 c in custard cup. Thaw and taste during the following lab. Taste remaining pudding.

Results: Rank on a 9-point hedonic scale: 9 = extremely thick, firm gel, extremely smooth, excellent flavor, to 1 = extremely thin, no gel, extremely lumpy, unacceptable flavor.

A. Commercial instant

Thickness	9	8	7	6	5	4	3	2	1
Gel	9	8	7	6	5	4	3	2	1
Smoothness	9	8	7	6	5	4	3	2	1
Flavor	9	8	7	6	5	4	3	2	1

B. Ultra-Tex 2 starch

Thickness	9	8	7	6	5	4	3	2	1
Gel	9	8	7	6	5	4	3	2	1
Smoothness	9	8	7	6	5	4	3	2	1
Flavor	9	8	7	6	5	4	3	2	1

C. Instant Pure-Flo F-1

Thickness	9	8	7	6	5	4	3	2	1
Gel	9	8	7	6	5	4	3	2	1
Smoothness	9	8	7	6	5	4	3	2	1
Flavor	9	8	7	6	5	4	3	2	1

D. H50-Modified Waxy

Thickness	9	8	7	6	5	4	3	2	1
Gel	9	8	7	6	5	4	3	2	1
Smoothness	9	8	7	6	5	4	3	2	1
Flavor	9	8	7	6	5	4	3	2	1

E. H50-Modified waxy with no phosphate

Thickness	9	8	7	6	5	4	3	2	1
Gel	9	8	7	6	5	4	3	2	1
Smoothness	9	8	7	6	5	4	3	2	1
Flavor	9	8	7	6	5	4	3	2	1

Conclusions: What is the difference in procedure when making a modified instant starch pudding vs. a non-instant starch?

How do the above starches effect flavor, consistency, viscosity, and mouthfeel of a chocolate pudding?

When would each be appropriate?

What is the affect of phosphate salts on gelation?

V. Effectiveness of Microwave Cooking on Blanc Mange

Cornstarch Pudding (Blanc Mange)
(2.6 g) 1 T cornstarch
(.7 g) 1/8 t salt
(25 g) 2 T sugar

(237 ml) 1 c milk
(2.5 ml) 1/2 t vanilla

Procedure: **Microwave Method.** In 2-c glass measuring cup, mix cornstarch, salt, and sugar. Stir in milk and vanilla. Cook on high 2 min. Stir. Cook on high 2 min more or until thick.

Evaluation Procedure: Compare with blanc mange on page 129.

Results: Rate thickness on a 9-point hedonic scale with 9 = extremely thick and 1 = extremely thin. Describe consistency.

Variable	Thickness	Appearance	Comments
1. Microwave cooked pudding cooked as directed			
2. Cooked on low power for 2 min longer			

Conclusions: Does microwave cooking influence flavor or consistency?

VI. Additional Starch-Containing Desserts

Tapioca Cream
(474 ml) 2 c milk
(76 g) 6 T sugar
(30 g) 2 2/3 T granular tapioca
(2.5 ml) 1/2 t vanilla

speck of salt
(33.2 g) 2 egg yolks
(66.8 g) 2 egg whites (pasteurized)

Procedure: Combine milk, 1/2 of sugar, tapioca, and salt. Cook in double boiler until slightly thick and tapioca is clear. Add tapioca to egg yolk. Put back into double boiler, and continue cooking until thickened. Remove from heat. Beat egg whites to form soft peaks. Gradually add remaining sugar and continue beating to make a meringue. Fold meringue into pudding mixture, cool slightly, and add vanilla.

Bread Pudding
4 slices stale bread
(14 g) 1 T butter or margarine
(50–100 g) 1–2 eggs, slightly beaten

(76 g) 6 T sugar
1 pinch salt
(474 ml) 2 c milk
(2.5 ml) 1/2 t vanilla

Procedure: Butter bread lightly, and cut into 1/2-in. cubes. Place in baking dish. Mix egg, sugar, salt, milk, and flavoring. Pour custard mixture over bread cubes. Set in pan of hot water and bake at 350°F (moderate oven) until firm, approximately 40 min.

Results: Record consistency.

Variable	Consistency	Appearance	Comments
Tapioca cream			
Bread pudding			

Fruits

Notes:

Goal: To observe principles in fruit preparation that maintain color and texture or give variety in products.

Objective: To identify products that undergo oxidative browning.
To identify antioxidants that will prevent oxidative browning.
To identify the role of the enzyme in oxidative browning and in the ripening of fruits and vegetables.
To observe the effect of solutes on diffusion and turgor in plant cells.
To taste a variety of fruits available, prepared by many methods.
To demonstrate preparation methods of fruits that maximize color, texture, and nutritive value.

Maintaining the nutrition, color, and flavor of fruit is of concern to the food processor and to those preparing fruit for the consumer. The respiration rate of raw fruit is a determining factor in maintaining quality during storage without further processing. Controlled atmosphere storage prolongs the quality of many fresh fruits. Changes in color may be attributed to enzymatic oxidation that occurs when fresh fruits such as apples, peaches, and pears are cut and exposed to oxygen. Antioxidants and methods to denature enzymes retard these changes. Not only do color and texture changes occur in raw fruit, but texture changes also occur with the heat of processing and cooking. Heat combined with various concentrations of solutes causing diffusion of liquid and solutes in and out of the plant cell will either soften or firm the fruit product.

❖I. Discoloration of Raw Apple and Banana Slices

Procedure: Prepare solutions and slice fruit directly into the solution being tested. Peel 2 Jonathan apples and cut into 8 wedges each. Cut one banana into 1/4-in. slices. Treat 2 apple wedges and 3 banana slices with each treatment as follows and expose to air.

Results: Rate color on a 9-point hedonic scale with 9 = natural color (*no* discoloration) to 1 = extremely dark.

Variable	Color After 1 Hour Apple	Banana	Explanation of Results
No treatment			
Dip in lemon juice for 5 seconds			
Dip in pineapple juice for 5 seconds			
Dip in ascorbic acid solution for 5 seconds [(1 g) 1/4 t ascorbic acid in (60 ml) 1/2 c water]			
Dip in salt solution [(2 g) 1/2 t salt in 60 ml) 1/4 c water]			
Dip in sugar solution [(8 g) 2 t sugar in 60 ml) 1/4 c water]			
Dip in Fruit Fresh (commercially prepared antioxidant; follow directions on container			

Conclusions: What substances are responsible for enzymatic oxidation?

What is the reaction of enzymatic oxidation of fruit?

Which treatments use an antioxidant to retard browning?

Which treatments are most effective?

❖II. A. Effects of Concentration of Sugar

Procedure: Pare 3 Jonathan apples and cut in sixths. Mix. Place 6 pieces in each of three saucepans and boil slowly (covered) for 10 min or until just tender. Time variable 1 and cook variable 2 and 3 for identical times. A toothpick may be used to test for doneness.

Variables:

1. Cook in (118 ml) 1/2 c water.

2. Cook in 1/2 c of 1:4 sugar syrup [(118 ml) 1/2 c water and (25 g) 2 T sugar].

3. Cook in 1/2 c of 1:1 sugar syrup [(118 ml) 1/2 c water and (100 g) 1/2 c sugar].

Results: Rank shape and textures: 9 = retains shape very well, firmest texture; 1 = retains shape least well, softest texture.

Variable	Shape	Texture	Translucency/ Opaque	Flavor Fruit	Juice
1/2 c water					
1:4 syrup					
1:1 syrup					

Conclusion: Which sugar concentration causes the greatest diffusion of water into the cell?

Which sugar concentration provides a firmer fruit? Why?

II. B. Effect of Adding Sugar Before or Following Cooking on Hydration of Cooked Fruit

Variables:

1. Sugar added after cooking. Cook prepared fruit in water (boil gently) in a covered pan for the specified length of time or until just tender. Add sugar, stirring gently until dissolved. Cool and examine.

2. Sugar added before cooking. Cook prepared fruit *with sugar* and water (boil gently) in a covered pan for the same length of time as in 1. Stir as in 1. Cool and examine.

Proportions for various kinds of fruit. For each variation, use:

a. (227 g) 1/2 lb rhubarb (cut in 1-in. pieces), (15 ml) 1 T water, and (50 g) 1/4 c sugar. Cook one half according to each variable above for 5 min. *Or*

b. 2 Jonathan apples (cut in sixths), (30 ml) 2 T water, and (25 g) 2 T sugar. Cook one half of fruit according to each variable above for 8 min. *Or*

c. (150 g) 1 c cranberries, (30 ml) 2 T water, and (50 g) 4 T sugar. Cook one half of fruit according to each variable above for 8 min.

Results: Rate appearance, color, and flavor on a 9-point hedonic scale, with 9 = best appearance, color, and flavor, and 1 = least attractive appearance, color, and flavor.

Variables: Time of Adding Sugar	General Appearance	Color	Flavor
Before cooking			
After cooking			

Conclusions: When did adding sugar cause fruit to become firm and shrink?

When did adding sugar caused fruit to become softer (water diffused in)?

II. C. Effect of Time of Adding Sugar on Hydration of Dried Fruits

Procedure: Use 10 medium prunes for each variant. Wash in warm water. Cook gently in enough water to cover in uncovered container.

Variables:

1. Cook as indicated above until tender. Add (75 g) 6 T sugar at end of cooking.

2. Cook with (75 g) 6 T sugar added at beginning. Cook in same amount of water, same heat, and for same time as variable 1. Remove both when prune with no sugar is barely tender.

Results: Rate appearance and texture with 9 = extremely plump and extremely tender to 1 = extremely shriveled and extremely tough.

Variables	Appearance	Texture	Flavor
Sugar added at the beginning of cooking			
Sugar added at the end of cooking			

Conclusions: To hydrate dried fruit, should sugar be added to water before or after cooking?

III. Effects of Sugar Concentration and Microwave Cooking Method

Procedure: Place apples in deep casserole. Cover or leave uncovered, depending on variable. Cook on high 1 min. Stir. Cook on high 1–3 min more until tender. Cook variables 2 and 3 for same time as 1.

Variables:

1. Cook 1 apple, sliced, with (15 ml) 1 T water, covered.

2. Cook 1 apple, sliced, with (15 ml) 1 T water and (12.5 g) 1 T brown sugar, covered.

3. Cook 1 apple, sliced, with (12.5 g) 1 T brown sugar and (15 g) 1 T butter, uncovered.

Results: Rank shape and textures: 9 = retains best shape, firmest texture; 1 = retains least shape, softest texture.

Treatment	Shape	Texture	Translucency	Flavor	
				Fruit	Juice
1 T water					
1 T each brown sugar and water					
1 T each brown sugar and water					

Conclusion: How do sugar and fat affect the texture of fruit cooked in the microwave?

❖IV. Effect of Apple Variety on Applesauce

Applesauce
4 apples* (1 of each variety)   water
(50 g) 4 T sugar   fg salt

*Suggest Jonathan, McIntosh, and Red Delicious to show differences.

Procedure: Wash, pare if desired, core, cut in equal width slices, and remove any decayed or bruised spots. Weigh smallest apple and use same weight for each apple. Cook in water 1/4 the weight. Add 1 T sugar. Stir until sugar dissolves. Cook 8 min or until at least 1 variety is tender. Compare.

Results: Rate the consistency from 9 = very hard to 1 = very mushy.

Variety	Consistency	Flavor
A.		
B.		
C.		
D.		

Results: Evaluate the flavor of apples using the hedonic scale.

	Extremely Tart	Tart	Slightly Tart	Very Slightly Tart	Neither Tart nor Sweet	Very Slightly Sweet	Slightly Sweet	Sweet	Extremely Sweet
A	❏	❏	❏	❏	❏	❏	❏	❏	❏
B	❏	❏	❏	❏	❏	❏	❏	❏	❏
C	❏	❏	❏	❏	❏	❏	❏	❏	❏
D	❏	❏	❏	❏	❏	❏	❏	❏	❏

Conclusions: Which variety breaks up into a sauce?

Which variety has the most flavor?

❖V. Effect of Apple Variety on Baked Apples

Baked Apples
(605.5 g) 4 apples* (1 of each variety)   (2.5 g) 1/2 t lemon juice
(50 g) 4 T brown sugar

*Suggest Red Delicious, Jonathan, and McIntosh for variety of results.

Procedure:

Conventional Oven: Wash, pare if desired, and core but not to bottom. Put into baking dish, fill cavities with sugar, add about 1/8 t lemon juice for each apple. Add water to depth of 1 in. Bake at 375°F until soft. Apples may be baked covered or uncovered. If uncovered, baste with syrup in pan. Compare apple variety.

Microwave:
(151.5 g) 1 apple   (.6 g) 1/8 t lemon juice
(12.5 g) 1 T brown sugar

Procedure: Wash, remove core, but not to bottom. Peel 1-in. strip at top and cut 1/4-in. slit half way down. Fill cavity with sugar and lemon juice. Place in casserole. Cover. Cook apple on high 2–4 min until tender.

Results: Describe consistency from extremely firm to extremely mushy.

Variety	Consistency
A.	
B.	
C.	
D.	
E. Microwave Baked	

Results: Evaluate the flavor of apples using the hedonic scale.

	Extremely Tart	Tart	Slightly Tart	Very Slightly Tart	Neither Tart nor Sweet	Very Slightly Sweet	Slightly Sweet	Sweet	Extremely Sweet
A	❏	❏	❏	❏	❏	❏	❏	❏	❏
B	❏	❏	❏	❏	❏	❏	❏	❏	❏
C	❏	❏	❏	❏	❏	❏	❏	❏	❏
D	❏	❏	❏	❏	❏	❏	❏	❏	❏
E.	❏	❏	❏	❏	❏	❏	❏	❏	❏

Conclusions: Which apple variety provides the best flavor for baked apples?

Which apple provides the most tart flavor?

Which apple provides the firmest texture?

VI. Fruit Jelly

(237 ml) 1 c grape jelly   (40 g) 1 1/2 oz liquid pectin
(350 g) 1 3/4 c sugar

Procedure: Wash jelly jar. Sterilize in boiling water for 10 min. Keep in hot water until used. Stir sugar into juice, and bring to rolling boil, stirring constantly. Add pectin and heat again to rolling boil and boil 1 min, stirring constantly. Remove from heat and skim off foam. Pour into sterilized jars. Process in a boiling water bath according to USDA canning instructions.*

Conclusions: What is pectin?

What function does pectin serve?

How do sugar and acid affect gelation?

*Complete Guide to Home Canning, Agriculture Information Bulletin No. 539, United States Department of Agriculture, Extension Service. U.S. Government Bookstore, Publication Department, 401 S. State St., Room 124, Chicago, IL 60605; (312) 353-5133.

Cooked Fruit Recipes

VI. Variety in Fruit Preparation

Broiled Grapefruit

2 grapefruit halves

(8 g) 2 t brown sugar

(.1 g) 1/16 t nutmeg

(5 g) 1 t butter

Procedure: Prepare halves of grapefruit. Sprinkle each half with brown sugar and a few grains of nutmeg. Add butter. Place on broiler pan 3 in. from flame or coil, and broil 5–10 min. Serve immediately.

Broiled Peaches

1 peach

(2 g) 1/2 t butter

(4 g) 1 t brown sugar

(2 ml) 1/2 t lemon juice

Procedure: Wash, cut in half, and remove stones from ripe peaches. Place in broiler pan with hollow side up. Fill each hollow with butter, brown sugar, a sprinkle of lemon juice, and a dash of cinnamon. Broil until peaches are tender.

Broiler Banana Split

(227 g) 2 bananas

(10 ml) 2 t lemon juice

(56 g) 1/4 c butter or margarine

(100 g) 1/2 c brown sugar

(1/8 cup) 2 T light cream

(15 g) 1/2 c corn flakes

vanilla ice cream

Procedure: Split bananas in half lengthwise, then halve crosswise. Place in shallow foilware pan. Brush with lemon juice. Melt butter; stir in sugar and cream. Cook and stir till bubbly.

Pour butter mixture over bananas. Broil for 1 min or until hot. Remove from heat; add corn flakes, spoon into dishes; top with scoops of ice cream. Serves 4.

Apple Brown Betty

(102 g) 1 c soft bread crumbs

(28 g) 2 T butter or margarine

(183 g) 1 1/2 c pared, sliced apples

(50 g) 1/4 c sugar

(.3 g) 1/8 t cinnamon

(.5 g) 1/4 t nutmeg, if desired

(10 ml) 2 t lemon juice

grated rind of 1 lemon

Procedure: Oil baking dish. Butter crumbs. Place 1/3 of crumbs in bottom of dish. Add half of apples, sugar, spices, water, lemon juice, and rind. Repeat. Cover top with remaining third of crumbs. Cover. Bake 30 min at 375°F. Remove cover; bake 30 min longer or until apples are tender and crumbs are brown.

Baked Pears

1 pear

(4 g) 1 t butter or margarine

(24 g) 2 T brown sugar

(2 ml) 1/2 t lemon juice

(.2 g) 1/8 t cinnamon

Procedure: Remove cores from ripe pear. Wash and cut in half. Place in baking dish with hollow side up. Fill each hollow with 1/2 t butter, 1 T brown sugar, a sprinkle of lemon juice, and a dash of cinnamon. Bake at 350°F until pears are tender, approximately 20 min.

Baked Bananas

1 banana

(4 g) 1 t sugar

(4 g) 1 t butter or margarine

(2 ml) 1/2 t lemon juice

Procedure: Slice banana in half lengthwise or leave whole. Place in oiled baking dish. Sprinkle sugar, butter, and lemon juice on each bottom. Bake at 350°F until tender and slightly translucent, 15–20 min.

Cranberry Sauce

(75.5 g) 1/2 c cranberries (59 ml) 1/4 c water
(50 g) 1/4 c sugar

Procedure: Pick over and wash cranberries. Add water and sugar. Cover. Boil gently 10 min or until skins burst. Skim. Cool. Mold as desired. Avoid long cooking since it makes cranberries bitter.

Rhubarb Sauce

(122 g) 1 c rhubarb (50 g) 1/4 c sugar

Procedure: Wash rhubarb; cut into 1/2-in. lengths, retaining skin. Add sugar. Cook *very slowly* without water until juice forms, then more rapidly until tender. A small amount of water may be added if thinner sauce is desired. It will require 3–5 min to cook young rhubarb after juice is formed. A small amount may be cooked in double boiler.

Fried Apples

(303 g) 2 apples (28 g) 2 T butter or margarine
(25 g) 2 T brown sugar

Procedure: Slice the apples in wedges. Saute in butter. Add sugar when tender; stir until dissolved.

Sauteed Pineapple Slices

2 pineapple slices, well drained (28 g) 2 T oil or margarine
flour

Procedure: Dip slices in flour. Saute in a well-greased skillet, turning once to brown both sides.

Glazed Apples

(303 g) 2 small to medium firm apples (1 g) ground cinnamon or nutmeg
(100 g) 1/2 c sugar (15 g) 1/4 t grated lemon rind (1 lemon)
fg salt *or* (15 ml) 1 T lemon juice (2/3 lemon)
(59 ml) 1/4 c water

Procedure: Wash, pare, and core apples. Cut into uniform pieces, wedges, or 3/4-in. slices, or leave whole. Combine sugar, water, salt, and desired flavoring. Place over low heat, stirring constantly until sugar is dissolved. Bring to boiling. Add apples and cook gently until apples are transparent and tender, 15–30 min. Turn them occasionally or baste with the syrup.

Glazed Cranberries

Procedure: Wash cranberries but do not drain thoroughly. Mix equal parts of sugar and berries by measure in upper part of double boiler. Cook over simmering water until sugar is a thick syrup, about 1 hour, and berries are glazed. Stir occasionally with a fork. Serve berries and syrup with meat.

Banana Foster

(340.5 g) 3 large bananas (56 g) 1/4 c margarine
(10 ml) 2 t lemon juice (.5 g) 1/4 t cinnamon
(100.5 g) 1/2 c brown sugar

Procedure: Peel the bananas and halve lengthwise, then brush with lemon juice. Melt brown sugar and butter in flat chafing dish. Add bananas. Cook just until tender. Sprinkle with cinnamon. Serve as is or with vanilla ice cream. May be flamed with liquor when serving.

Fresh Fruit Recipes

Fresh Fruits: Paring and sectioning fresh fruit will be demonstrated.

A wide variety of fruits such as the fruit mango, kiwi, bing cherries, papaya, plums, apples, and strawberries contribute color, texture, and a variety of nutrients.

Fresh Fruit Fondue

5 oz frozen strawberries	1/2 apple
4 oz cream cheese	1/2 fruit mango
1/2 banana	1/2 kiwi

Procedure: Blend together frozen strawberries and cream cheese. Place in fondue dish. Chill. Dip pieces of fresh fruit into dip.

Guacamole

salt	(5 ml) 1 t lemon juice
1 clove garlic, cut	(5.5 g) 2 t minced onion
1 large ripe avocado, pitted	mayonnaise
(.5 g) 1/4 t chili powder	corn chips or tostadas

Procedure: Sprinkle a bowl with a little salt and rub with the garlic. Mash the avocado in the bowl and season with 1/4 t salt, chili powder, and lemon juice. Stir in the onion. If desired, the fleshy part of ripe tomatoes, diced, or sliced ripe olives or crisp crumbled bacon may be added. Mix well. Cover with a thin layer of mayonnaise to keep the mixture from darkening. Just before serving, stir well. Serve with corn chips or tostadas.

Preparation and Evaluation of Various Fruits

Results: After tasting, describe appearance and palatability of each product.

	Comments
Fresh (by demonstration) Grapefruit halves and sections	
Orange slices and sections	
Pineapple points	
Fruit cups	
Fresh fruit fondue	
Guacamole	
Fruit mango	
Papaya	
Broiled Grapefruit halves	
Peaches	
Bananas	
Broiler banana split	
Baked Apple brown betty	
Pears	
Bananas	
Stewed Cranberry sauce	
Rhubarb	
Apples	
Fried Pineapple, sliced	
Apples	
Glazed Apples	
Cranberries	
Banana Foster	

Vegetables

Notes:

Goals: To observe results of experiments that illustrate maintenance of color, textures, and flavor of vegetables.

Objectives: To taste the effect of cooking sulfur containing vegetables.
To observe flavor, texture, and color changes of vegetables due to pH and heating time.
To observe flavor changes due to cutting vegetables before cooking.
To observe effects of a variety of cooking methods on flavor, texture, and color of vegetables.

Nutritional merits of vegetables continue to be explored. Chlorophyll, carotenoids, and fiber as well as phytochemicals such as indoles and isothiocyanates in cruciferous vegetables are being studied for their anticarcinogen effects. The high-fiber, low-fat content of most vegetables meets cardiovascular disease dietary guidelines. USDA (United States Department of Agriculture) dietary guidelines are emphasizing consumption of a variety of vegetables.

Maintaining texture and color of vegetables is a major goal of the food processor and of those preparing food for the consumer. Chlorophyll is unstable to acid and excess heat. Anthocyanins and anthoxanthins are stable to acid. These concepts should be utilized in choosing cooking and heat preservation methods..

Vegetables have a wide variety of textures, colors, and nutrients. Eggplant, okra, acorn and zucchini squash, broccoli, green pepper, and turnips are but a few of the many varieties.

I. Effect of Cooking Time on Flavor
Cauliflower
1/2 head cauliflower

Procedure: Cut florets from 1/2 head cauliflower. Wash thoroughly with running water. Cut into florets of uniform size. Divide into 3 equal portions. Start longest-cooking variable first to have all done at same time.

Variables:
A. Cook 1 portion 40 min in water of same weight with lid.
B. Cook 1 portion 15 min in water of same weight with lid.
C. Cook 1 portion 10 min in water of same weight with lid.

Evaluate the cauliflower by marking the square that best represents the flavor, texture, and color.

Flavor	Strongest Flavor			Neither Strong nor Mild			Mildest Flavor		
A. 40 min	❑	❑	❑	❑	❑	❑	❑	❑	❑
B. 15 min	❑	❑	❑	❑	❑	❑	❑	❑	❑
C. 10 min	❑	❑	❑	❑	❑	❑	❑	❑	❑

Texture	Firmest Texture						Softest Texture		
A. 40 min	❑	❑	❑	❑	❑	❑	❑	❑	❑
B. 15 min	❑	❑	❑	❑	❑	❑	❑	❑	❑
C. 10 min	❑	❑	❑	❑	❑	❑	❑	❑	❑

Color	Most Natural						Least Natural		
A. 40 min	❑	❑	❑	❑	❑	❑	❑	❑	❑
B. 15 min	❑	❑	❑	❑	❑	❑	❑	❑	❑
C. 10 min	❑	❑	❑	❑	❑	❑	❑	❑	❑

Evaluation: Set up a triangle test using 2 samples of A and one sample of B. Label as below.

Example: Sample Sample Sample
062 396 487

Which sample is different? Which sample has the stronger flavor?

Conclusions: Which cooking time gives the mildest flavor?

Which cooking time gives the strongest flavor?

Which cooking time gives the best texture?

❖II. Effect of pH and Heat on Pigments and Texture of Cooked Vegetables

Procedure: Use the same size pan for all variables. Use 1 qt saucepan, 1 c deionized water, and 1/4 t salt. Have water boiling before vegetable is added and bring back to a boil as quickly as possible after vegetable is added. Regulate heat to keep water boiling steadily but avoid high heat that will scorch juices and cause excessive evaporation. Cook all variables 8 min except the last.

To compare cooking water, pour cooking water into 1-c measure and add deionized water as necessary to make 1 c; fill a test tube and place in rack.

Directions for Vegetable Preparation

Broccoli—Cut all heads at point where easily cut with sharp knife. Wash 1 large bunch thoroughly, preferably in running water. Look carefully for insects. Cut into serving-size pieces by cutting from bottom of stalk up toward blossom. The blossom part may be pulled in two, leaving buds attached to a portion of the stalk. Divide into 7 equal portions. Use same size of pieces for all variables.

Red cabbage—Wash 1/2 of a medium head and remove outer leaves if necessary. Using a large knife and a cutting board, shred into strips about 1/3-in. wide. Toss together and divide into 7 equal portions.

Carrots—Wash and scrape 6 carrots; cut into uniform slices. Toss all slices together and then divide into 7 equal portions.

Onions—Remove dry outer skins from 6 yellow skinned onions. Slice. Divide each onion into 7 equal portions.

❖Vegetable Pigment and Texture Results

Identify color and texture differences according to the scale on the next page.

Variables	Chlorophyll Example: Broccoli	Carotenoid Carrots	Anthocyanin Red Cabbage	Anthoxanthin Onions
Uncovered	Color* □□□□□□□□ Texture* □□□□□□□□	Color* □□□□□□□□ Texture* □□□□□□□□	Color* □□□□□□□□ Texture* □□□□□□□□	Color* □□□□□□□□ Texture* □□□□□□□□
Covered	Color □□□□□□□□ Texture □□□□□□□□	Color □□□□□□□□ Texture □□□□□□□□	Color □□□□□□□□ Texture □□□□□□□□	Color □□□□□□□□ Texture □□□□□□□□
Lid off first 3 min on for remainder of cooking time	Color □□□□□□□□ Texture □□□□□□□□	Color □□□□□□□□ Texture □□□□□□□□	Color □□□□□□□□ Texture □□□□□□□□	Color □□□□□□□□ Texture □□□□□□□□
Same as above but put 1/4 t soda to water before adding vegetables	Color □□□□□□□□ Texture □□□□□□□□	Color □□□□□□□□ Texture □□□□□□□□	Color □□□□□□□□ Texture □□□□□□□□	Color □□□□□□□□ Texture □□□□□□□□
Same as above but add 1/2 t vinegar to water before adding vegetables	Color □□□□□□□□ Texture □□□□□□□□	Color □□□□□□□□ Texture □□□□□□□□	Color □□□□□□□□ Texture □□□□□□□□	Color □□□□□□□□ Texture □□□□□□□□
Covered, but use tap water in place of deionized water	Color □□□□□□□□ Texture □□□□□□□□	Color □□□□□□□□ Texture □□□□□□□□	Color □□□□□□□□ Texture □□□□□□□□	Color □□□□□□□□ Texture □□□□□□□□
Cook covered for 16 min instead of 8	Color □□□□□□□□ Texture □□□□□□□□	Color □□□□□□□□ Texture □□□□□□□□	Color □□□□□□□□ Texture □□□□□□□□	Color □□□□□□□□ Texture □□□□□□□□

See next page for color and texture scale.

Scale for color:

Extremely Bright Natural	Very Bright Natural	Bright Natural	Slightly Bright	Neither Natural nor Greatly Discolored	Slightly Discolored	Discolored	Very Discolored	Extremely Discolored
❏	❏	❏	❏	❏	❏	❏	❏	❏

Scale for texture:

Extremely Firm	Very Firm	Firm	Slightly Firm	Neither Firm nor Mushy	Slightly Mushy	Mushy	Very Mushy	Extremely Mushy
❏	❏	❏	❏	❏	❏	❏	❏	❏

Conclusions: Which method maintained a true chlorophyll pigment?

Why should baking soda not be added?

Which method maintains anthocyanin and anthoxanthin pigment?

Which methods produced a soft texture? Explain why.

Which methods produced a firm texture?

Is tap water more alkaline or acidic? How does tap water affect pigment?

How does heat affect color and texture? Why?

Which pigments were not stable?

Describe a cooking procedure that best maintains each pigment.

❖III. Effect of Size on Cooking Time

Use 2 medium-size carrots and 1/3 c water for each variant. Have cover on pan entire cooking period. Bring to boil, turn to low heat to simmer only until tender, and record cooking time.

Results: Record the cooking time, and rate tenderness and flavor on a scale with 9 = extremely firm to 1 = extremely mushy. Rate flavor from 9 = extremely flavorful to 1 = extremely bland.

Variable	Time for Cooking	Tenderness	Flavor
Whole			
1/8-in. slices			

Conclusions: Which preparation and cooking process retained the most flavor?

How does heat affect color and texture?

❖IV. Comparison of Methods of Preparation

A. Effect of preparation method on color, flavor, and texture of green beans

Start so all variables finish cooking together. Snip tips of beans and cut in half.

Boiled (fresh)—Place (114 g) 1/4 lb green beans with (118 ml) 1/2 c boiling water. Cook on medium for 15 min, covered after first 3 min.

Pressure cooked (fresh)—Place (114 g) 1/4 lb green beans with (118 ml) 1/2 c water in pressure cooker. Cook 3 min after control jiggles. Reduce pressure immediately by placing pan under faucet or in pan of cold water. Remove lid.

Microwave oven (fresh)—To (114 g) 1/4 lb green beans, add (30 ml) 2 T water in a 1-qt covered casserole. Cook on high 2 min. Stir. Cook 3 min more. Stir. Cover.

Steamed (fresh)—Place (114 g) 1/4 lb green beans in top of steamer filled with (474 ml) 2 c boiling water in bottom. Cook for 15 min, covered.

Canned—Heat contents of commercially canned beans to boiling.

Frozen—Place (140 g) 5 oz green beans in (118 ml) 1/2 c boiling water. Cook 8 min covered.

Results: Describe texture: very firm to very soft, color from bright green to olive green, and flavor on a 9-point hedonic scale from 9 = most flavorful to 1 = least flavorful.

Variable	Texture	Color	Flavor
Fresh—boiled			
Fresh—pressure cooked			
Fresh—microwaved			
Fresh—steamed			
Frozen—boiled			
Canned—boiled			

Conclusions: Which methods maintained the most flavor?

Which methods maintained a crisp texture?

Which methods caused the greatest texture loss?

What is the pigment in green beans?

Which methods caused the greatest color change?

Why is the pigment less stable in some cooking methods?

B. Effect of preparation method on color, texture, and flavor of carrots

Start so all variables finish cooking together. Scrape surface of carrots with vegetable peeler.

Fresh baked—Place 2 carrots cut in half lengthwise in covered glass baking dish with (59.25 ml) 1/4 c water. Bake covered for 30 min or until tender.

Fresh boiled—Place 2 carrots in (59.25 ml) 1/4 c boiling water. Cover. Cook covered 15 min.

Fresh microwaved—Add (59.25 ml) 1/4 c water to 2 carrots cut in half lengthwise. Cook on high 6–8 min in covered casserole. Stir halfway through. Allow to stand 5 min.

Pressure cooked—Slice 2 carrots in half lengthwise. Add (59.25 ml) 1/4 c water to carrots in pressure cooker. Cook 2 1/2 min after control jiggles. Reduce pressure immediately by placing pan under faucet or in pan of cold water. (If carrots are large, cut into 4 strips.)

Canned—Heat contents to boiling.

Frozen—Place (140 g) 5 oz in (118.5 ml) 1/2 c boiling water and cook 5 min.

Results: Describe texture: very firm to very soft, color from bright orange to pale, dull orange, and flavor on a 9-point hedonic scale from 9 = most flavorful to 1 = least flavorful.

Variable	Texture	Color	Flavor
Baked			
Boiled			
Microwaved			
Pressure cooked			
Canned			
Frozen			

Conclusions: Compare cooking times for each method.

Compare total carrot flavor for each method.

What is the pigment in carrots?

How stable is the pigment in each method?

Why does texture change in frozen product?

Preparation Methods for Less Starchy Vegetables

Goals: To utilize principles that maintain color, texture, and nutrients in preparation for tasting a wide variety of vegetables.

Objectives: To become familiar with a large variety of vegetables.
To gain skill in a variety of vegetable cooking methods.
To taste a wide variety of vegetables.
To gain a repertoire of a large variety of vegetables and their preparation for use in menu planning.

Baked

Savory Onion

(150 g) 1 large sweet onion
(34 g) 2 T catsup

(8 g) 2 t brown sugar
(14 g) 1 T melted margarine

Procedure: Slice onion into 1/4-in. slices and place in a baking dish. Mix together catsup, brown sugar, and melted margarine and pour over the onion. Bake at 350°F until tender.

Boiled

Boiled Artichoke with Sauce

Preparation: Cut off the stems. Pull off the tough bottom row of leaves and cut off 1/4 of the top of leaves with scissors. To avoid discoloration, dip the cut ends in lemon juice. Steam or place upright in 1–2 in. water. Cook for 45 min or until tender.

Serving: The leaves are dipped one at a time in a sauce and the lower end is pulled through the teeth to extract the tender portion. When a cone of young leaves appears, pull this off, lift the fuzzy center out and discard it. Cut the remaining heart with a fork. Suggested sauces are melted butter, mayonnaise, hollandaise sauce or Bechamel. Go back to Fats, Emulsions, and Salads, page 48 for hollandaise sauce recipe.

Green Beans with Dill Sauce
Fresh Green Beans

(228 g) 1/2 lb green beans

1/2 c water

Procedure: Bring water to a boil. Wash and stem green beans. Add green beans to water. Bring back to a slow boil. Cook 3 min. Cover and cook 12 min longer. Add dill sauce when served.

Dill Sauce

(57.5 g) 1 oz cream cheese
(5 ml) 1 t half & half cream

(.5 g) 1/4 t dill
(1.5 g) 1/4 t salt

Procedure: Blend together cream cheese, cream, dill, and salt. Serve with green beans.

Ham Hocks and Collard Greens

(168 g) 1/2 ham hock
1 medium onion, sliced

(170 g) 6 oz collard greens
(237 ml) 1 c water

Procedure: In pressure cooker place ham hock with medium onion and water. Cook for 30–40 min. Exhaust. Meanwhile wash collard greens thoroughly, remove hard center vein, and then chop coarsely. Add greens to pressure cooker and cook 12 min. Season with salt and pepper.

Turnip and Mustard Greens

(56 g) 2 oz salt pork
(237 ml) 1 c water
(112 g) 4 oz mustard greens

(112 g) 4 oz turnip greens
1/4 red pepper
(2 g) 1/2 t sugar

Procedure: In pressure cooker place salt pork with water. Cook 15 min. Meanwhile wash mustard greens and turnip greens 5 or 6 times. Drain. Cut into small pieces. Cool pressure cooker under water before removing pressure gauge and lid. Add greens and place meat on top of greens. Add 1/4 red pepper and sugar. Cook in pressure cooker 12 min, then simmer with lid off until liquid cooks down.

Cheesy Mustard Cauliflower

(908 g) 1 medium head cauliflower (about 2 lbs)   (9 g) 1 1/2 t salt
(711 ml) 3 c water   (118.25 g) 1/2 c mayonnaise
(8.25 g) 1 T finely chopped onion   (5.5 g) 1 t prepared mustard
(56 g) 1/2 c shredded cheddar cheese   paprika

Procedure: Trim leaves from cauliflower. Leaving head whole, remove as much of core as possible by cutting a cone-shaped piece from bottom of head. Combine water and salt in 4-qt Dutch oven and bring water to boil. (Place cauliflower in boiling water, stem side down.) Cook until water boils again. Reduce heat to low and cook, uncovered, 5 min. Cover and simmer 10–15 min more or until cauliflower is tender. Drain in colander. Return cauliflower to Dutch oven.

     Combine mayonnaise, onion, mustard, and cheese in bowl and mix to blend. Spread mayonnaise mixture over cauliflower. Steam covered over low heat 5 min or until cheese melts. Transfer cauliflower to serving platter, using two pancake turners. Sprinkle with paprika.

Scalloped

Scalloped Egg Plant

(151.5 g) 1/3 egg plant   (2 g) 1/2 t sugar
1/2 clove garlic   (.3 g) 1/8 t pepper
(27 g) 2 T salad oil   (.1 g) 1/8 t basil
(4.5 g) 2 t flour   (.5 g) 1/4 t paprika
(170 g) 3/4 c canned tomatoes   (12 g) 2 T grated Parmesan cheese

Procedure: Preheat oven to 375°F. Lightly grease 10-oz casserole. Wash and peel egg plant. Cut into 2-in. cubes. Simmer, covered in small amount of boiling salted water 10 min. Drain. In skillet, saute garlic, finely chopped, in salad oil for 3 min. Add flour, then canned tomatoes, sugar, paprika, pepper, and basil. Cook over medium heat until mixture boils.

     In casserole, layer egg plant cubes alternately with tomato mixture; top with grated Parmesan cheese. Bake 15–20 min until lightly browned.

Au Gratin

Asparagus

(453 g) 1 16-oz can or 3/4 lb fresh asparagus   (113 g) 1 can mushrooms
(16.5 g) 2 T chopped onion   (14 g) 1 T margarine
(1.5 g) 1/4 t salt   (14.5 g) 2 T flour
(237 ml) 1 c milk   (56.5 g) 1/2 c grated cheddar cheese
(100 g) 2 hard-cooked eggs (sliced)—see   (35 g) 1/2 c cracker crumbs
     page 82 for cooking directions

Procedure: Wash fresh asparagus. Cut off tough ends. In a 2-qt casserole dish place tips of asparagus toward center and add 1 c water. Cover. Cook in microwave 7 min. Turn at least once. Let stand 3 min. Melt margarine; saute onions in margarine until tender; mix flour into margarine and onion well. Add milk and bring to boiling temperature. Lower heat and cook for 5 min, stirring occasionally.

     In 2-qt casserole dish layer 1/2 of asparagus, 1/2 of the sauce, 1/2 of the cheese, and 1 hard-cooked egg. Continue with layers of second half. Top with crumbs. Bake in microwave for 5 min.

Flavored Sauce

Harvard Beets

(±400 g) 2–3 beets
(118 ml) 2 T vinegar   (25 g) 2 T sugar
(118 ml) 1/2 c water   (3.5 g) 1 1/3 T cornstarch

Procedure: Cut tops from beets leaving 1 1/2-in. stems. Retain roots. Wash. Cook 30–45 min. Drain and remove skins, stems, and roots. Dice or slice.

     Mix sugar and cornstarch. Add water and vinegar. Bring to a boil. Turn heat to low and cook 5 min stirring occasionally. Mix beets with sauce.

Stir Fry

Stir-Fry Cabbage

(113 g) 1/4 head cabbage
(42 g) 3 T margarine
(.5 g) 1/4 t celery seed

(1.5 g) 1/4 t salt
(.2 g) 1/8 t pepper

Procedure: Slice cabbage in 1/8-in. slices. Melt margarine in skillet. Add salt, pepper, celery seed, and cabbage to skillet. Fry 3–5 min, stirring constantly, until slightly tender. Serve.

Sauteed

Zucchini and Tomato

(150 g) 1 zucchini
(28–42 g) 2–3 T margarine or butter
dash pepper

(1.5 g) 1/4 t salt
(.1 g) 1/2 t basil
(113.5 g) 1 tomato

Procedure: Slice zucchini in 1/4-in. slices. Place margarine or butter in skillet. Saute zucchini until slightly tender. Add salt, pepper, basil, and tomato cut into chunks. Heat to warm.

Celery Oriental

3–4 ribs celery
(21 g) 1 1/2 T margarine

(34 g) 1/2 c sliced mushrooms
(19 g) 1/8 c slivered almonds

Procedure: Cut large, outside celery ribs diagonally. Cook in a little boiling salted water until just crisp-done (you have to taste); drain. Saute mushrooms in butter; add the celery and slivered almonds. Toss around lightly till heated.

Broiled

Tomato

(113.5 g) 1 tomato
(13 g) 2 T bread crumbs

(28 g) 2 T butter or margarine
(5.5 g) 1 T parmesan cheese

Procedure: Cut tomato in half. Sprinkle cut side with salt and pepper. Saute bread crumbs in butter. Sprinkle over tomato. Add cheese. Arrange cut side up in boiler pan or in shallow baking dish. Broil until crumbs are brown and tomatoes are tender.

Pan Fried

Pan-Fried Okra

(170.5 g) 6 oz fresh or frozen okra
(50 g) 1 egg
(118 ml) 1/2 c milk

(70 g) 1/2 c yellow cornmeal
vegetable oil

Procedure: Slice fresh or frozen okra in 1/2-in. slices. Dip in mixture of egg and milk. Coat with cornmeal. Fry in 1/2-in. vegetable oil until tender.

Microwave

Broccoli in Chicken Dill Sauce

(454 g) 1 lb fresh broccoli
(59 ml) 1/4 c water
(28 g) 2 T butter or margarine
(33.5 g) 1/4 c chopped onion

(296 ml) 1 can cream of chicken soup
(158 ml) 2/3 c milk
(.5 g) 1/4 t dill seed
dash pepper

Procedure: Cut broccoli in serving size pieces, removing tough stem ends. Place in a 2-qt glass casserole with water in microwave oven 8–10 min. Drain well. Place onion and butter or margarine in a glass mixing bowl, cover with waxed paper, and cook in microwave oven 2 min or until onion is tender. Remove from oven; stir in soup, milk, dill, and pepper. Stir to blend. Pour over broccoli; return to oven. Cook uncovered 4 min or more.

Results: Comment on color, texture, and palatability.

Variable	Comments
Baked Savory onion	
Boiled Artichoke	
Greens	
Cheesy mustard cauliflower	
Green beans and dill sauce	
Scalloped Eggplant	
Au Gratin Asparagus	
Flavored Sauce Harvard beets	
Panned/Stir Fry Cabbage	
Sauteed Zucchini and tomato	
Celery oriental	
Steamed Artichoke	
Broiled Tomatoes	
Pan Fried Okra	
Microwave Broccoli in chicken dill sauce	

Conclusions: Describe cooking procedures above: boiled, scalloped, stir fry, au gratin, saute, and broil.

Identify the pigment in each vegetable above.

Methods of Preparation of High Protein or Starchy Vegetables and Legumes

Goal: To utilize principles that maintain color, texture, and nutrients in preparation for tasting a wide variety of high starch and high protein vegetables and legumes.

Objectives: To recognize some vegetables and legumes as a protein source.
To gain skill in a variety of vegetable and legume cooking methods.
To taste a wide variety of vegetables and legumes.
To gain a repertoire for a large variety of vegetables and legumes for use in menu planning.

Legumes are the dried seeds of plants such as beans, peas, and lentils. They provide about one fifth of the world's protein and are high in carbohydrates and fiber and low in fat. Before cooking, the beans are generally hydrated by soaking. Soaking times are dependent on temperatures. At 20°C, a 16-hour soak is equivalent to 5 hours at 40°C or 1 1/2 hours at 60°C. Lentils and split peas do not require soaking.

Legumes may be processed into a variety of products such as dried soup mixes and dips. Soy is processed into soy flours, texturized soy products, soy protein concentrates, and isolated soy protein products, as well as tofu.

Vegetables
Baked

Acorn Squash

1/2 acorn squash	pepper
(15 ml) 1 T water	(14 g) 1 T margarine
(.5 g) 1/8 t salt	(25 g) 2 T brown sugar

Procedure: Place 1 half upside down on paper towel or baking dish. Bake on high in microwave 3 min. Turn over. Bake 2–5 min more until nearly tender. Add water, salt, margarine, and sugar. Bake 1 min. Let stand 5 min.

Sweet Potatoes and Apples

(464 g) 2 cooked sweet potatoes, sliced	(50 g) 1/4 c sugar, brown or granulated
(56 g) 1/4 c butter or margarine	(1 g) 1/4 t salt
(227 g) 1 1/2 medium tart apples, pared and sliced	(29 ml) 2 T hot water

Procedure: Alternate layers of potatoes and apples in a 1 1/2-qt shallow casserole. Dot each potato layer with butter or margarine. Sprinkle each layer of apples with sugar and salt. Add water. Cover. Bake in a moderate oven (375°F) about 45 min or until liquid is evaporated. Uncover during the last 20 min of baking to brown the top.

Baked Potato

Procedure: Wash 1 each: Idaho, red, and sweet potato. Bake uncovered in 350°F oven approximately 1 hour until tender.

Creamed
Creamed Turnips and Potatoes
Procedure: Boil 1 cubed red potato in 1/2 its weight of water, covered, until tender (approximately 15 min). Boil 1 peeled and cubed turnip in 1/2 its weight in water until tender (approximately 15 min).

White Sauce

(14 g) 1 T margarine	(2 g) 1/2 t salt.
(7 g) 1 T flour	(118 ml) 1/2 c milk

Procedure: Melt margarine; add flour and salt. Stir well. Add milk and bring to boil to thicken. Add cooked potato and turnip to this white sauce. Serve.

Mashed

Mashed Potato

(150 g) 1 Idaho or red potato   (1 g) 1/4 t salt
(30–60 ml) 2–4 T milk   (5 g) 1 t margarine

Procedure: Peel and quarter potatoes. Boil each potato according to principles for white vegetables. Use 1/2 the weight of vegetable of water. Heat to boiling. Add potato and cover with a lid until potato is tender (about 15 min). Mash and weigh smallest potato. Use the same amount of potato for each potato variety. Add equal quantities of milk, salt, and margarine to each mashed potato. Whip briefly. Microwave 15 seconds if cold.

Instant Mashed Potato

2/3 c water   (59 ml) 1/4 c milk
(14 g) 1 T margarine   (24 g) 2/3 c instant potato flakes
(.5 g) 1/4 t salt

Procedure: Heat water, margarine, and salt to boil. Remove from heat. With fork, stir in milk and flakes until potatoes are desired consistency.

Mashed Acorn Squash

1/2 acorn squash   pepper
(15 ml) 1 T water   (14 g) 1 T margarine
(.5 g) 1/8 t salt   (25 g) 2 T brown sugar

Procedure: Slice squash into halves. Boil in 1/2 its weight of water, covered with lid until slightly tender. Take squash from peel. Mash with mixer; add salt, pepper, margarine, and brown sugar. Heat in casserole dish in oven 15 min at 350°F.

Riced

Riced Potatoes and Rutabaga

(227 g) 2 small white potatoes   (.5 g) 1/2 t salt
(±150 g) 1/2 rutabaga   (.1 g) 1/16 t pepper
(10 g) 2 t butter or margarine

Procedure: Quarter the potatoes and cube the rutabaga. Measure water to equal 1/2 the weight of the vegetable. Bring water to a boil. Using the principles for cooking white and yellow vegetables, place vegetable in boiling water, cover with lid, and cook until tender (potato = 15 min, rutabaga = 25 min). Press through the ricer. Season with butter or margarine, salt, and pepper.

Legumes

Legumes as shown are purchased canned, dried, or processed such as tofu. Red beans and rice entree is shown.

Stir Fry

Stir-Fried Tofu (soy protein)

(14 g) 1 T oil
(.5 g) 1 t fresh grated ginger
(.5 g) 1/4 t pepper
(224 g) 8 oz tofu, cut in 1-in. squares

(30 ml) 2 T soy sauce
1/2 head Chinese cabbage, cut in 1 x 2-in. pieces
(113 g) 4 oz fresh sliced mushrooms
(170 g) 1 c cooked rice

Procedure: Marinate tofu in 1 T soy sauce. Heat oil and saute ginger briefly. Add Chinese cabbage. Saute. Add tofu, pepper, and mushrooms. Stir fry, stirring gently. Add remaining soy sauce. Serve over 1 c rice (see page 128 for directions for cooking rice).

Baked

Honey Baked Lentils

(128 g) 2/3 c cooked lentils or
    (454 g) 1 lb uncooked
(0.6 g) 1/4 t dry mustard
(.2 g) 1/16 t powdered ginger
(5 ml) 1 t soy sauce

(16.5 g) 2 T chopped onion
(59 ml) 1/4 c water
(19 g) 1 slice bacon
(31 g) 1 1/2 T honey

Procedure: Cook lentils in 1 c water for 20 min. Mix together mustard, ginger, and soy sauce. Add onions and water. Stir into cooked lentils. Cut bacon in 1-in. pieces. Sprinkle the bacon over the top. Pour honey over all. Cover tightly. Bake for 1 hour in 350°F moderate oven. Uncover last few min to brown the bacon. Bacon may be partially cooked if desired.

Microwave method: Bake on high, covered, for 10 min. Stir. Bake on medium for 10–20 min or until tender. Add water as needed.

Boiled

Black-Eyed Peas

(90 g) 1/2 c drained black-eyed peas
(56 g) 2 oz pork
(3 g) 1/2 t salt
dash pepper

1/2 pepper pod
(6 g) 1/2 T sugar
(237 ml) 1 c water

Procedure: Soak dried black-eyed peas overnight. Cook pork, cut in small pieces, with peas, pepper pod, sugar, salt, pepper, and water until peas are tender. This will take approximately 15 min in a pressure cooker or 50–60 min in sauce pan.

Boiled (Canned)

Boiled Red Beans with Rice (Louisiana)

(187 g) 1 c canned red beans

(14 g) 1 T bacon drippings

1/2 small onion, chopped

1/2 bay leaf, crushed

(37.83 g) 1/4 green pepper, chopped

1/2 rib celery, chopped

(1.5 g) 1 T parsley, chopped

(12 g) 1 T sugar

(170 g) 1 c cooked rice

Procedure: Cook rice (see page 128 for cooking directions). Season canned red beans with bacon drippings. Add onion, green pepper, celery, parsley, and bay leaf. Cook for at least 1/2 hour. Add sugar. Serve on a mound of rice.

Boiled

Ham and Great Northern Beans

(95 g) 1/2 c dried great northern beans

(355 ml) 1 1/2 c water

(14 g) 1/2 oz ham

Procedure: Soak dried great northern beans in water overnight. Place beans and ham (cubed) in pressure cooker with water. Cook for 20 min.

Salad

Kidney Bean Salad

(140 g) 3/4 c cooked or canned kidney beans

(29.5 g) 2 T mayonnaise or cooked
  salad dressing

(30 g) 1/4 c diced celery

2 small sweet pickles, chopped

Procedure: Combine. Serve on lettuce and garnish with slices of hard cooked egg.

Vegetable Cookery

Results: Describe consistency from very smooth to coarse to lumpy and describe palatability.

	Consistency	Palatability
Baked Potatoes : Idaho		
Red		
Sweet		
Acorn squash		
Sweet potatoes and apples		
Boiled		
Creamed Turnips and potatoes		
Mashed Potatoes (Idaho, red, instant)		
Rice Potatoes and rutabaga		
Stir fry Tofu		

Legume Cookery

Results: Record volume and comment on palatability.

	Original Volume	Soaked Volume	Cooked Volume	Comment
Baked legumes Honey baked lentils				
Boiled legumes Black-eyed peas				
Red beans with rice				
Ham and great northern beans				
Salad Kidney bean salad				

Conclusions: Compare textures of Idaho and red potatoes. How do they differ?

Describe the composition of tofu. From what is it made?

Describe soaking times and temperatures appropriate for legumes.

Describe cooking and preparation procedures: boil, rice, stir fry.

Identify the volume increases in legumes, from soaking and from cooking.

In what cultures are the above vegetables and legumes most common?

Batters

Notes:

FLOURS

Goal: To observe the effect of protein and bran content on structure and hydration.

Objectives: To observe affect of flour type on gluten ball formation.
To observe the difference in hydration capacity of various flours.

❖I. Characteristics of Gluten Balls Made from Different Flours
Gluten Balls

Procedure: To (58 g) 1/2 c flour, add just enough water to make a *stiff* dough and knead 10 min; wash under water (have pan full of cool water and change often) until all starch has been removed: water will be clear. Form dough into a ball. Bake at 450°F for 15 min, then 300°F for 30 min.

Results: Indicate which flours pack most readily, which feel very fine, and which have a more granular feel.

Type of Flour	Packing When Pressed in Hand	Granulation (Feeling Between Fingers)	Volume and Structure of Gluten Ball
Cake			
All-purpose			
Bread flour			
Whole wheat (graham)			
Rye			

Conclusion: What is the composition of flour?

How does the composition of cake, all-purpose, bread, whole wheat, and rye flour differ?

Which flour—cake or all-purpose—will pack and hold shape when pressed in hand?

Which flour gives the largest volume gluten ball? Why?

(Photo: Courtesy of the Wheat Flour Institute)

Hydration Capacity of Different Flours

Procedure: Use 50 g flour for each variable. Add the amount of water specified. Compare the consistencies of batters and doughs. (Proportions are based on volumes rather than weights.)

Results: Record which batters have the least viscosity (are thinnest) and which have the most viscosity (are thickest) when comparing each type of flour.

Type of Flour	Pour Batter 1:1 118 ml Water	Drop Batter 1:2 59 ml Water	Soft Dough 1:3 39 ml Water
Cake			
All-purpose			
Whole wheat			
Rye			

Conclusions: Which flour contains more protein?

Which flour contains more fiber?

Which component absorbs the most water?

BAKING POWDERS AND BAKING SODA

Goal: To identify ingredients and action of both baking soda and baking powder.

Objectives: To observe action of single-acting powders without heat.
To observe effect of heat on double-acting powders.
To observe the effect of acid on leavening with baking soda.
To list ingredients in each of the above leavening agents.

I. Comparison of Speed of Reaction

Mix 1/4 t of each type of baking powder and baking soda listed in the table with of cold water in a test tube. Cover immediately with a balloon. Note the speed of gas evolution. Let the beakers stand until one or more have ceased to be active. **Note the minutes required.** Next stir and permit the gas to escape. Warm each and record results whether there is further evolution of gas. Taste the solution after the reaction has ceased, and make a test with litmus paper.

Results: Record data on table below using balloon size as indicator of quantity of gas produced.

| Type | Brand Name | Gas Formation | | | Gas Ceases | | Reaction to Litmus | Equation for Reaction |
		at Once	on Standing	When Warmed	Cold Min	Hot Min		
Tartrate								
Phosphate*								
SAS phosphate								
Baking soda								

II. Information from the Labels on the Cans of Baking Powders and Baking Soda

Type	Brand Name	Acid Ingredients	Amount Recommended per C Flour	Retail Package Size, Cost per Oz	Cost per Lb
Tartrate					
Phosphate					
SAS phosphate					
Baking soda					

Conclusions: Name the two major types of ingredients in baking powder.

Name the ingredient in baking soda.

What causes a single-acting baking powder to produce CO_2?

What causes a double-acting baking powder to produce CO_2?

What causes baking soda to produce CO_2?

Source is listed in Appendix B.

BATTERS

Goal: To observe the quality of products made from pour batters; functions of ingredients and taste.

Objectives: To observe the functions of eggs in popovers and cream puffs.
                To observe the leavening effect of liquid in batters near the 1:1 flour to liquid proportion.
                To observe the effect of mixing on gluten formation.
                To taste regional pour batters such as spoon bread and brown bread.

The ingredients in batters and doughs commonly include flour, liquid, leavening, salt, egg, sugar, and fat. The proportions of these ingredients and the mixing methods determine the type product produced. Each ingredient has specific functional properties. Below are listed the common ingredients and some of the basic functional properties.

Flour:	Forms gluten when hydrated and mixed, contributing to structure when coagulated.
	Starch gelatinizes and thickens product when cooked.
Liquid:	Hydrates flour and forms gluten when mixed, dissolves leavening, sugar, and salt.
	May produce steam for leavening, especially in batters with a 1:1 flour to water ratio.
Leavening agents:	Produce a gas to make product rise.
Salt:	Added for flavor primarily but may affect gluten.
Egg:	Provides structure as it coagulates.
	Emulsifies fat and liquid.
	Provides color and flavor.
	Holds air for leavening when beaten.
Sugar:	Tenderizes and contributes to browning reaction.
	Provides flavor.
Fat:	Tenderizes and may provide flavor and mouthfeel.

Type of mixing and amount of mixing will also affect the structure of the product.

The batters below are pour batters having a 1:1 flour to water ratio. High temperatures producing steam from the water contribute leavening.

I. Effect of Mixing and Ingredients on Popovers and Cream Puffs

❖A. **Popovers**

    (116 g) 1 c flour   (100 g) 2 eggs
    (3 g) 1/2 t salt   (237 ml) 1 c milk

Procedure: Sift salt and flour into mixing bowl. Add unbeaten eggs and 1/2 of the milk. Beat until smooth, using rotary beater or whisk. Add remainder of milk and mix well. Fill well-oiled deep muffin pans, popover pans, or glass custard cups 1/3 to 1/2 full. Place 35 g in each cup. Avoid excess fat in pans, as it reduces volumes and gives misshapen products. Bake at 400°F about 20 min, until they are well risen and brown, then quickly slash the top with a paring knife. Turn off heat, and allow popovers to dry in the oven, approximately 10 min. Popovers should be firm to the touch when removed from oven, or they will collapse. Serve promptly.

Variables:

1. Prepare as directed. Place 1/2 in pan and bake.

2. Beat other half with rotary egg beater for 3

   min after batter is smooth.

3. Prepare one recipe with 1 egg rather than 2.

Results: Rate volume on hedonic scale with 9 = largest volume and 1 = smallest volume. Comment on thinness of shell and size of cavity.

Variable	Volume	Appearance Interior	Exterior	Palatability
1. Standard recipe mixed until smooth (2 eggs)				
2. Standard recipe mixed 3 min after batter is smooth				
3. 1 recipe with 1 egg				

Conclusions: What are the quality characteristics of a popover?

How does excessive mixing affect volume of popovers?

What function does the egg serve in a popover?

❖B. Cream Puffs

(118 ml) 1/2 c water   (58 g) 1/2 c flour
(51 g) 1/4 c fat   (100 g) 2 eggs
(1.5 g) 1/4 t salt

Procedure: To bake in a conventional oven, preheat oven to 400°F. Heat water, fat, and salt to boiling point. Add flour all at once. Stir vigorously until mixture leaves sides of pan and clings to spoon. Remove from heat. Cool slightly. Then add unbeaten eggs, 1 at a time, beating thoroughly after each addition. Make into cream puffs each weighing 45 g. Drop mixture by spoonfuls onto oiled baking sheet 1 1/2 in. apart, or shape into rounds about 2 in. in diameter. Bake 25 min at 400°F. Cut slit in top and bake 10 min longer.

❖Variables: 1/2 recipe for each variable baked in conventional oven as directed in procedure above.
  1. Control: standard product.
     a. Use whole egg
     b. Use Egg Beaters
  2. Egg undermixed with cooked starch and fat mixture.
  3. Formula using 1/2 of egg quantity.

Variables 4a and 4b: 1 recipe: 2 cream puffs baked in each oven.

4a. Convection: Bake in convection oven: 400°F with convection *on*. Bake 18 min. Cut slit in top. Bake 10 min longer.

4b. Conventional oven: Bake at 400°F for 18 min in conventional oven (not convection). Cut slit in top. Bake 10 min longer.

Results: Rate volume on a hedonic scale with 9 = largest volume and 1 = smallest volume. Describe appearance and palatability.

Variable	Volume	Appearance		Palatability
		Interior	Exterior	
1a. Control: Whole egg				
1b. Control: Egg Beaters				
2. Egg undermixed				
3. 1/2 standard egg quantity				
4. Effect of type of oven a. Baked in convection oven				
b. Bake in conventional for only 18 min				

Conclusions: What are the quality characteristics of cream puffs?

What is the function of egg in a cream puff?

What is the leavening agent of a cream puff?

What effect does a convection oven have on baking cream puffs?

❖II. Effect of Source of Leavening and Type of Flour on Griddle Cakes
A. Griddle Cakes Using Sour Milk and Baking Soda vs. Sweet Milk and Baking Powder

(58 g) 1/2 c flour
(1.5 g) 1/4 t salt
(1 g) 1/4 t soda
(4 g) 1 t sugar

(118 ml) 1/2 c buttermilk or thick sour milk
(25 g) 1/2 egg, well beaten
(27.5 g) 1/2 T liquid fat

Procedure: Sift dry ingredients together. Add buttermilk, egg, and fat. Mix just to combine ingredients; leave slightly lumpy. Drop mixture by spoonfuls on a hot griddle that may or may not be oiled, according to kind. When cakes are risen, full of bubbles, and cooked on edges, turn them and cook other side. Serve at once.

Variables
1. Recipe above using sour milk and baking soda.
2. Recipe above substituting milk for sour milk and 1 t baking powder for 1/4 t baking soda.

B. Griddle cakes using all-purpose flour vs. cake flour
Variables
1. Use all-purpose flour in above recipe.
2. Use cake flour in above recipe.

Results: Rate texture and tenderness on a hedonic scale with 9 = fine texture and extremely tender and 1 = coarse texture and extremely tough.

Variables	Appearance	Texture	Tenderness	Palatability	Thickness of Baked Product
A.1. Sour milk: All-purpose flour					
A.2. Sweet milk: All-purpose flour					
B.1. Sour milk: All-purpose flour					
B.2. Sour milk: Cake flour					

Conclusions: Why is leavening agent changed when sour milk is replaced with milk?

What is the chemical reaction of sour milk mixed with baking soda?

What is the function of each ingredient?

Is the liquid a source of leavening? Why?

How does replacing all-purpose flour with cake flour affect batter viscosity and final product?

III. Waffles

A. Standard Waffles

(72 g) 1/2 c + 2 T flour
(3.8 g) 1 t baking powder
(1.5 g) 1/4 t salt
(6 g) 1/2 T sugar, if needed

(118 ml) 1/2 c milk
(30 ml) 2 T oil
(16.6 g) 1 egg yolk, beaten thick
(33.4 g) 1 egg white, beaten stiff

Procedure: Sift dry ingredients together. Mix milk and fat with egg yolks. Combine milk mixture with dry ingredients. Stir only until blended. Fold in egg whites. Pour into center of hot waffle iron that may or may not be oiled, according to kind. Close top of iron. For a crisp waffle, use larger amount of fat and cook longer.

B. Toaster Waffle

Procedure: Toast frozen waffle as indicated on directions.

Results: Rate texture and tenderness on a hedonic scale with 9 = fine texture and extremely tender and 1 = coarse texture and extremely tough.

Variables	Exterior Appearance	Texture	Tenderness	Palatability	Cost
Standard waffles					
Toaster waffles					

Conclusions: What are the leavening agents in waffles?

Is this a pour batter?

Compare costs and quality of home prepared vs. frozen waffles.

❖IV. Steamed Boston Brown Bread

(35 g) 1/4 c yellow cornmeal

(29 or 32 g) 1/4 c white or rye flour

(33 g) 1/4 c graham flour

(1.5 g) 1/4 t salt

(1 g) 1/4 t soda

(118 ml) 1/2 c sour milk

(57.5 g) 3 T molasses

Procedure: Sift dry ingredients together. Blend milk and molasses. Add to dry ingredients. Mix. Turn into well-oiled molds (1-pt, wide-mouth canning jars), filling no more than 2/3 full. Cover. Place in pressure cooker with 2 c water. Cook on rack with 2 in. water in pressure pan at 5 lbs pressure for 50 min. Then remove from jars, and dry in oven 10 min. If served hot, slice (with a string). Bread may be baked as a loaf instead of steamed. In that case, add 1 T melted fat. Bake 1 hour at 375°F.

Results: Rate texture and tenderness on a hedonic scale with 9 = fine texture and extremely tender to 1 = coarse texture and extremely tough.

Variable	Exterior Appearance	Texture	Tenderness	Palatability
Boston brown bread				

Conclusions: What batter consistency is Boston brown bread?

What are the leavening agents?

V. Spoon Bread

(26.25 g) 3 T yellow cornmeal

(79 ml) 1/3 c milk, scalded

(28 g) 2 t butter or margarine

(50 g) 1 egg, separated

(1.5 g) 1/4 t salt

(.95 g) 1/4 t baking powder

Procedure: Place baking dish sprayed with non-stick coating on the bottom in a pan of hot water and heat in oven at 375°F. Add cornmeal slowly to milk, stirring constantly. Cook in double boiler or over low heat until consistency of mush, 5–8 min. Blend in butter or margarine. Remove from heat and set aside to cool.

Meanwhile, add salt to egg whites and beat until stiff but not dry. Beat egg yolks; add cornmeal mixture and baking powder and blend thoroughly. Fold cornmeal mixture into stiffly beaten egg whites.

Pour into a *heated* 10-oz casserole greased only on the bottom and set in a pan of hot water. Bake in a moderate oven (375°), about 30 min or until a knife inserted halfway between the center and the outside edge comes out clean. Serve by dipping large spoonfuls from casserole.

Results: Rate texture and tenderness on a hedonic scale with 9 = fine texture and extremely tender to 1 = coarse texture and extremely tough.

Variable	Exterior Appearance	Texture	Tenderness	Palatability
Spoon bread				

Conclusions: What are the leavening agents in this product?

What is the function of the cereal?

VI. Rosettes
Procedure: Make 1/2 recipe popover batter. Add 1/2 t oil to liquid ingredients and 1/2 t sugar to the dry ingredients. Heat oil in deep fat fryer to 365°F. Heat rosette iron in fat to 365°F. Drain iron on paper towel, then dip into batter nearly to top of iron. Fry until brown. Remove, drain, and sprinkle with powdered sugar.

VII. Crepes
(58 g) 1/2 c sifted flour
(3 g) 1/2 t salt
(12 g) 1 T sugar

(158 ml) 2/3 c milk
(14 g) 1 T butter or margarine
(100 g) 2 eggs, well beaten

Procedure: Sift salt and sugar with flour. Combing eggs, milk, and butter. Add to flour mixture. Blend with wire whip or beater until smooth. Pour 1 T batter on hot griddle, tilt to make thin. Bake until light brown on both sides.

Results: Comment on appearance, tenderness, and palatability.

Variable	Exterior Appearance	Tenderness	Palatability
Rosettes			
Crepes			

Conclusions: What is the ratio of flour to liquid in rosette and crepe products?

Is steam a leavener?

What is the function of each ingredient?

Drop Batters

Notes:

DROP BATTERS: MUFFINS

Goal: To using prior knowledge of functions of ingredients in a batter, to identify the functions of each ingredient and of the combining and mixing process of the muffin formula.

Objectives: To identify muffin batter as a pour batter, drop batter, or soft dough.
To observe the effect of mixing on muffin batter.
To identify the effect on structure, tenderness, and volume of each ingredient.
To observe the effect of convection, microwave, and conventional baking on the product.
To compare products prepared from commercial mix and a conventional recipe.
To observe the gluten development due to excess stirring.
To compare the results of using different baking powders in a simple quick bread.

❖Muffins

(120 g) 1 c flour
(5.7 g) 1 1/2 t baking powder
(12 g) 1 T sugar
(3 g) 1/2 t salt

(125 ml) 1/2 c milk
(25 g) 1/2 egg, well beaten
(13 g) 1 T oil

Procedure: Use formula above and variable below. Sift dry ingredients together. Add oil and milk to egg mixture. Combine dry and liquid mixture. *Stir only enough to mix ingredients slightly—no more than 15 strokes. Batter will still be lumpy.* Take out 45 g batter for each of 2 muffins and place in oiled muffin tin. Stir 10 more strokes. Take out batter for 2 more muffins. Stir 35 strokes more and place batter for last 2 muffins in pan. Mark pans with wax pencil for identification. *Conventional baking:* at 218°C (425°F) for 15–20 min. Remove from pans at once.

I. Effect of Number of Strokes of Stirring and Type of Leavening
Variables:
Phosphate baking powder

1. 15 or less strokes (still lumpy)
2. 25 strokes
3. 60 strokes

SAS phosphate baking powder

1. 15 or less strokes (still lumpy)
2. 25 strokes
3. 60 strokes

Commercial baking mix

1. 15 strokes
2. 25 strokes
3. 60 strokes

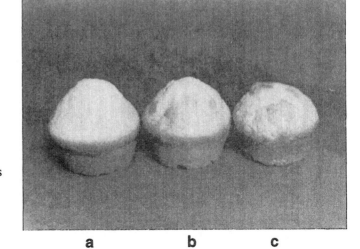

Beating muffin batter excessively produces a peaked appearance and a tunneled texture (a). Less beating in (b) and even less in (c) produces an uneven, slightly rounded surface with a finer and more tender texture.

a   b   c

II. Effect of Fat and Sugar Ratio in Microwave Muffins
Variables:
1. Standard formula

2. Double fat

3. Double fat and sugar

Procedure: Use procedure above, mixing only 15 strokes. Place batter into microwave muffin pans. Bake 6 muffins on high for 2 1/2 min.

III. Effect of Microwave vs. Convection vs. Conventional Baking
Variables:
1. Conventional: Bake 2 muffins in 6-cell muffin tin at 375°F for 15 min with 50 g in each muffin tin and 25 g water in empty cells.

2. Microwave: Effect of power setting. Put 50 g muffin mix in each of two cells in a 6-cell muffin tin. Add 25 g water to each empty tin.

   a. Bake 2 muffins at 100% power (10) for 2 min.

   b. Bake 2 muffins at 80% power (8) for 2 min.

   c. Bake 2 muffins at 70% power (7) for 2 min.

3. Microwave / convection combination

   a. Bake 6 muffins on combination 4 for 5 min (directions may vary for specific brands of ovens).

❖IV. Effect of Added Ingredients on Microwave Muffins
Microwave Raisin Bran Muffins

(66 g) 1 1/8 c raisin bran cereal	(38.5 g) 1/3 c flour
(79 ml) 1/3 c milk	(37.5 g) 3 T packed brown sugar
(45 ml) 3 T oil	(5.7 g) 1 1/2 t baking powder
(50 g) 1 egg, beaten	(.5 g) 1/4 t cinnamon

Procedure: Combine cereal, milk, oil, and eggs. Stir until cereal is moistened. Let stand 5 min. Combine flour, sugar, baking powder, and cinnamon. Add cereal mixture; stir until blended. Use oiled 6-hole microwave muffin pan. Fill each cup with 45 g of batter. Cook at medium-low (7) for 6 1/2 min.

Results: Rate texture and tenderness on a 9-point hedonic scale with 9 = very fine texture and extremely tender and 1 = very coarse texture and extremely tough. Comment on appearance, volume, and flavor.

Variable: Baking Powder Type/No. of Stirring Strokes	Appearance				Volume	Texture	Tenderness	Flavor and Moistness
	Browning	Glaze	Shape	Top				
Tartrate Baking Powder A.1. 15 strokes								
A.2. 25 strokes								
A.3. 60 strokes								
SAS Phosphate Baking Powder A.1. 15 strokes								
A.2. 25 strokes								
A.3. 60 strokes								
Commercial Mix 15 strokes								
25 strokes								
60 strokes								
Variable: Oven type								
Micro Baking B.1. Std. recipe								
B.2. Double fat								
B.3. Double fat and sugar								
C.1. Conventional								
C.2a. Microwave 100% power								
C.2b. Microwave 80%								
C.3. Microwave/ Convection								
D. Microwave Raisin Bran								

Conclusions: How does stirring muffin batter affect appearance (smoothness of surface, peaked tops)?

How does stirring affect tenderness and appearance of tunnels?

How does flavor vary due to leavening agents?

How does microwave or convection baking affect the product?

What is the function of each ingredient in a muffin?

How does the ratio of sugar and fat to flour affect the amount of stirring desirable?

CAKES WITH SHORTENING

Goal: To prepare quality shortened cakes and observe effects on texture, tenderness, and mixing methods of higher ratio of sugar and standard formula cakes.

Objectives: To compare mixing methods with and without air beaten into egg whites.
To observe the functions of sugar and fat in tenderizing and in producing a fine crumb.
To use mixing methods commensurate with formulas of either conventional or high sugar ratio.
To compare the effects of changing type of flour and proportion of sugar on tenderness, texture, and volume.
To compare conventional and microwave baking methods.
To compare reduced fat and conventional formulas.

I. Effect of Methods of Mixing and Formula on Time and Effort Involved and Quality of Product

A. Shortened Cake: Conventional Formula and Mixing

(100 g) 1/2 c sugar	(50 g) 1 egg
(5.7 g) 1 1/2 t baking powder	(90 ml) 3/8 c milk
(2.5 ml) 1/2 t vanilla	(51 g) 1/4 c hydrogenated fat
(3 g) 1/2 t salt	(96 g) 1 c sifted cake flour

Variables:

❖1. Conventional Method of Mixing: Whole Egg

Procedure: Cut and place a piece of waxed paper in the bottom of 8-in. round cake pan. Preheat oven to 375°F. Sift salt, baking powder, and flour together. Set aside. Place fat and sugar in mixer and mix for 5 min on high. Add whole egg. Beat at medium speed for 2 min more.

Reduce to lowest speed. Add about 1/4 c sifted dry ingredients. When mixed, add about 2 T milk and flavoring. Continue alternating dry and wet ingredients until all is mixed. The beater does not need to be turned off until total mixing time is 3 min.

Bake at 375°F for 25–30 min or until a toothpick inserted comes out clean. When done, remove from oven, cool slightly, remove from pan, and take paper off bottom. Place on rack to cool.

2. Conventional Method of Mixing: Egg Separated

Procedure: Cut and fit a piece of waxed paper in bottom of 8-in. round cake pan. Preheat oven to 375°F. Sift salt, baking powder, and flour together. Set aside. Remove (25 g) 2 T sugar from the 1/2 c and set aside. Place fat and remaining sugar in mixer and mix for 5 min on high. Add egg yolk. Beat at medium speed 2 min more.

Reduce to lowest speed. Add about 1/4 c sifted dry ingredients. When mixed, add about (30 ml) 2 T milk and flavoring. Continue alternating dry and wet ingredients until all is mixed. The beater does not need to be turned off during the addition of dry and liquid ingredients. Continue beating at low speed until total mixing time is 3 min.

Beat egg white to soft peak. Add remaining sugar; beat to stiff peak. Fold into batter. Bake at 375°F for 25–30 min or until a toothpick inserted comes out clean. When done, remove from oven, cool slightly, remove form pan, and take paper off bottom. Place on rack to cool.

❖B. Shortened Cake: Quick Formula and Method and Mixing

(116 g) 1 c sifted cake flour	(134 g) 2/3 c sugar
(109 ml) 1/3 c + 2 T milk	(50 g) 1 egg, unbeaten
(3 g) 1/2 t salt	(5.7 g) 1 1/2 t baking powder
(51 g) 1/4 c hydrogenated fat	(2.5 ml) 1/2 t vanilla

Procedure: Cut and fit a piece of waxed paper in bottom of 8-in. round cake pan. Preheat oven to 375°F. Have ingredients at room temperature. Sift all dry ingredients into mixing bowl. Add fat and half of milk and flavoring. Beat with electric mixer on medium speed for 2 min. Scrape bowl frequently.

Add remaining liquid and unbeaten whole eggs (yolk and whites), and continue beating 2 more min, scraping bowl frequently. Bake at 375°F for 25–30 min or until toothpick comes out clean. When done, remove from oven, cool slightly, remove from pan, and take paper off bottom. Place on rack to cool.

Variables:
1. Formula above.
2. Use margarine instead of hydrogenated fat.

C. Shortened Cake: Commercial Mix
Procedure: Mix and bake cake according to box directions

❖D. Shortened cake with fat replacer
1. **Yellow Cake with Fat Replacer**

   (113 g) 1/2 c + 1 T sugar   (101 g) 1 c + 1 T cake flour
   (12 g) 1 1/2 T N-FLATE*   (8.5 g) 2 t baking powder
   (6.25 g) 1 T + 1 t dextrose   (1.5 g) 1/4 t salt
   (132 ml) 1/2 c water   (83 g) 1/3 c whole eggs
   (3 ml) 1/2 t vanilla

Procedure: Blend dry ingredients well with mixer. Add water, vanilla, and whole eggs to dry mix. Beat on low speed for 30 seconds. Whip on high speed for 4 min minimum. Pour into 8-in. round cake pan lined with waxed paper. Bake at 350°F (177°C) for 28–35 min.

2. **Yellow Cake Mix, Fat Free (Commercial)**

Characteristics of Shortened Cakes

Shape: Symmetrical in shape and slightly rounded layer cake; almost flat on top; free from cracks.

Crust: Thin, tender, soft, golden brown; no spots; neither crisp nor shiny.

Volume: Large volume in proportion to the ingredients; feels light.

Texture: Crumb is light, moist, velvety; grain is fine, uniform.

Tenderness: Tender; does not crumble excessively; when cut, holds shape.

Color: Uniform.

Flavor and Odor: Characteristic; pleasing.

*Source listed in Appendix B

Comparison of Methods of Mixing of Shortened Cakes

Results: Identify color and thickness of crust. Rank texture, tenderness, and flavor on a hedonic scale of 9 = very fine texture, extremely tender, and most flavorful and 1 = very coarse texture, extremely tough, and least flavorful.

Method of Mixing	Prep Time (Min)	Shape	Crust	Volume	Texture	Tenderness	Flavor	Color
A.1. Conventional mixing, whole egg added								
A.2. Conventional mixing, egg separated								
B. Quick method 1. Use hydrogenated fat								
2. Use margarine for hydrogenated fat								
C. Commercial mix								
D.1. Shortened cake: Fat replacer								
D.2. Commercial mix: Fat free								

Conclusions: How did adding beaten egg whites affect texture and volume of the cake?

How do formulas of conventionally mixed and quick mixed cakes vary?

Describe the function of each ingredient.

In which cake mixing method would gluten development be greatest?

How do formulas vary to compensate for the mixing method?

Describe a quality shortened cake by shape, texture, tenderness, crust, and volume.

How does the quality differ in cakes made with fat replacers?

Why does the cake volume and tenderness change when using a margarine spread?

II. Effect of Varying Sugar Proportions and Type on Cake Quality

Variables:

A. Use conventional formula and mixing (I.A.) but reduce sugar to 1/4 c.

B. Use conventional formula and mixing (I.A.) but increase sugar to 3/4 c.

C. Use conventional formula and mixing (I.A.) but use 1/2 c high fructose corn syrup*.

D. Compare to control: I.A.

Cakes with various amounts and types of sugar

Results: Identify color and thickness of crust. Rank texture, tenderness, and flavor on a hedonic scale of 9 = very fine texture, extremely tender, and most flavorful and 1 = very coarse texture, extremely tough, and extremely poor flavor.

Amount of Sugar	Shape	Crust	Volume	Tenderness	Flavor	Color
A. (50 g) 1/4 c						
B. (150 g) 3/4 c						
C. High fructose corn* syrup: (118 ml) 1/2 c						
D. (100 g) 1/2 c (control)						

Conclusions: How does high fructose corn syrup affect quality?

What is the function of sugar in a cake?

How does sugar affect coagulation temperature?

Why did one of the variables rise and then fall?

III. Effect of Cake Flour vs. All-Purpose Flour on Cake Quality

Variables:

A. Conventional mixing and formula (I.A.), but substitute all-purpose flour for cake flour.

B. Conventional mixing and formula (I.A.) using cake flour.

Results: Identify color and thickness of crust. Rank texture, tenderness, and flavor on a hedonic scale of 9 = very fine texture, extremely tender, and most flavorful and 1 = very coarse texture, extremely tough, and extremely poor flavor.

Variable	Shape	Crust	Volume	Tenderness	Flavor	Color
A. All-purpose flour						
B. Cake flour						

Conclusion: Does cake flour give a finer texture and a more tender cake? Why?

SPONGE, ANGEL, AND CHIFFON CAKES

Goal: To recognize and prepare high quality sponge and chiffon cakes and observe the relationship of mixing method to ingredient functions.

Objectives: To compare characteristics and formulas of true sponge, angel food, and chiffon cakes.
To apply knowledge of egg white foams, starch, and flours to procedures for making sponge and chiffon cakes.

In contrast to most of the previous batters and doughs, sponge and angel cakes contain no added fats or oils other than that in the egg. Tenderization is attributed to a low-gluten flour (cake flour), to the sugar, and to minimal mixing of the flour (folding). In traditional formulas, leavening comes from steam and air rather than from chemical leaveners.

❖I. True Sponge Cake

(66 g) 1/3 c sugar
(100 g) 2 eggs
(23.5 ml) 1 T + 1 t water
(2 g) 1/2 t grated lemon rind

(5 g) 1 t lemon juice
(32 g) 1/3 c cake flour, sifted
(.8 g) 1/8 t salt

Variables:

A. Sponge: whole egg

Procedure: Preheat oven to 400°F. Sift together cake flour, salt, and 2/3 of the sugar. Beat whole eggs and water until thick and lemon colored. Add remaining sugar. Fold flour mixture into egg mixture. Pour into 6-in. unoiled tube pan or unoiled 4 x 6-in. loaf pan. Bake at 400°F for 20 min. When done, turn pan upside down and let stand until cold. Loosen cake from sides of tin.

B. Sponge: egg separated

Procedure: Preheat oven to 400°F. Sift together cake flour, salt, and 1/3 of the sugar. Set aside. Beat egg whites until soft peak. Beat in lemon juice. Gradually add 1/3 of the sugar. Beat to stiff peak. Set aside. Beat egg yolk with water until lemon colored. Add remaining sugar. Fold egg whites into yolks, then fold in flour gradually. Fold until well mixed. Pour into 6-in. unoiled tube pan. Bake at 425°F for 20 min. When done, turn pan upside down, and let stand until cold. Loosen cake from sides of tip with spatula.

1. Angel Food Cake

Variables:

A. Procedure below

B. Angel food cake mix

(100 ml) 3/8 c + 1 T egg whites
(26 g) 1/4 c cake flour
(2.5 ml) 1/2 t vanilla

(82 g) 1/3 c + 1 T sugar
(1.6 g) 1/2 t cream of tartar
(.8 g) 1/8 t salt

Procedure: Preheat oven to 400°F. Sift 1/2 of sugar with flour and salt. Set aside. Beat egg whites until foamy. Add cream of tartar. Beat to soft peak. Add 1/2 of sugar and vanilla. Beat to stiff peak. Fold in flour-sugar mixture. Pour into 6-in. unoiled angel cake pan or ungreased 4 x 6-in. loaf pan. Bake at 400°F for 20–25 min. Loosen cake from sides of tin with a spatula.

III. Chiffon Cake

(48 g) 1/2 c cake flour	(24.9 g) 1 1/2 egg yolks
(3.8 g) 1 t baking powder	(33 ml) 2 T + 2 t cold water
(63 g) 1/3 c sugar	(2.5 ml) 1/2 t vanilla
(1.5 g) 1/4 t salt	(50 ml) 1/4 c egg whites
(30 ml) 2 T salad oil	(.4 g) 1/8 t cream of tartar

Procedure: Preheat oven to 375°F. Sift flour, baking powder, sugar, and salt together. Mix together and pour in salad oil, egg yolks, water, and vanilla. Beat with electric mixer 2 min on medium speed. Set aside. Beat egg whites until foamy. Add cream of tartar. Beat until stiff. Fold flour mixture into egg whites. Pour into 7-in. unoiled tube pan or 4 x 6-in. unoiled loaf pan and bake until top springs back: about 15 min. Turn pan upside down and let stand until cold. Loosen cake from sides of tin with spatula or knife.

Quality Characteristics of Sponge Cakes:

- Symmetrical in shape
- Crust tender, but not sticky
- Color, flavor, and odor: delicate lemon
- Delicately browned
- Light in weight for size
- Texture: silky, tender, moist, and resilient
- Grain: fine, uniform
- Evenly and slightly rounded

Results: Rank texture, tenderness, and flavor on a hedonic scale of 9 = extremely fine texture, extremely tender, and most flavorful and 1 = very coarse texture, extremely tough, and extremely poor flavor.

Variable	Shape	Volume	Crust	Color Interior	Exterior	Texture	Tenderness	Flavor
Sponge cake Egg separated								
Whole egg								
Angel food cake								
Angel cake mix								
Chiffon cake								

Conclusions: How do the formulas of sponge, angel, chiffon, and shortened cakes differ?

Why are pans unoiled for sponge, angel, and chiffon cakes?

What is the major tenderizing ingredient in sponge and angel cakes?

What mixing method prevents too much gluten development?

What are the characteristics of quality sponge, angel, and chiffon cakes?

What are the leavening agents of sponge and angel cakes?

Doughs

Notes:

SOFT DOUGH: BISCUITS

Goal: To observe and taste flakiness and tenderness in quality biscuits and to recognize mixing and ingredient functions that yield these qualities.

Objectives: To compare the extent of kneading on the characteristics of rolled biscuits.
To use mixing methods and formulas that produce quality biscuits.
To observe the effect of fat replacers on quality of biscuits.

❖I. Effect of Kneading on Baking Powder Biscuits

Biscuits

(230 g) 2 c sifted flour	(65 g) 5 T fat
(11.4 g) 3 t baking powder	(177 ml) 3/4 c milk
(3 g) 1 t salt	

Procedure: Preheat oven to 425°F. Sift dry ingredients together. With pastry blender, cut in fat until mixture resembles coarse cornmeal. Add milk all at once, mixing until dough clings together. Turn onto a lightly floured board. Knead as directed in variable below. Shape into a ball, pat, and roll into a sheet 1/2-in. in height. If available, use 1/2-in. wooden gauges placed on each side of dough. Roll the dough to the depth of the wooden gauge to give more uniformity to each variable. Cut with a floured cutter. Place on baking sheet and bake at 425°F for 12–15 min. Do not re-roll trimmings for experimental biscuits.

Variables:

A. Before kneading, pinch off 1/4 of the dough for 2 biscuits. Do not knead. Roll and cut as directed below.

B. Knead remaining dough 10 times, take out 1/3 of the dough, roll, and cut as directed below.

C. Knead remaining dough 10 more strokes, take out 1/2 of the dough, roll, and cut as directed below.

D. Knead remaining dough 10 more strokes, roll, and cut as directed below.

❖II. Effect of Fat Replacer on Biscuit Quality

Low-Fat Biscuits

(93 g) 1 c cake flour	(14 g) 2 T LoDex 10 Maltodextrin (Amaizo)*
(10 g) 2 T sweet whey*	(5 g) 1 t granulated sugar
(3.5 g) 1 t baking soda	(3.5 g) 1 t baking powder
(1.2 g) 1/4 t Bealite 3401-L*	(2 g) 1/2 t amalean II instant starch*
(2.4 g) 1/2 t butter flavor*	(1.6 g) 1/2 t butter milk flavor*
(1.5 g) 1/4 t salt	(60 ml) 1/4 c water

Procedure: Blend all dry ingredients. Add water and blend until thoroughly wetted and mixture is of uniform consistency. Roll to 1/2-in. thickness between wooden gauges if available. Cut in 2-in. biscuits. Bake in convection oven at 350°F for 10 min or in conventional oven at 425°F for 12–15 min.

III. Effect of Convection and Microwave Baking on Biscuit Quality

Procedure: Use 1/2 of biscuit dough recipe in Experiment I. Knead 10 strokes, roll, and cut into 6 biscuits.

Variables

A. Bake 2 biscuits in preheated convection oven at 425°F for 10 min.

B. Bake 2 biscuits in preheated 425°F conventional oven for 10 min.

C. Bake 2 biscuits in combination convection/microwave for 2 min at 475°F with convection on and microwave on low for 2 min. Continue baking with only convection on for 5 min longer.

*Source listed in Appendix B

IV. Refrigerated Biscuits: Commercial

Procedure: Bake one package as directed on package.

Results: Rate on a 9-point hedonic scale with 9 = extremely fine texture, extremely tender, and extremely moist to 1 = extremely coarse texture, extremely tough, and extremely dry. Comment on volume, crust, and flakiness.

Variable	Volume	Crust	Flakiness	Texture	Color	Tenderness	Moistness	Flavor
I. Kneading Variables A. 0 strokes								
B. 10 strokes								
C. 20 strokes								
D. 40 strokes								
I. Biscuit using fat replacer								
III. Oven Variable A. Convection								
B. Conventional								
IV. Refrig. (precut)								

Conclusions: What are the functions of kneading biscuit dough?

Identify quality differences when fat is reduced and fat replacer used.

Which biscuits had both characteristics of quality: tenderness and flakiness?

Compare the effect on appearance and baking time of convection, microwave, and conventional baking.

STIFF DOUGH: PASTRY

Goal: To prepare, taste, and evaluate quality pastry using a variety of methods and ingredients.

Objectives: To compare tenderness and flakiness of pastry prepared with various fats and mixed by different methods.
To prepare one- and two-crust pies.

I. Effect of Mixing Method and Type of Fat on Pastry Quality

A. Variables in method

❖1. Plain Pastry

(115 g) 1 c flour	(63 g) 1/3 c fat
(3 g) 1/2 t salt	(29 ml) 2 T cold water

Procedure: Sift flour and salt together. With pastry blender cut fat into flour mixture until particles are the size of peas. Sprinkle water over flour mixture and stir lightly with fork until particles stick together and will form a ball when pressed in palms of hands. Amount of water varies with temperature, type of flour, fineness of division of ingredients, and rate at which water is added. If dough will not form ball, add 1–2 T more water. Roll as indicated in directions below.

❖Variables in type of fat:

a. Use hydrogenated fat.

b. Use lard

c. Use margarine or butter.

2. Water Whip Pastry

(116 g) 1 c flour	(29 ml) 2 T boiling water
(3 g) 1/2 t salt	(68 g) 1/3 c hydrogenated fat

Procedure: Sift flour and salt together. Set aside. Beat water and fat with a fork until mixture is creamy and fluffy. Add to sifted dry ingredients. Stir lightly with fork until particles stick together and form a ball when pressed in palms of hands. Amount of water varies with temperature, type of flour, fineness of division of ingredients, and rate at which water is added. If dough will not form ball, add 1–2 T more water. Roll as indicated in directions below.

3. Water Paste Pastry

(116 g) 1 c flour	(29 ml) 2 T water
(3 g) 1/2 t salt	(68 g) 1/3 c hydrogenated fat

Procedure: Sift flour and salt together. Remove 3 T and mix to a paste with water. Cut fat into remaining flour and salt mixture. Stir the two mixtures together lightly with fork until particles stick together and form a ball when pressed in palms of hands. Amount of water varies with temperature, type of flour, fineness of division of ingredients, and rate at which water is added. Roll as indicated in directions below.

❖4. Oil Pastry

(116 g) 1 c flour	(3 g) 1/2 t salt
(80 ml) 1/3 c oil	(29 ml) 2 T water

Procedure: Sift flour and salt together. Pour water and oil together. Mix and quickly pour liquid into dry ingredients, and stir lightly with a fork until particles stick together and form a ball when pressed in palms of hands. Amount of water varies with temperature, type of flour, fineness of division of ingredients, and rate at which water is added. Roll as indicated in directions below but roll between 2 sheets of waxed paper.

B. Rolling pastry for pie

Procedure: Above recipes make one 9-in. pie crust or two 6-in. pie crusts. Use 1/2 of pastry for one 6-in. pie crust and 1/2 of pastry for experimental samples (C, below). Refrigerate dough for 10 min to facilitate rolling. Sprinkle flour very lightly on board or pastry cloth. Pat and roll out dough as lightly and as circular as possible, rolling from center to outside. Roll to 1/8-in. thickness until slightly larger than pan. Fold in halves or quarters and place loosely in pan. If pastry breaks, press back together rather than re-roll.

For single crust baked separately, trim edges and flute. Prick sides and bottom with a fork to prevent shrinkage. To insure a well-shaped pie crust when baked, a pie pan identical in size and shape may be placed on top of fitted crust. This pan is removed after crust sets to permit browning.

For two-crust pie, after placing bottom crust in pan, add filling, then roll top crust. Cut openings in this crust, then fold in quarters or halves and place over filling. Press edges firmly together. Flute.

C. Rolling pastry for experimental samples

Procedure: Roll above recipes to 1/8-in. thickness (roll between metal gauges if available to maintain constant thickness). Cut samples into 1 x 1 1/2-in. rectangles. Prick with a fork. Bake on baking sheet at 425°F until light golden brown. Evaluate samples using a sensory scale and/or by using a shortometer to test for tenderness.

Quality Evaluation Characteristics of Pastry:

Exterior—slightly uneven, small blisters, large blisters, smooth, dry, slightly greasy, golden brown, pale, burned

Interior—tender, crisp, crumbly, tough, soggy, flaky, compact, mealy, smooth

Palatability—crisp, well cooked, burned, raw, greasy, tender, tough, pleasing

Results: Rate each sample on a hedonic scale with 9 = extremely flaky and 1 = no flakiness.

Methods	Flakiness
A. Plain	
1. Lard	
2. Hydrogenated fat	
3. Margarine	
B. Water whip	
C. Water paste	
D. Oil	

Results: Rate each pastry on the following scale.

	Extremely Tender	Moderately Tender	Slightly Tender	Neither Tender nor Tough	Slightly Tough	Moderately Tough	Extremely Tough
Plain: lard	❏	❏	❏	❏	❏	❏	❏
Plain: hydrogenated fat	❏	❏	❏	❏	❏	❏	❏
Plain: margarine	❏	❏	❏	❏	❏	❏	❏
Water whip	❏	❏	❏	❏	❏	❏	❏
Water paste	❏	❏	❏	❏	❏	❏	❏
Oil	❏	❏	❏	❏	❏	❏	❏

Conclusions: Which fat is plastic?

What characteristics of fat contribute to tenderness?

What characteristics of fat contribute to flakiness?

At what stage of mixing in the plain pastry method may you mix to much and cause toughness?

What characteristics would water whip, water paste, and oil methods contribute?

What conditions may cause pastry to shrink?

II. Effect of Baking Method on Pastry
Use 2 frozen crusts.
A. Bake in Pyrex pan in microwave for 5 1/2 min on power level 8.
B. Bake in convection at 400°F for 12 min.

Results: Rate each pastry on the following scale.

	Extremely Tender	Moderately Tender	Slightly Tender	Neither Tender nor Tough	Slightly Tough	Moderately Tough	Extremely Tough
A.	❏	❏	❏	❏	❏	❏	❏
B.	❏	❏	❏	❏	❏	❏	❏

III. Pies

A. One crust, custard filling

Pumpkin Pie

(681 g) 1 1/2 c pumpkin, cooked	(.5 g) 1/4 t nutmeg
(150 g) 3/4 c sugar	(.5 g) 1/4 t cloves
(3 g) 1/2 t salt	(150 g) 3 eggs, slightly beaten
(1 g) 1/2 t ginger	(296 ml) 1 1/4 c milk
(2 g) 1 t cinnamon	(177 ml) 3/4 c evaporated milk

Procedure: Use pastry as in I.A. Combine sugar, salt, pumpkin, and spices. Add eggs and milk and blend. Pour into pastry. Bake at 450°F for 10 min. Continue baking at 325°F for 45 min or until knife comes out clean. Yield: one 9-in. pie.

B. One crust, cooked cream filling

Chocolate Cream

(100 g) 1/2 c sugar	(33.2 g) 2 egg yolks, well beaten
(22 g) 3 T flour	(14 g) 1 T butter or margarine
(3 g) 1/2 t salt	(2.5 ml) 1/2 t vanilla
(296 ml) 1 1/4 c milk, scalded	(42. 55 g) 1 1/2 squares, unsweetened chocolate

Procedure: Use pastry as in I.A. Beat egg yolks in medium bowl. Set aside. Mix dry ingredients well. Add milk slowly while stirring. Add chocolate. Heat on direct heat until boiling. Immediately turn down heat. Add thickened flour mixture to egg yolks in bowl a little at a time. Stir well. Put back in saucepan. Heat 5 min on low. Stir only occasionally. Add margarine (or butter) and vanilla. Pour into pie shell. Cover with meringue. Bake at 350°F for 15 min until golden brown. Yield: one 9-in. pie.

Meringue

(66.8 g) 2 egg whites	(50 g) 4 T sugar

Procedure: Beat egg whites until soft peak. Add sugar gradually, beating until stiff peak. Spread over pie filling. Bake at 350°F for 15 min

C. Two-crust, fruit-filled pie

Cherry

(133 g) 3/4 c canned sour cherries, drained	(3.9 g) 1 1/2 T cornstarch
(180 ml) 3/4 c cherry juice	(21 g) 1 1/2 T margarine
(200 g) 1 c sugar	

Procedure: Use double pastry recipes as in I.A. Use 1/2 of pastry to line pan. Combine sugar and cornstarch. Add cherries and cherry juice, and place in pastry. Dot top with margarine. Roll 1/2 of pastry and place over fruit, press edges together, and flute. Bake at 425°F for 30–40 min. Yield: one 9-in. pie..

❖IV. Use of Frozen Crusts: Custard Pie

Variables:

A. Fill frozen crust with 1 recipe of custard pie filling mix. Bake at 450°F for 10 min; continue baking at 325°F for 45 min or until knife comes out clean.

B. Bake frozen crust as for single crust, then fill with custard pie filling mix. Bake at 450°F for 10 min; continue baking at 325°F for 45 min or until knife comes out clean.

Results: Record baking temperature and describe firmness/sogginess of crust and palatability of pie.

Pie Variable	Baking Temperature	Crust	Pie
Pumpkin			
Chocolate			
Cherry			
Custard, frozen crust			
Custard, baked crust			

Conclusions: What contributes to a crust that is not soggy?

For what fillings are fillings and crust baked together?

When is crust pricked? When is it left solid?

Soft Dough: Yeast Doughs

Notes:

Goal: To prepare yeast leavened products and to understand the requirements for CO_2 production and for gluten development in yeast doughs.

Objectives: To observe the effect of temperature on yeast production of CO_2 and on volume increase of dough.

To prepare yeast dough: observing proofing and practicing kneading and shaping dough.

To manipulate yeast dough for use in a variety of products.

To observe the effects on time of preparation and quality of yeast product due to baking in conventional, convection, or microwave oven.

To make yeast bread without gluten as may be necessary in clinical situations.

Yeast is a microorganism that utilizes sugar to produce carbon dioxide. Presence of moisture, type of sugar, temperature, and whether the yeast is in dry or compressed form all determine the speed of carbon dioxide production.

Doughs made with yeast generally use a flour that will form more gluten when mixed, thus providing more structure for the product. All-purpose or bread flour is used. The dough is mixed more to give elasticity.

❖I. Effect of Various Temperatures upon the Growth of Yeast

Variables:

A. Mix 1/2 cake of yeast with 60 ml lukewarm water and 5 g sugar. Mix in 45 g flour. Put in a warm place, keeping the temperature about 80°F for 1 hour.

B. Mix 1/2 cake yeast with 60 ml rapidly boiling water and 5 g sugar. Mix in 45 g flour. Hold at 80°F for 1 hour.

C. Mix 1/2 cake yeast with 60 ml ice water and 5 g sugar. Mix in 45 g flour. Hold in refrigerator for 1 hour. Note volume, then hold at 80°F for 1 hour.

D. Mix 1/2 cake yeast with 60 ml ice water and 5 g sugar. Mix in 45 g flour. Hold at 80°F for 1 hour. Compare to C.

Results: Record the time it takes for each to double in bulk and indicate which do not rise.

Variable	Time to Double in Bulk	Comparison of Volume When First Has Doubled in Bulk
A. Lukewarm ingredients—80°F proofing		
B. Boiling water—80°F proofing		
C. Ice water—refrigerator proof 1 hour		
D. Ice water—80°F proof		

Conclusions: What is yeast?

Write the equation of CO_2 production from yeast action on sugar.

What liquid temperature and proofing temperature produced the greatest volume increase?

Did boiling water stop yeast action?

Did ice water stop yeast action? Delay action?

II. Proofing and Shaping Yeast Products

A. Microwave Proofing of Yeast Dough

Procedure: Place 4 c water in a 4-c glass measure. Cook water on 100% power (HIGH) for 6 1/2–8 1/2 min until it boils. Move water to back of oven. Place kneaded dough in a greased microwave-safe bowl, turning once. Cover dough with waxed paper and place in microwave oven *with hot water.* Heat dough and water at *10% power (LOW)* for 10–13 min or until dough has almost doubled. Punch dough down; shape.

If making loaves, place shaped loaves in 8 x 4 x 2-in. microwave-safe dishes and cover with waxed paper. Return to microwave with *3 c water.* Heat on low for *5–8 min* until nearly doubled in size.

B. Proofing at 80°F

Procedure: Place in lightly oiled bowl and cover. Set in warm place, approximately 80°F, until doubled, then punch down. Let rest 10 min and shape as desired. Let shaped rolls or loaves rise again.

C. Shaping:

1. Pan rolls—Shape dough into balls about 1 1/2-in. in diameter. Brush with melted butter. Place close together in a greased pan. Bake 20–25 min at 350°F.

2. Finger rolls—Shape dough into 4-in.-long strips. Brush with butter. Place side by side in a greased pan. Bake 20–25 min at 350°F.

3. Cloverleaf rolls—Shape dough into small balls a little less than 1-in. diameter; place 3 balls in each greased muffin cup.

4. Speedy cloverleaf rolls—Shape dough into balls about 2 in. in diameter; place in greased muffin cups. With kitchen shears cut balls almost to bottom in half, then in quarters.

5. Bow knots—Roll small pieces of dough into 9-in. strips about 1/2 in. thick. Tie in loose knots. Place on greased cookie sheet.

6. Braids—Roll out dough on lightly floured surface to 1/4 in. thickness. Cut into strips 1/2 in. wide and 5 in. long. Pinch together ends of 3 strips to seal braid; braid 3 strips, and fasten other ends. Place on greased cookie sheet.

7. Curlicues or pinwheels—Roll out dough, 1/2 at a time, on lightly floured surface into a 15 x 9-in. rectangle 1/4 in. thick. Brush with melted butter. Cut crosswise into twelve 9 x 1 1/4-in. strips and place in greased muffin cups, cut-side down.

8. Fan-Tans—Roll out dough, 1/2 at a time, on lightly floured surface to a 15 x 9-in. rectangle 1/4 in. thick. Brush with melted butter. Cut into 9 x 1 1/2-in. strips. Stack 5 strips together; cut into 1 1/2-in. pieces. Place each stack, cut-side down, in greased muffin cup.

9. Crescents—Roll out dough, 1/2 at a time, on lightly floured surface to a 12-in. circle about 1/2 in. thick. Brush with melted butter. Cut each round into 12 wedges. Starting with wide end, roll each wedge to point. Place on greased cookie sheet, point-side down. Curve ends.

10. Quick Parker House rolls—Roll dough into a rectangle 1/4-in. thick, cut rolls with a biscuit cutter. Flatten with palm of hand into ovals. Brush with melted butter to within 1/4 in. of edge. Fold each circle over to make a half circle; press edge to seal. Place on greased cookie sheet.

11. Bread loaves—Roll dough into a 12 x 18-in. rectangle. Fold in thirds as shown.

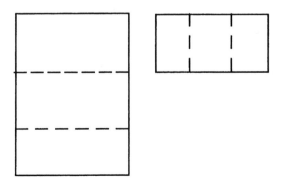

D. Baking:

Bake loaves at 325° for 35–40 min. Test for doneness. Loaves should sound hollow when tapped. Bake individual rolls at 400° for 10 min.

III. Preparation of Quality Yeast Products

❖A. **Basic Sweet Dough**

    (7 g) 1 pkg. active dry yeast
        softened in 1/4 c water
        (105–110°F, 41– 44°C) *OR*
        (17 g) 1 cake compressed yeast
        crumbled in 1/4 c water
        (80–85°F, 27–30°C)

    (118 ml) 1/2 c scalded milk, lukewarm*
    (50 g) 1/4 c sugar
    (25 g) 2 T fat, softened
    (6 g) 1 t salt
    (261 g) 2 1/4 c flour, approximately
    (50 g) 1 egg

*Heat milk to scalding temperature (just below boiling). Cool scalded milk to lukewarm.

Procedure: Soften yeast in the water and let stand 5–10 min. Combine cooled milk, sugar, fat, and salt. Add enough flour to make a thick batter. Mix well. Add softened yeast and eggs. Mix.

    Continue beating in flour until dough is smooth and can be lifted in a mass on the spoon, leaving the bowl clean. Turn dough onto lightly floured board, and knead until smooth and satiny. If kneaded with mixer and dough hook, knead on slow speed for 3 min. Keep as soft as can be handled. Proofing may be done by microwave method or at 80°F (II A or B above). Shape dough into rolls or a loaf. Proof again until near double in volume. Bake at 400°F for 10 min if made into rolls. Bake at 350°F for 35–40 min if made into a loaf.

❖B. **Whole Wheat Bread**

    (7 g) 1 pkg. active dry yeast
    (59 ml) 1/4 c water (lukewarm)
    (177 ml) 3/4 c hot water or scalded milk
    (6.3 g) 1/2 T soft shortening

    (12.5 g) 1 T brown sugar
    (6 g) 1 t salt
    (133 g) 1 c whole wheat flour
    (116–154.5 g) 1–1 1/3 c all-purpose flour

Procedure: Soften yeast in 1/4 c water for 5 min. Stir to dissolve. Pour 3/4 c hot liquid over sugar, salt, and shortening. Stir. Cool to *lukewarm*. Add yeast and enough flour to make a stiff batter; beat well. Add additional flour to make a soft dough. Turn out on lightly floured board or place in mixer for kneading.

    Knead dough, working in additional flour only if necessary to keep dough from sticking to board. Knead until light and elastic, about 5 min. If kneading by machine, knead 3 min on second lowest speed. Place in warm oiled bowl, turning dough over once to bring greased side up. Cover with damp cloth. Proof at 80°F or in microwave.

    Dough may be shaped into rolls or loaves, as indicated in II.C. For loaf, place in greased 8 1/2 x 4 1/2 x 2 1/2-in. loaf pan; oil top lightly; let rise again to almost double in bulk, 50–60 min or until dough does not spring back when lightly touched with finger tip. Bake loaf in moderate oven (350°) 35–40 min or until the loaf is lightly browned. Tip loaf out of pan and thump bottom or sides of loaf with fingers or knuckles. A hollow sound indicates doneness. If made into individual rolls, shape, let rise until double in bulk, bake at 400°F for 10 min. Cool on rack before storing.

C. **Bagels**

    (232–290 g) 2–2 1/2 c unsifted all-purpose flour
    (9 g) 1 1/2 t salt
    (18 g) 1 1/2 T sugar

    (3.5 g) 1/2 pkg. active dry yeast
    (177 ml) 3/4 c very warm tap water (105–115°F)
    (33.4 g) 1 egg white, beaten with (14.5 ml) 1 T cold water

Procedure: In a medium-sized bowl, thoroughly mix 3/4 c flour, sugar, salt, and undissolved yeast. Gradually add warm tap water to dry ingredients and beat 2 min at medium speed with electric mixer, scraping bowl occasionally. Add 1/4 c flour. Beat at high speed 2 min, scraping bowl occasionally. Stir in enough additional flour to make a soft dough.

    Turn out onto lightly floured board; knead until smooth and elastic, about 8–10 min. Place in ungreased bowl. Cover with a piece of plastic wrap and let rise in moist proofing cabinet 20 min. (Dough will not be doubled in bulk.) Punch down. Roll dough into rectangle 1/2-in. thick. Cut dough into 6 equal strips, and roll strips into ropes. Twist ropes and pinch ends together to form circle. Place on ungreased baking sheet. Cover and let rise in warm place 20 min. Boil in 1 3/4-in. water in an electric skillet. Add a few bagels at a time. Simmer 7 min. Remove from water and place on towel to cool. Cool 5 min.

Place on greased baking sheets. Bake at 375°F for 10 min. Remove from oven. Brush with combined egg white and cold water. Return to oven; bake about 20 min longer or until done. Split and serve toasted with margarine or cream cheese.

D. Pita Bread

(290–348 g) 2 1/2–3 c unsifted flour   (3.5 g) 1/2 pkg. active dry yeast
(6 g) 1 1/2 t sugar   (237 ml) 1 c very warm tap water (105–115°F)
(6 g) 1 t salt

Procedure: Preheat oven to 450°F and place baking sheet in to heat. In medium-sized bowl, thoroughly mix 1 c flour, sugar, salt, and undissolved yeast. Gradually add tap water to dry ingredients and beat 2 min at medium speed of electric mixer, scraping bowl occasional. Add 3/8 c flour. Beat at high speed 2 min, scraping bowl occasionally. Stir in enough additional flour to make a soft dough. Turn out onto lightly floured board; knead until smooth and elastic, about 8–10 min. Place in a greased beaker, turning to grease top. Cover with a piece of plastic wrap; let rise by proofing methods II.A. or II.B. until doubled in bulk.

Punch down; turn out onto lightly floured board, and divide dough into 3 equal pieces. Shape each into a ball; let rest 30 min on a lightly floured board; roll each ball into an 8-in. circle. Place on a lightly floured baking sheet.

Slide the circle directly onto the other baking sheet, which had been placed in preheated oven. Be careful not to burn yourself! Place on the lowest rack of the very hot oven. Bake about 5 min, or until done. (Tops will not be brown.) Lightly brown tops of bread by placing under hot broilers 3 in. from source of heat for about 1 min, or until browned.

IV. Effect of Oven Type on Loaves of Bread

Use formula for recipe of dough as given in III.A. Directions may vary with oven brand and size.

Variables:

A. Use 280 g of dough. Roll flat and shape into loaf. Let rise. Bake in convection oven at 325°F for 30 min.

B. Use 280 g of dough. Roll flat and shape into loaf. Let rise. Bake in Thermodore convection/microwave/bake at 425°F for 6 1/2 min. (Other brands of ovens will require different directions.)

1. Set oven at 425°F.

2. Press *on.*

3. Set microwave on low.

4. Set time for 6 1/2 min.

5. Press microwave and convection on.

6. Move lever to microwave position.

C. Use 280 g of dough. Roll flat and shape into loaf. Let rise. Bake in conventional oven at 325°F for 30 min.

Conclusions: Which method takes the least time?

Were all products done?

Which product had the best texture?

Were any products tough?

Which product had the best appearance?

❖V.   Effect of Reduced Salt on Gluten Development in Yeast Dough

Prepare dough as directed in III.A., but with no salt.

VI. Effect of No Gluten on Yeast Bread

Low-Protein, Yeast Leavened Bread

(7 g) 1 pkg. active dry yeast	(51 g) 1/4 c shortening
(37 g) 3 T sugar	(352 g) 2 3/4 c DPP wheat starch*
(296 ml) 1 1/4 c warm water (110–115˚)	(3 g) 1/2 t salt

Procedure: Grease loaf pan, 9 x 5 x 2 3/4 in. Dissolve yeast and sugar in warm water in large mixing bowl. Let stand 5 min. Blend in shortening and part of DDP wheat starch on low speed, scraping bowl frequently. Gradually blend in remaining DPP wheat starch. Mixture should fall in a ribbon from scraper. If too thick, blend in water, 1 T at a time, until mixture is smooth and creamy. If too thin, blend in DDP wheat starch, 1 T at a time.

    Beat 1 min on high speed. Pour into pan. Let rise in very warm place (100˚F) until batter is 1/2 in. from top of pan, 30–45 min. Leave bread in oven. Turn oven control to 425˚F and bake 30–35 min or until golden brown. Immediately remove from pan; cool.

Results: Describe texture of products as fine, coarse, very coarse, or open and describe as extremely light, light, neither light nor heavy, heavy, or extremely heavy. Comment on color and flavor.

Variable	Baking Time	Texture	Light/Heavy	Color	Flavor
III. A. Sweet roll					
III. A. Sweet bread					
III. B. Whole wheat bread					
III. C. Bagels					
III. D. Pita bread					
IV. A. Bread—convection	30 min				
IV. B. Convection/microwave	6 1/2 min				
IV. C. Conventional	30 min				
V. Low-salt bread					
VI. No-gluten bread					

Conclusions: Why is milk heated (scalded) before making yeast dough?

What is the function of sugar in yeast dough?

Yeast dough should be kneaded with very little additional flour. Why?

What conditions provide greatest CO_2 production from yeast?

*Source of ingredient listed in Appendix B.

What conditions slow or retard CO_2 production?

What is the purpose of kneading yeast dough?

Why is yeast dough proofed before and after shaping into rolls or loaves?

Why does pita bread develop a pocket?

The absence of gluten reduces what expected quantities in bread?

How does the absence of salt affect the volume, texture, and flavor of bread?

What is the leavening agent in yeast bread?

SOFT AND STIFF DOUGH: COOKIES

Goal: To observe the quality of cookies and to understand the functions of flour and fat in these products.

Objectives: To observe cookies made with and without gluten.

I. Effect of No Gluten on Sugar Cookies
Variables
A. No-gluten sugar cookie

Sliced Sugar Cookies

(250 g) 2 1/4 c Dietetic Paygel baking mix*   (37 g) 3 T sugar
(113 g) 1/2 c margarine, softened   (5 ml) 1 t vanilla
(80 ml) 1/3 c light corn syrup

Procedure: Heat oven to 400°F. In medium bowl, mix all ingredients thoroughly. Refrigerate 1 hour. Shape dough on waxed paper into a roll about 2 in. in diameter. Cut into 1/4-in. slices. Place on ungreased baking sheet. Bake about 12 min or until edges are golden. Store in tightly covered container. Makes about 3 1/2 dozen.

B. Sugar cookies, refrigerated dough
Procedure: Cut six 1/4-in. slices of sugar cookie. Bake refrigerated sugar cookie according to package directions.

C. No-gluten ginger cookies

Ginger Cookies

(113 g) 1/2 c margarine, softened   (4 g) 2 t ginger
(67 g) 1/3 c granulated sugar   (1.9 g) 1/2 t baking powder
(25 g) 2 T brown sugar (packed)   granulated sugar
(220 g) 2 c Dietetic Paygel baking mix•

Procedure: Heat oven to 400°F. In medium bowl, mix margarine and sugars thoroughly. Stir in baking mix, ginger and baking powder. Mix with hands to blend thoroughly. Dough should be stiff, but if it seems crumbly, add water, 1 t at a time. Roll into 1-in. balls; place about 2 in. apart on ungreased baking sheet. Flatten with bottom of glass, which has been dipped in granulated sugar. Bake about 10 min. Store in tightly covered container. Makes 2 dozen cookies.

D. No-gluten applesauce cookies

Applesauce Cookies

(102 g) 1/2 c shortening   (3.8 g) 1 t baking powder
(150.5 g) 3/4 c brown sugar (packed)   (1 g) 1/2 t cinnamon
(50 g) 1 egg   (1 g) 1/2 t nutmeg
(220 g) 2 c Dietetic Paygel baking mix•   (1 g) 1/2 t cloves
(170 g) 2/3 c applesauce   (73 g) 1/2 c raisins

Procedure: Heat oven to 400°F. In medium bowl, mix shortening, brown sugar, and egg thoroughly. Stir in remaining ingredients. Drop by teaspoonfuls about 2 in. apart onto ungreased baking sheets. Bake 10–12 min. Store in tightly covered container. Makes about 4 dozen cookies.

*Source listed in Appendix B.

Results: Comment on tenderness, texture, color, and palatability.

Variable	Tenderness	Texture	Color	Palatability
Sugar cookie, no gluten				
Sugar cookie, refrigerated				
Ginger cookie				
Applesauce cookie				

Conclusion: With no gluten, was product tender and palatable?

STIFF DOUGH: NOODLES

Noodles
(50 g) 1 egg or (66 g) 2 egg yolks, slightly beaten   (2 g) 1/2 t salt
flour to make a very stiff dough

Procedure: Add salt to egg. Stir in flour. Knead until smooth. Roll as thin as possible, like thin paper. Cover with clean towel. Let stand 1/2 hour to dry. Roll. Cut into 1/8-in. slices. Shape out rolls into strips. Cut into desired lengths. Cook as for boiled macaroni. Noodle paste may be cut into fancy shapes instead of strips if preferred. Noodles may be dried and kept for some time before using. Yield: 1 c, uncooked.

Food Preservation and Food Safety

Notes:

FOOD PRESERVATION: CANNING

Objectives: To understand the safety function of processing as related to microbial growth and enzyme action.
To develop an understanding of the commonly used methods of canning acid and low-acid foods.
To have reliable sources of information about canning.

Activities: Note display of different kinds of jars, closures, and processing equipment.

Procedure: For each group of 2, can and process 1 pt vegetable (low-acid) or fruit (acid) using the USDA "Guide to Home Canning." Complete the seal; label the jar with name, date, and processing method used.

To successfully store food, many methods of food preservation are used. One of the most common methods is canning (or retorting, as used in the food industry). It is imperative to process foods when canning by a method that assures safety from pathogenic microorganisms. Temperature and time of heat exposure determines destruction of pathogenic bacteria. The length of time and degree of temperature needed is determined by the pH of the food and the consistency of the food. In foods that have a near neutral pH, some microorganisms require heat above the boiling point for destruction. For these foods a pressure canner must be used. Research conducted by the United States Department of Agriculture has determined safe methods for canning in the home. These instructions and methods are published in the "Complete Guide to Home Canning, Agriculture Information Bulletin No. 539." Following carefully the USDA Guide is the safest way to assure safety from pathogens in canned foods.
For each product, follow the times and temperatures recommended in the U.S.D.A. Bulletins.*

Results: Record pH, packing method, and processing method and comment on presence of seal, fill of container, and appearance of final product.

Product	pH	Packing Method (Raw or Hot)	Processing Method (Boiling Water Bath or Pressure)	Comments
				—

*Complete Guide to Home Canning, Agriculture Information Bulletin No. 539, United States Department of Agriculture, Extension Service.

U.S. Government Bookstore
Publication Department
401 South State Street, Room 124
Chicago, IL 60605
Phone: 312-353-5133

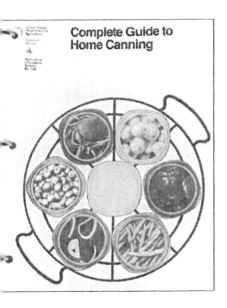

Complete Guide to
Home Canning

FOOD PRESERVATION: FREEZING

Objectives: To understand factors important in producing good quality frozen foods:
1. Slow growth of microorganisms by freezing.
2. Protect from moisture loss by use of suitable packaging material.
3. Prevent discoloration of some fruits.
4. Prevent changes in vegetables due to enzyme action.

To be familiar with equipment and procedures used in processing frozen foods.

Storage of food by freezing requires following guidelines to prevent exposure of food to air during the storage period. Air may cause sublimation of the water in the food and freezer burn of the surfaces. Oxidation of fats in frozen foods will cause rancidity, and enzymatic oxidation of fruits such as peaches or apples will cause discoloration. Other enzymatic reactions may cause texture and flavor changes. To avoid these undesirable changes in frozen foods, packaging and seals should be air tight and as much air as possible removed from the package. Antioxidants may be added to the product or the food may be blanched (heated in steam or water) to denature enzymes before freezing. Freezing temperatures below 0°F (−18°C) are also important to minimize texture changes, retard oxidation, and assure quality. Following the USDA Guidelines for "Home Freezing of Fruits and Vegetables" will provide direction for maintaining quality.

Activities: Note display of different kinds of rigid and nonrigid containers and methods of sealing.

Procedure: For each group of 2, prepare and freeze 1 pt of fruit or vegetable. For each product, follow the directions in USDA bulletins.

Results: Comment on prefreezing treatment and absence of air in type of container and seal used. After storage, evaluate ice crystal formation in package.

Product	Pretreatment	Container	Comments

*Home Freezing of Fruits and Vegetables, Home and Garden Bulletin No. 10, United States Department of Agriculture, Extension Service.
U.S. Government Bookstore
Publication Department
401 South State Street, Room 124
Chicago, IL 60605
Phone: 312-353-5133

EXPERIMENTAL LABORATORY IN FOOD SCIENCE

Procedure:

1. Choose a problem related to material covered in this course. The problem should be an extension of one already covered or a problem that had no experiment.

2. Develop the laboratory experiment with a hypothesis to be tested.

3. Obtain approval from laboratory instructor for the experiment.

4. Write a market order on the correct form for needed food and equipment.

5. Write a paper in 2 parts, including the following information:

Part I + market order page

Title of experiment

Hypothesis

Objectives (purpose) of experiment

Review of literature (summary of readings)

    Discuss functions of ingredients altered

Experimental procedure

    Formula plus variables (use grams and milliliters)

    Procedure for making products (write number of mixing strokes, time of mixing, etc.)

    Procedure for evaluation (include evaluation forms)

Bibliography

Part II

Graph or table of results

Results and conclusions—discuss *why* product changes occurred

SCORECARD

Name _____

Part I	Possible Points	Points Received
Are objectives clearly defined?	2	_____
Review of literature pertinent to topic?	2	_____
Is experimental procedure accurate?	2	_____
Evaluation procedures	2	_____
Bibliography (3 references minimum)	2	_____
Is market order complete and specific?	2	_____
Part II		
Are results clearly presented?	4	_____
Are results clearly explained?	4	_____
TOTAL POINTS	20	_____

Assignment late = −1 point/day

Example of Special Project
Developed in part by Rachael Geik and Liza Szucs

Effect of Fat Replacement on Muffin Quality

Hypothesis: Substitution of margarine with either pureed prunes or applesauce will provide muffins with equal quality to those with margarine in tenderness, appearance, and flavor.

Objectives: To replace fat with applesauce and prune puree in muffin formula.
To evaluate muffins using a 7-point consumer preference hedonic scale on tenderness, appearance, and flavor.
To evaluate muffins using a penetrometer to assess compression.
To evaluate texture by comparing copies of cross sections.

Formula and Procedure:

Apple Muffins

(77 g) 2/3 c all-purpose flour	(80 ml) 1/3 c milk
(37.5 g) 3 T granulated sugar	(15 ml) 1 T beaten egg
(5.2 g) 1 1/2 t baking powder	(13 g) 1 T margarine
(.7 g) 1/8 t salt	(45 g) 1/3 c raw apples
(.6 g) 1/4 t cinnamon	

Topping

(12 g) 1 T sugar	(.6 g) 1/4 t cinnamon

Procedure: Mix together flour, sugar, baking powder, salt, and cinnamon. Stir 10 strokes. In separate bowl, combine milk, egg, and fat, beating 1 min on medium speed of portable mixer. Add dry ingredients to liquid ingredients and mix with spoon 6 strokes. Fold in apples with 6 strokes. Fill muffin tins using 1/4-c measure to dip batter. Fill each tin with 35 g batter and sprinkle with 2 g sugar-cinnamon mix. Bake 12 min in 425°F oven on center shelf.

Variables:

1. Control

2. Substitute 1/4 c applesauce for 1 T margarine

3. Substitute 1/4 c pureed prunes for 1 T margarine

Procedure for Evaluation:

1. Using the calipers, measure the height of each muffin.

2. Split muffin in half. Take an overhead picture of muffin texture. Compare size and texture.

3. Using a metal corer, cut a circle from 1/2 muffin. Measure compression with a penetrometer.

4. Using a 9-point hedonic scale (as attached), measure sensory qualities of flavor, appearance, tenderness, moistness, and overall quality by having 8 students rank the muffins.

Review of Literature:

For this experiment discuss topics such as the functions of fat in baked products and previous research reported in the literature on fat replacement in baked products.

References:

Review of literature should cite food science textbooks and scientific journals such as *Journal of Food Science, Food Technology,* and *Cereal Science.*

Appendix A
SENSORY

Prepare the following solutions for the Sensory Laboratory. Place each solution in a coded container from which the student may pour their sample.

Series A

a-1 (372)	Bitter .... quinine sulfate or caffeine	.1 g/liter (0.1%)
a-2 (569)	Salt .... NaCl	4 g/liter (.4%)
a-3 (825)	Sweet .... Sucrose	50 g/liter (5%)
a-4 (798)	Sour .... Citric Acid	2 g/liter (.2%)
a-5 (281)	Unami .... Monosodium glutamate	2 g/liter (.2%)

Series B

b-1 (293)	Sucrose	50 g sucrose/liter (5%)
b-2 (142)	Sucrose + citric acid	50 g sucrose + .3 g citric acid/liter

Series C

c-1 (621)	Sucrose	50 g sucrose/liter
c-2 (256)	Sucrose + salt	50 g sucrose + .3 g NaCl/liter
c-3 (879)	Sucrose	50 g/liter

Series D

d-1 (190)	salt	4 g NaCl/liter
d-2 (876)	salt + sugar	4 g salt + 7 g sucrose/liter

Series E

e-1 (186)	Citric acid	2 g citric acid/liter
e-2 (453)	Citric acid + sugar	2 g citric acid + 7 g sucrose/l

Series F

f-1 (739)	Quinine or caffeine	.1 g quinine sulfate or caffeine/l
f-2 (468)	Quinine or caffeine + sugar	.1 g quinine sulfate + 7 g sucrose/l

Series G

g-1 (907)	Sucrose	50 g sucrose/l
g-2 (345)	Sucrose	50 g sucrose/l
g-3 (868)	Fructose	50 g fructose/l

Series H

h-1 (308)	Sucrose	50 g sucrose/l
h-2 (reference)	Sucrose + NaCl	50 g sucrose + .3 g NaCl/l
h-3 (129)	Sucrose + NaCl	50 g sucrose + .3 g NaCl/l

Series I

i-1 (470)	Reconstituted frozen lemonade
i-2 (598)	Reconstituted dried lemonade mix
i-3 (229)	Fresh Lemonade: 1/4 c lemon juice extracted from 1 lemon, 1/4 c sugar, 1 1/3 c water, mix

Series J

j-1 (092)	Lemonade: yellow
j-2 (338)	Lemonade: red
j-3 (876)	Lemonade: green
j-4 (923)	Lemonade: blue

Appendix B
INGREDIENT SOURCES FOR LABORATORIES

Ingredient	Source, Address, Phone Number

Sensory Quality Laboratory

| Caffeine | Sysco Food Services |
| Monosodium Glutamate | Cincinnati, Ohio 45241 |

Frozen Desserts

Sea Kem	FMC Corporation 1735 Market St. Philadelphia, PA 19103 1-800-526-3649
CMC	Hercules, Inc. Research Center 500 Hercules Rd. Wilmington, Delaware 19808 1-800-722-7072
Passeli SA2	AVEBE American, Inc. 4 Independence Way CN-5307 Princetown, NJ 08543-5307
Kontrol	Germantown (U.S.A.) Co. 505 Parkway, P.O. Box 405 Broomall, PA 19008 1-800-345-8209
Corn Syrup (36 and 42 DE)	A.E. Staley Mnf. Co. Decatur, IL 62525
N-Lite D	National Starch & Chemical Co. 10 Finderne Ave. Bridgewater, NJ 08807-3300 908-685-5350
Sherex 302	Quest International 1937 7th Street, NW Rochester, MN 55901
Frozen Pasteurized Egg White	Crystal Lake P.O. Box 1058 Warsaw, IN 46581-1058 219-267-3101

Solutions with Sugar
Sea Gel GP 713

FMC Corporation
2000 Market St.
Philadelphia, PA 19103
1-800-526-3649

Fats, Emulsions, and Salads
Keltrol T Xanthan Gum
Kelcoloid LVF propylene glycol alginate

Kelco, Division of Merck and Co., Inc.
75 Terminal Ave.
Clark, NJ 07066
1-800-535-4141

Tween 60

ICI
Concord Plaza
3411 Silverside Rd.
P.O. Box 15391
Wilmington, DE 19850
302-886-3000

Oleorecin liquid paprika

McCormick
Hunt Valley, MI 21031
1-800-632-5847

Bealite 3401-L

Beatreme Foods
352 E. Grand Ave.
Beloit, WI 53511
1-800-328-7517

Frozen egg yolk

Crystal Lake
P.O. Box 1058
Warsaw, IN 46581-1058
219-267-3101

Thermflo
Purity 420
Nlite L
N-Lite L

National Starch & Chemical Co.
10 Finderne Ave.
Bridgewater, NJ 08807-3300
908-685-5350

Whey protein

Milk and Cream
Sea Gel
Gelcarin GP 359

FMC Corporation
2000 Market St.
Philadelphia, PA 19103
1-800-526-3649

Starchy Sauces and Desserts
Polar gel 18W
Polar gel 15
Polar gel 10W
Amalean I starch

Amaizo
1100 Indianapolis Blvd.
Hammond, IN 46320-1094
1-800-348-9896

Tetrasodium Pyrophosphate
Disodium Phosphate

FMC Corporation
1735 Market St.
Philadelphia, PA 19103
1-800-526-3649

Myvacet 9-45

Eastman Chemical Co.
P.O. Box 431
Kingsport, TN 37662
1-800-327-8626

Ultra Tex 2
Instant Pure Flo F-1
H-50 Waxy Cornstarch

National Starch & Chemical Co.
10 Finderne Ave.
Bridgewater, NJ 08807-3300
908-685-5350

Baking Powders and Baking Soda
Phosphate

FMC Corporation
1735 Market St.
Philadelphia, PA 19103
1-800-526-3649

Cakes with Shortening
N-flate

National Starch & Chemical Co.
10 Finderne Ave.
Bridgewater, NJ 08807-3300
908-685-5350

High Fructose Corn Syrup

A.E. Staley Mnf. Co.
Decatur, IL 62525

Soft Dough: Biscuits
Sweet whey
Bealite 340-L

Kerry
352 E. Grand Ave.
Beloit, WI 53511
1-800-328-7517

Butter Flavor

Universal Flavors
265 Harrison Ave.
Kearny, NJ 07032

LoDex 10 Maltodextrin
Amalean II Instant Starch

Amaizo
1100 Indianapolis Blvd.
Hammond, IN 46320-1094
1-800-348-9896

Buttermilk

Soft Doughs: Yeast Doughs
DPP Wheat Starch
Dietetic Paygel baking mix

Dietary Specialties Inc.
P.O. Box 227
Rochester, NY 14601